It's All Greek To Me

greektome.co
Original series on God TV

It's All Greek To Me

DAY-BY-DAY DEVOTIONAL TO KINDLE YOUR FAITH AND CAUSE YOU TO WALK IN VICTORY

Christos Demetriou

Published by ACTS International Limited, West Sussex, England
www.greektome.co

The Greek words used in this book; their definitions and phonetic spelling are based on the author's own understanding of the Greek language and not deemed to be completely accurate. No claims of absolute originality are made for the material in this book. The words contained herein are not intended to replace personal study of the *Holy Bible*. The author envisioned that the ideas, opinions and thoughts expressed will stimulate and inspire 'own thinking' and lead the reader to a deeper relationship with God.

It's All Greek to Me - Devotional / Christos Demetriou. —1st ed.

ISBN 978-0-9557280-7-5 (Paperback)
ISBN 978-0-9557280-8-2 (Kindle)

Dedicated to the blessed Holy Spirit.
Thank you for being my source of inspiration.
Not just for this book, but for everything in life.

To my dearest wife Loraine and my daughter Xana.
The two bright starts in my universe.

Thank you for being with me... along every path, upon every mountain top and in every valley. It's been an exciting journey and I couldn't have done it without you.

Contents

"Without some knowledge of Greek, you cannot understand the critical commentaries on the Scriptures, and a commentary that is not critical is of doubtful value."

George Ricker Berry

Author of the Interlinear Greek to English New Testament

It's All Greek to Me

CHAPTER 1

Foreword

THE GREEK LANGUAGE IS VERY DESCRIPTIVE. It has the unique ability to express thoughts, ideas and concepts accurately and concisely. We are probably all familiar with the saying "the Greeks have a word for it!" In the context of New Testament scripture, I believe this to be true. It would be unwise and inadvisable to assume that any Greek word can be translated throughout the Bible using the same English word. Take for instance that word "master." This word "master" is used in the Authorised Version to translate *six* different Greek words, all bearing different shades of meaning. The word "judgment" stands for *eight* different Greek words in the original; and so, of many others. Consequently, the English translation can only provide a *word* that is the nearest literal equivalent and is often misleading in its spiritual application.

This Day-by-Day Devotional is not intended to teach people Greek, though it may be used to good advantage for that purpose. It is designed to help the reader discover some of the immense treasure that is embodied in the original Greek text with a view to releasing God's word to speak prophetically into people's lives.

By placing certain Greek words into their correct setting, and thereafter elaborating and expounding on the translation, I have endeavored to reveal a clear and accurate perspective to the meaning of each individual "word" as sited in a particular verse of scripture.

The Apostle Paul wrote much of the New Testament, and his depth of thinking and depth of feeling is expressed so beautifully in the original text. His mastery of the Greek language literally parts the clouds and allows the brilliance of Christ to shine through almost every Greek word. The intensity of Paul's devotion to Christ and the sheer force of his commitment has challenged me to seek more insight and dig deeper.

I have also been astounded by his use of *words*, often borrowed from the secular arena and on occasion only used once in order to make a specific point. I am convinced that this kind of supreme inspiration could only originate in God Himself, and that the Holy Spirit must have imparted it to Paul.

In his own words, Paul considered himself a 'Jew's Jew' and a 'Pharisee' (Philippians 3:4-6). However, many of us imagine that he viewed the world as post-industrial, urban, individualistic Westerners do and that he consequently behaved as we do. But he lived in the 1st Century, in the Eastern Mediterranean, in a group-oriented society. Many translations of his writings today speak the theological language of two millenniums later! Thus, it is important to have some understanding of the ancient culture and traditions into which he was born. On occasion, in order to fully comprehend the meaning of certain *words*, I have drawn on my Greek Cypriot upbringing that is steeped in Eastern Mediterranean culture. For this unique privilege, I am truly grateful to God.

Lastly, when undertaking to write this Daily Devotional, I became aware that each word has the power to penetrate the challenging realities we face from day to day, and in so doing, manifest the life and love of God.

I pray that you will gather wisdom, knowledge and understanding from these pages, but more than that, I pray that God breathes His life (Zoe) and releases His love (Agape) into your very existence.

Did Jesus Speak Greek?

Palestine was multilingual in the time of Christ. Aramaic was the language of the remnant of Israel, a remnant of the Babylonian captivity some 300 years prior to Christ. Jesus spoke Aramaic as is seen in the Gospel record, Hebrew was the language of the rabbinic circle, but it was Greek that was common to all in that region. *Koine* means 'common' or 'everyday' and was the language of the Hellenistic world. Jesus and His disciples would most likely have spoken Greek, which unquestionably was a practicality and of necessity at the time. Furthermore, there existed in Jerusalem a Greek speaking Jewish synagogue (Acts 6:9), which no doubt used the Greek Old Testament Septuagint in their services.

My great uncle, an Archbishop in the Greek Orthodox church in New York, was a theology scholar of much notability. I was told that he wrote a thesis on whether Jesus spoke Greek, and this in turn, led to him to write a book on the subject. Therefore, I may have thought it was acceptable to simply agree that Jesus spoke Greek, but rather, I decided to dig deeper. As a result, I was very pleased when I discovered that one of the premier New Testament scholars had directly taken up this question: Stanley Porter, in *"Did Jesus Ever Teach in Greek?"* (*Tyndale Bulletin 44, no. 1 [1993]: 199–235*).

Did Jesus speak Greek? The New Testament doesn't directly answer all the questions we like to ask it. But when combined with archaeological evidence, Stanley Porter concludes;

"In the light of this accumulated evidence, which is overwhelming when compared to the equivalent Aramaic evidence, it is surprising that many scholars have not given more consideration to the hypothesis that Jesus spoke and even possibly taught in Greek.

The evidence regarding what is known about the use of Greek in ancient Palestine, including the cosmopolitan Hellenistic character of lower Galilee, the epigraphic and literary evidence, including coins, papyri, literary writers, inscriptions and funerary texts, but most of all several significant contexts in the Gospels, all points in one direction.

Whereas it is not always known how much and on which occasions Jesus spoke Greek, it is virtually certain that He used Greek at various times in His itinerant ministry."

CHAPTER 2

Day-by-Day Devotional

WELCOME TO THE 365 DAY DEVOTIONAL **"IT'S ALL GREEK TO ME"** - a Greek word for each day of the year that will fortify your faith and cause you to live a victorious life.

When Ward Simpson the CEO of God TV asked me to do a series that would encourage and strengthen the precious people watching the channel, I immediately knew he had heard from God. Unbeknown to Ward, I had already started writing a book titled "It's All Greek to Me," and therefore, it is not an accident that you now have a copy of this book in your hands.

As you take the time to read and meditate on the distinctive message each Greek 'word for the day' uncovers, I believe that the Holy Spirit will breathe life onto that *word* and cause you to walk in victory in whatever circumstances you may find yourself in. The reason I wrote this book is simply to provide God with a channel though which He may bless and encourage you.

I would advise that you start or end each day with one of the 365 words contained in this devotional. Or perhaps you may find the time during your daily schedule to stop and *meditate* on the revelation you have received by using this book.

"The entrance of Your words gives light; and it gives understanding to the simple."
(Psalm 119:130)

If you devote your time, on a regular and disciplined basis, to feed upon the truths presented in the following pages, I am fully persuaded you will be nourished and begin to flourish and prosper in all areas of life.

"When you see this, your heart shall rejoice, and your bones shall flourish like grass; the hand of the Lord shall be known to His servants."
(Isaiah 66:14)

Please note, you do not need to start this devotional at the beginning of any week, month or year. The 365 days are written in a way that you can engage at any time. However, when you choose a start date, that will become "Day 1."

Day 1

Love

ἀγαπάω = *'agapaho'*
To love dearly, to be well pleased with, to love deeply, to love unconditionally and constantly

Love has its perfect expression in the relationship between Christ and His church (Ephesians 5:25). The word *ἀγαπέ* (*agape*) has such a distinctive meaning that it is very difficult to find a general definition. Love can only be known by the actions it prompts. God's love is seen in the wonderful gifts He has given to mankind – the gift of His Son and the gift of His Holy Spirit. This special kind of love, that is completely unconditional, expresses the deep and constant affection God has towards unworthy people. *Agape*, is unique in that it's based entirely on the character of God, not on the worthiness or qualifications of the person at the receiving end. And it is certainly not based on the feelings one may or may not have when dispensing love. The feelings are optional, they may come and go, but the 'God-kind of love' is eternal, and will never change.

Not only does God's love never change, it never fails! Today, the unchangeable, unfailing love of God will saturate your mind and heart and cause His supernatural peace to manifest in a fresh and profound way. What's more, nothing can separate you from His love. As a husband is joined to his wife, and they become "one," so too are you joined to God's love.

DAY 2

MERCY

ἐλεήμονες = *'ellehimones'*
To show mercy, be merciful, tenderhearted, forgiving, benevolent, lenient.

When we read that God is merciful or that He has mercy, we may be assured that He is feeling our heartache just as intensely as we are. As the writer in Hebrews taught us, the reason we can *"come boldly to the throne of grace that we may obtain mercy and find grace to help in time of need,"* is because the occupant of that throne is a merciful High Priest who is touched with the feeling of our frailties. He is one who sympathizes with us in all our weaknesses (Hebrews 4:15-16). Those divine affections are the foundation of His mercy.

Throughout the day remind yourself that God's mercies endure forever, and they are new every morning. That means there is a *mercy* for every situation you may encounter today. God's mercies are fresh every morning! He won't apply yesterday's mercies to today's circumstances. God is touched by your human frailties, He understands and identifies with your weaknesses.

Knowing this truth, start confessing: "When I am weak, I'm at my strongest in Him." That way, His mercies will become the foundation upon which you build every day.

DAY 3

SOUND MIND

σωφρονισμοῦ = *'sohfronnismou'*
A well-behaved mind, an admonishing or calling to soundness of mind, to moderation and self-control, self-control, moderation.

A sound mind or wise discretion in the Greek is literally *'a well-behaved mind'* (2 Timothy 1:7). Therefore, when we remember our past victories, and have an attitude of thanksgiving towards God in the midst of adverse conditions, this state of mind reflects one that is 'exercising good judgment, is disciplined, and has the ability to make the right decisions under pressure'.

We are not to have any fears except to fear the Lord. He has given us the Holy Spirit, who is the Spirit of power, love and a sound mind. A *sound mind* is one that is clear, focused on God and truth, not confused or muddied, and not distracted. We get clarity from the Holy Spirit. If we live in fear, or entertain any type of fear, that is evidence that we are not trusting God. We must lay our fears at His feet and leave them there.

Doing this will fill you with the power of God and you will become more like Him. This is a promise for today. If you stand on it and lay your fears down right now, you will discover the power of Christ in our life and acquire a well-behaved mind that has the ability to make right decisions under pressure.

DAY 4

SUFFICIENT

ἱκανότης = *'hikanotis'*
To be or make sufficient, render fit, to make able, to be more than adequate, to equip one with adequate power to perform.

The Lord our God is not only *all-sufficient* in and of Himself, but He is also able to make you all-sufficient in all things. 2 Corinthians 9:8-11 proclaims, *"And God is able to make all grace abound toward you; that you, always having all sufficiency in all things, may abound to every good work."* Furthermore, the Lord will make you an able and affective servant in His kingdom. However, you must understand that 'in yourself' you are certainly not sufficient in all things. You must learn this truth, purposefully set your mind and heart upon this truth, and live according to this truth.

Yet, the Lord our God is *all-sufficient*! We are to find all our sufficiency in Him, and when we do find all our sufficiency in the Lord; He, in His all-sufficient grace, will make us able servants that are all-sufficient in all things.

You must learn not to lean upon your own capability. Rather, learn to set all your focus and faith upon our Lord Jesus Christ. That way, you will become fully-equipped with 'more than adequate power' to accomplish the plans and purposes God has laid out for you today.

DAY 5

EPISTLE

ἐπιστολή = *'epistolli'*
A letter, written message, epistle, dispatch, correspondence

2 Corinthians 3:2, *"You are our epistle, written in our hearts, known and read by all men."* The Greek word translated *epistle* is derived from the word *epistelo* which means *'to send to'*. That is why it can also be translated *message*. Therefore, this verse could read, "*You are our message sent to all men, written on our hearts, known and read by all.*" We in fact are individual 'living' messages, sent from the Author of Life to all men. And in a qualified sense, we are just as much 'one' with the Author (Jesus Christ).

For that reason, as we continue to abide in Him, we are just as permanent, as enduring, and as eternally fixed in God as Christ is. So, remember, we all have the same message written on our hearts (inscribed permanently by the power of the Holy Spirit), and this love-letter simply reads, *"For God so loved the world that He gave His only begotten Son, that whosoever believes in Him will not perish but have eternal life"* (John 3:16).

Each of us carries a communication that can have an effect on people for eternity! Why not let others see what is written on your heart with the blood of Jesus today! Let them see and read the message that God loves them as a father loves his child, and desires to take care of them day-by-day (from glory-to-glory).

Day 6

Blessed

μακάριος = *'makahrios'*
Blessed, exceedingly blessed and fortunate, favoured by God, privileged, envied, happy, elated

People with the qualities listed in the Beatitudes gain God's approval, and because God thinks well of them, they are *blessed.* Note, God's blessing is far broader and exceedingly more important than merely being happy! It all hinges on whether God thinks well of us or not. Quite simply, we are *blessed* because God is pleased with us!

Blessings are a result of God's response to our actions and attitudes. You will also notice that the second half of each Beatitude reveals what the blessing is; *"for they..."* or *"for theirs..."* Surely all eight of these qualities listed should be part of each of us, so each of us should share in all eight blessings. Just as each of the eight qualities provides us with a broad overview of our responsibilities, the eight blessings also give us insight into the privileges that come to us because we are meeting those responsibilities.

Our privileges (blessings) are only there because God is well-pleased with us. The main reason why we can be called *blessed* is because our Heavenly Father has seen something in you and me that has caused Him to be delighted. This day, God the Father will see something in you that will cause Him to rejoice and be glad. Acknowledge Him when He does that with praise and thanksgiving!

Day 7

Ask

αἰτέω = *'ehteho'*
To ask, request, petition, demand, beg, call for, crave, desire, require

If you are operating in faith it doesn't matter how many times you ask! Let's examine James 4:2, *"Yet you do not have because you do not ask."* A literal translation reads, *"You do not have what you want because you are not asking."* Notice, it does not say, *"Because you have not asked"* (singular). Rather, *"Because you do not ask; or, "Are not asking."* This suggests an ongoing request or petition.

Therefore, when you ask God for His abundant blessings, focus on the fact that He wants to do so much more for you, rather than letting your faith be determined by your circumstances. Remind yourself that God is not limited by your circumstances. If you are rich in faith, there are no limits to what God can accomplish for you!

Today, I'm going to join my faith with yours, and let's believe together that God is going to give you above and beyond what you ask from Him. So don't limit God in any way; His blessings are limitless and immeasurable.

Receive that blessing right now - in Jesus Name!

DAY 8

ABILITY

ἰσχύος = *'ischoos'*
Ability, force, strength, might, inherent personal capability

When our *abilities* are used in everyday situations for true service to God, it gives an added dimension to the word *purpose*; at which point, every one of us can experience fulfillment and joy.

Do you know that God the Father has already placed within you the 'attitudes' that will inspire you to develop the right 'attributes' that will bring Him glory? Do you know that God the Father has placed within you the 'talents' that can be molded into the right *abilities* that bring Him glory? And do you know that God the Father is constantly at work in you bringing about the fullness of both your intrinsic qualities and your personal *abilities*? But remember, you cannot do it in your own strength. You can do it only in His strength and supply. What's more, only God knows your true potential, and only God can help you fulfil it.

Therefore, throughout the day, try not to rely on your own strength, learn to depend entirely on the *ability*: the inherent personal proficiency that God has supplied through the power that is at work in you. *"Now to Him who is able to do exceedingly abundantly above all that we ask or think, according to the power that works in us"* (Ephesians 3:20). This power or *ability* (that is at work in you) will cause you to feel satisfied and be filled with joy.

DAY 9

WORRY

μεριμνᾶτε = *'merimnahte'*
To worry, be anxious, be troubled with cares, be distracted by worry, be nervous or tense, to carry a burden for the future,

The Greek word used here and translated *worry* is derived from another ancient Greek word that means, *'to divide into parts'*. Worry is something that divides our focus, something that causes us to be preoccupied with things that add stress and pressure to life. In Philippians 4:6 Paul recommends that we, *"Be anxious for nothing, but in everything by prayer and supplication, with thanksgiving, let your requests be made known to God."* Paul is urging his readers to break an established pattern of anxiety! He is probably speaking of imaginary troubles or phantom anxieties.

Therefore, he tells his readers to stop worrying, and not to be overtly anxious over anything; leaving them no exceptions! Note also, the language is as comprehensive as it can be: *"not... about anything, but in everything..."* No anxiety, real or potential, is excluded! From personal experience Paul had learned that "the way to be anxious about nothing was to be prayerful about everything."

You have an opportunity right now to stop the cycle of worry – the very thing that has been dividing your life into parts and causing you to be anxious. So, stop worrying and start praying!

DAY 10

QUICKEN

ζωοποιήσει = *'zohopeesi'*
To quicken, accelerate, hasten, stimulate, give life to, excite, arouse, rouse, stir up, activate, galvanize, inspire or kindle

Romans 8:11: *"But if the Spirit of Him who raised Jesus from the dead dwells in you, He who raised Christ from the dead will also give life to* (quicken) *your mortal bodies through His Spirit who dwells in you."* The Greek word translated *quicken* literally means "to infuse with new life." The same Spirit that resurrected Jesus Christ dwells in us, and that very same Spirit will also infuse with new life our mortal bodies. This is resurrection power at work in you and me; to equip us for every eventuality.

The resurrection of Jesus Christ is all about power and authority! The King rules and reigns, and He is seated at the right hand of God with His enemies under His feet. And because He has *new life*, we as joint-heirs have the very same privileges. If Jesus never rose from the dead there would be no victory to enjoy. His resurrection caused us to be more than conquerors. God's word tells us to know Christ and the power of His resurrection (Philippians 3:10).

The same power that resurrected Jesus from the dead is infusing your mortal body with the "God-kind-of-life." Yes, you can receive your healing today! Let your body be quickened with power!

Day 11

Perfect

τελέω = *'teleho'*

Perfect, to bring to a close, to finish, to end, to perform, execute, complete, fulfil, to bring to a successful conclusion, put the finishing touches to

2 Corinthians 12:9: ***He said to me, "My grace is sufficient for you, for My strength is made perfect in weakness."*** It's thought provoking to find the word *τελεῖται* (perfect) used because it literally means "to bring to an end" or "to bring to a close." Implying that the Lord's strength (*δύναμις*) requires our weaknesses and imperfections to be complete! Human weakness provides the opportunity for divine power to succeed. This is one of the most important lessons we can learn in life.

So, remember this: His strength comes to a successful conclusion in your weakness (literal translation) - resulting in His grace being manifested and magnified. When you are feeling weak in yourself, then you are in fact strong in the grace of Jesus Christ. Whenever you feel frail or fragile, you must go to Christ, receive strength from Him, and enjoy the abundant supply of divine strength and grace. The apostle Paul rejoiced in his weaknesses because he fully understood this principle.

God has you covered! Your success does not depend on your natural abilities but on God's *perfect* power working in and through you. Not just for today but every day!

Day 12

Hidden

κρύπτω = *'kripto'*
Hidden, to hide, to be hid, to escape notice, to conceal (that it may not become known)

God is *hidden* until He decides to reveal Himself to you (Matthew 11:25). He opens your mind by His Spirit, and changes your heart, and enlightens your understanding about Himself. The Son desires to reveal the Father in a special and personal way in which it will not always be the same. Paul's experience in Acts 9 on the Damascus road was far different than Lydia's conversion in Acts 16. The belief of some of the Jews on the day of Pentecost in Acts 2 was radically different than the outpouring upon Cornelius' house in Acts 10. The arguments about Paul's conversion, which had hardened Felix, almost convinced Agrippa to be saved.

God discloses Himself personally, uniquely and individually to each one of us. God shrouds Himself in a *hidden* place and reveals Himself only to those who the Son chooses to reveal Him to. God surrounds Himself in a cloud of glory and allows only His *elect* to enter in and see Him. Psalm 91:1, *"He who dwells in the secret* (hidden) *place of the Most High, shall abide under the shadow of the Almighty."*

God wants to reveal Himself to you today; He wants to interrupt your daily plans and cause His blessings to flow beyond measure!

Day 13

Leave

ἀφῆκες = *'ufikes'*
To leave alone, forsake, abandon, to let go or give up, to disregard, neglect

Revelation 2:4: *"Nevertheless, I have this against you, that you have left your first love."* The church at Ephesus had forgotten the most important aspect of a church. This may also mean they had bad attitudes, and that they were once enthusiastic but are now apathetic. Yet, more importantly, the love that they had for Christ, and for one another, had diminished. They had forsaken their first love. The Greek word *ἀφῆκες* can have a very strong meaning: "to abandon or disregard," as in abandoning a child. In this instance, we are told that their love was *let go, left out*, and *neglected*. It implies that their first love was severely disrespected! As we all know, love can sometimes grow faint.

The question this verse raises is... "Have I neglected my first love?" Do I love Jesus today as much as I did when I first met Him? And, what exactly does it mean to give up my first love? God defines love as the first and second greatest commandments. Therefore, if you leave your first love, you disrespect the most important of all God's commandments: "to love God with all your heart."

Why don't you examine your heart today, and make sure your love for God is as deep and as impassioned as it can be. You'll be blessed!

DAY 14

GUARD

φρουρήσει = *'froorehsi'*

To guard, protect by a military guard, either to prevent hostile invasion or to keep the inhabitants of a besieged city from flight

Philippians 4:7: *"And the peace of God, which surpasses all understanding, will guard your hearts and minds through Christ Jesus."* God's peace will protect our hearts and minds. God's peace, like a garrison of soldiers, will guard over our thoughts and feelings; making them as protected as a fortress against the evil assaults of anxiety, worry and fear. Let's take heart, because our deep emotions and inner feelings, that part of us which is often so vulnerable to attack by the enemy, is the very place that God's peace is being established. Like a battle-ready battalion of soldiers the *peace of God* will protect us!

How do you find supernatural peace? First, you trust the Lord with your everyday cares (the small things), and once you have practiced this daily, you will be able to trust Him with the major problems and concerns that come along. But you need to articulate your anxieties to Jesus all the time; and roll every care on to Him. This child-like trust opens the door to supernatural peace.

Remember, the peace of God is meant to *guard* and protect you from further attacks of anxiety and fear. And, it is God's will for you to abide in His wonderful peace. Today, trust Him and receive His peace!

DAY 15

FILLED

πληροῦσθε = *'pliroosthe'*

To be filled, to make full, to fill up, to fill to the full, to cause to abound, to furnish or supply liberally, to make complete

Ephesians 5:18: *"And do not be drunk with wine, in which is dissipation, but be filled with the Holy Spirit.* In the Greek, the verb *"be filled"* is in the imperative mode. That means the infilling of the Spirit isn't an optional part of the Christian life. Every Christian is to be *filled* with the Spirit all of the time. If you aren't, you are out of God's will. Also, the verb is in the 'present tense'. This insight is particularly helpful because the Greek present tense has the idea of continual action; you doing something that is ongoing. It's not a one-time event.

This sentence could easily be translated, *"Be continually filled with the Holy Spirit," or, "keep on being filled constantly and continually."* That is why the *filling* of the Spirit is not primarily a one-time experience. It's supposed to be the normal way of life for the Christian – a lifestyle!

Yes, you need to develop a lifestyle of being continuously filled with the Spirit of God. A fresh anointing for every circumstance. You probably need a fresh anointing right now! So, why not ask the Holt Spirit to fill you to overflowing? You will be amazed at His response. God will get all the glory and you will get all the benefits.

DAY 16

CONFIDENCE

παρρησίαν = *'parrisian'*
Confidence, boldness, cheerful courage, unreserved utterance, assertiveness, self-assurance, fearlessness, audacity, daring

Confidence is extremely important in almost every aspect of life, yet so many people struggle with it. Hebrews 10:35 says, *"Therefore do not throw away your confidence, which has a great reward."* The word *παρρησίαν* is literally "all speech" and it denotes "unreserved utterance" or "speaking boldly without fear." It is a difficult word to accurately translate into the English language. An expounded translation of this verse could read: "Do not throw away your unreserved boldness and fearless declaration of your faith, which has great reward." Your confidence must be rooted and grounded in faith, and as a result of that, you will be able to fearlessly and boldly declare God's word.

This is a faith exercise! You are openly told to hang on to the confidence you already have. The reason? If you do not hang on to your confidence, the rich rewards that are due will be hindered from getting to you. Simply put, don't through away what you already have! Use your faith and place complete trust in God's faithfulness. Decide today, to be confident and courageous in everything you say and do! And be encouraged by the fact that you will be richly rewarded for your efforts.

Day 17

Children

παιδιά = *'pehthia'*
A young child, a little boy or little girl, infants, children, little ones

Matthew 18:3: *"I tell you the truth, unless you change and become like little children, you will never enter the kingdom of heaven."* What did Jesus mean when He told us to become 'just like little children'? The word *παιδιά* (little children) is used, which does not mean "a babe in arms" or "a teenager." It is usually a small child, an infant maybe aged 4 to 6, therefore, *παιδιά* (little children) refers to kids who have not started any serious schooling so they spend much of the day playing and enjoying themselves. Bear in mind that becoming like a *little child* does not mean you revert to childhood or become childish.

Have you noticed how children find the time to ponder? It's wonderful to watch children as they ponder the beauties of the world; new animals, sunsets and night skies. We miss out on these wonders because we don't take the time to discover new things. Why don't you find the time today to contemplate the wonders of God's creation? All around you is evidence of His splendor!

One of the greatest gifts you can give yourself is time. Time to enjoy life like a little child; time to gaze upon the beauty of God's majestic handiwork. So take time out today to enjoy this gift!

Day 18

Abide

μένω = *'meno'* / ὑπομένω = *'iepomeno'*
To remain, abide, dwell, tarry, not to depart, to continue to be present, to continue to be, not to perish, to last, to endure

1 John 4:15: *"Whoever confesses that Jesus is the Son of God, God abides in Him, and he in God."* In the Modern Greek *"μένω"* (meno) means *to stay* or *remain.* However, in the New Testament it is usually translated *abide* or *dwell.* For this verse, the modern Greek translation is probably better because it denotes a permanent state within an intimate relationship: *"God stays (or remains) in you, and you in God."*

In its strengthened form *ἐπιμένω* implies a perseverance or tolerance in continuing or remaining. That being the case, God has chosen to persevere and be tolerant in order to remain (continue to be present) in you, and you in Him!

Be conscious of this special relationship. During every moment in every day, the Almighty God has chosen to remain with you, and be in you, no matter what! He perseveres to keep the promise, and His mercies endure forever. You may be going through some very challenging times, but He will never leave you or forsake you.

Take comfort in this knowledge, and never feel abandoned or lonely. God is ever-present in you, and you in God!

Day 19

Build

οἰκοδομέω = *'oikodomeo'*
To build a house, to erect something, to build up or edify

Matthew 7:24: *"Therefore whoever hears these sayings of Mine, and does them, I will liken him to a wise man who built his house on the rock."* Our lives are likened to a building that is built on a rock (the person of Jesus Christ), and the building materials can only be found in God's word. When our lives are built on the Word of God the storms of life cannot bring about any destruction. Remember, we are not intended to live a storm-free life, but rather a destruction-free life!

Concerning your spirituality, encouraging and edifying those around you is a key to operating in the Gifts of the Holy Spirit. In fact, unless what you say and do builds others up, you are not being spiritual, nor being led by the Holy Spirit. Love always builds, it never pulls down.

Make a concerted effort to encourage and edify everyone you come into contact with. Enrich the lives of others and your life will be enriched. This is the best practice for genuine self-improvement. And, you will feel it's benefits immediately!

Try it right now! Make sure you encourage and inspire someone today!

DAY 20

DAUGHTER

θυγάτηρ = *'thugatir'*

Natural or spiritual relationship, the acceptance and approval of God, descendants or posterity, inhabitants of a region

Daughter, in a sense, is the practical realization of acceptance with, and the approval of God Himself. It is clearly demonstrated by the way Jesus addressed the woman with the issue of blood. *"Daughter, be of good cheer; your faith has made you well. Go in peace"* (Luke 8:48). Here is a woman that was rejected, banished and severely ostracized by the entire community, yet, Jesus calls her "daughter!" How secure she must have felt. The sense of belonging, which she desired for so many years, was suddenly fully satisfied. At last, she felt accepted and truly loved.

If you have low self-esteem or lack confidence with others, you can take heart from this touching remark. In the past, you may have been spoken down to, excluded by those you had feelings for, or even shunned by family members. But Jesus will always look you in the eye and address you as daughter or son. This is a fully inclusive title. It represents total acceptance and complete approval. And Jesus strengthens this precious spiritual relationship every day. He intends to express His unconditional love for you - no matter what the circumstances, no matter how disappointed you may be feeling. Like the woman with the issue of blood, touch Him today!

Day 21

Enlighten

φωτίζω = '*photizo*'

To be enlightened or illuminated, to give light or shine, to make to see

Photizo, from *phos*, 'light' is used intransitively, and it signifies "to give light, to shine, or illuminate." Ephesians 1:18, talks metaphorically of spiritual enlightenment: *"I pray that the eyes of your heart may be enlightened, so that you will know what is the hope of His calling, what are the riches of the glory of His inheritance in the saints."* When the eyes of your heart are enlightened you will see what God sees. What's more, you will know what He wants you to do. The way the apostle Paul puts it is that you must have "the eyes of your hearts enlightened, that you may know." This may seem strange, but the heart does have eyes. Most people speak of "the heart" as nothing more than the blood-pumping organ in the chest. Yes, this *heart* is very real to us and necessary to keep us alive. But intuitively we know that there is more to us than flesh and bones.

That is why you must pray this way. You need to know (really know), the plans and purposes of God, and the only way this can happen is if you receive enlightenment through the heart. We all need clarity in our lives, and the only way to get this is to be *enlightened*. Pray that God's divine light shines into your heart today, conveying true clarity in all matters of life. Ask God to flood your heart with light!

Day 22

Kneel

γονυπετέω = '*gonupeteo*'
To bow the knees, to fall prostrate, to express reverence and honour

Gonupeteo denotes "to bow the knees, kneel," and "to fall prostrate." This word describes the act of one that is desperate for relief, as in Mark 1:40: ***And a leper came to Jesus, beseeching Him and falling on his knees before Him, and saying, "If You are willing, You can make me clean."*** But you don't have to be despairing to kneel before the Lord.

Kneeling before the Lord can reflect a state of hopelessness; however, it is far more beneficial to see it as an act of reverential worship. Reverence in worship signifies a spiritual attitude and disposition of your soul that, when entering into God's presence in worship, causes you to humble yourself in the sight of His majesty and glory. In fact, you are bowing down in your heart. Embracing such an attitude of reverence brings about a spiritual disposition of submission (from the heart), which causes you to kneel. The reality of who God is and who we are shapes all true worship. As a true worshipper, you can surrender and kneel before the King of Kings whenever you choose. This does not necessarily change your outward posture, although it sometimes can, it allows you to embrace the presence of God anywhere and at any time.

DAY 23

OBEDIENCE

ὑπακοή = '*hupakoe*'
To obey, obedience of faith, fulfilment of God's commands

Romans 1:5 talks about the "obedience of faith." Since faith is one of the main subjects of the Book of Romans, it is therefore the primary act of obedience in the new life that brings about spiritual maturity. Obedience of faith however, must be accompanied by obedience to the truth. It is pointless knowing the truth without obeying the truth. This is the only way to true freedom and liberty.

When it comes to obedience there is no greater example than the Lord Jesus Christ. As children of God, we ought to obey our Father in heaven as Jesus obeyed His Father in heaven. We are called to live a life of obedience by carefully following God's commands, by setting our hearts on God's word, and by walking in God's ways. More than anything else, our obedience is what matters most to God. Remember, "Obedience is far better than sacrifice". When King Saul disobeyed God, this is what the Prophet Samuel said to him in 1 Samuel 15:22: *"Does the Lord delight in burnt offerings and sacrifices as much as in obeying the voice of the Lord? Obedience is better than sacrifice."*

Today, you can choose to be obedient to God's word, and please your Heavenly Father, or choose to make sacrifices that He doesn't receive. The way to God's heart is to obey His instructions - very moment of every day!

Day 24

Abba

Ἀββᾶ = '*abba*'
The unquestioning trust of a child, confidence framed by the lips of infants

Abba is an Aramaic word found in Romans 8:15: *"For you did not receive the spirit of bondage again to fear, but you received the Spirit of adoption by whom we cry out, 'Abba, Father'."* Abba Father is the only One who personally and intimately knows your greatest strengths and weaknesses. This is the main reason why you should view God as Abba (Daddy) every day of your life. Abba, as conveyed through Jesus and Paul, reveals a profound understanding that God knows you infinitely better than you know yourself.

Accepting that God knows everything about you (past, present and future), and is never unsettled by what you may think, say or do, will provoke an extraordinary level of security. You will feel secure in every aspect of life; in family matters, in your business affairs, and in service to God. Mostly, you will feel secure in your relationships.

Being reassured in your relationships truly enriches your life because stressful relationships can become toxic. When you turn to Abba Father and take shelter under the shadow of His wings, you will always feel loved, cared for and secure. So, always turn to the One who knows you better than you know yourself!

DAY 25

ALMIGHTY

παντοκράτωρ = '*pantokrator*'
Always powerful, forever ruler of all, holding all strength or power eternally

In 2 Corinthians 6:18 we hear God declare: *"I will be a Father to you, and you shall be My sons and daughters," says the Lord Almighty.* God's omnipotence, His all-powerfulness as El Shaddai, (Almighty God), is a predominant theme of the Bible. All of the heroes we read about, at some time or other, have faced impossible situations. Yet, God comes up with the answer every time. Why? Because He is the omnipotent God, the Supreme Ruler of heaven and earth. Remember this: God is always in control. Should He choose, He can exercise absolute authority over very circumstance. After all, He alone is the Almighty: "forever holding all strength and power in His hands!"

When you have revelation of the eternally powerful Person who has chosen to represent you in challenging times, you can never contemplate or embrace thoughts of defeat. For, if God be for you who can be against you (Romans 8:31). And greater is He who is in you than he who is in your circumstances (1 John 4:4).

Make a positive confession today, say to yourself: "I am more than a conqueror, through Christ who loves me" (Romans 8:37); "and I have a heavenly Father who is also God the Almighty."

DAY 26

BURDEN

βάρος = '*varos*'
A weight or anything pressing on one physically, something heavy or burdensome

2 Corinthians 4:17: *"For our light affliction, which is but for a moment, is working for us a far more exceeding and eternal weight of glory."* Whatever you may be suffering right now is working for you and is subject to change. Yet, when compared to the exceeding weight of the glory which is to come, it should be considered a light affliction.

Nevertheless, there are burdens that we cannot avoid. Often the burdens and stresses of life cause you to feel like a weight is pressing down on you physically. Anxiety feels like a big load has been placed on your chest. These are signs that you need someone to lift the weight off you. Someone to remove the burdens that you are unable to cope with, burdens that are holding you back. Jesus came to do exactly that! He is the burden lifter; He is the burden carrier. All you have to do is role your cares onto Him, because He cares for you (1 Peter 5:7).

Jesus has already sent out this invitation: *"Come to Me, all you who labour and are heavy burdened, and I will give you rest"* (Matthew 11:28). This tender offer is directed specifically at anyone who is carrying burdens. If that's you, accept His invitation and come to Him today. Jesus really cares for you!

DAY 27

DELAY

χρονίζω = 'chronizo'
To delay and waste time, to linger or procrastinate

Chronizo literally means "to while away time," that is, by way of lingering, tarrying, delaying. Hebrews 10:36-37: *For you have need of endurance, so that after you have done the will of God, you may receive the promise: "For yet a little while, and He who is coming will come and will not delay. Now the just shall live by faith; but if anyone draws back, My soul has no pleasure in him."* Notice, there is a direct correlation between faith and endurance, but what hinders you from receiving the promise is "drawing back" or "procrastinating." Why? Because wasting time or hesitating is displeasing to God.

Faith is active and decisive! Faith believes and then receives! It never waists time thinking about the "what if's." God does not procrastinate therefore, He expects the same from you. The Lord has already provided specific 'covenant' promises that can be applied to your life today. God Almighty has given you immediate and unlimited access to His promises, and by exercising your faith right now you can receive them.

Don't delay any longer, receive the promise that God has put aside for you today. He wants you to prosper in all matters of life, and be in good health, just as your soul prospers (3 John 1:2).

Day 28

Double Minded

δίψυχος = *'thixichos'*
To have two souls, to be double minded

James 1:6-8: *"But let him ask in faith, with no doubting, for he who doubts is like a wave of the sea driven and tossed by the wind. For let not that man suppose that he will receive anything from the Lord; he is a double-minded man, unstable in all his ways."* The term double-minded comes from the Greek word meaning "a person with two minds or souls." It's interesting that this word appears only in the book of James (James 1:8; 4:8). Bible scholars conclude that James might have coined this word from a secular term.

In this passage, James says a doubting person is like a wave of the sea, blown and tossed by the wind. Such a man should not think he will receive anything from the Lord because he is *double-minded* and unstable in all he does. Clearly, doubter is a double-minded person. In addition, a doubter cannot expect to receive anything – yes anything – from God. But it's the other characteristic that you should be aware of. A person who has two-minds is also a person who is unstable in all his ways (not just some of his ways).

Instability in one area is bad enough, but instability across all areas is tragic and needs to be avoided. The remedy is quite simple, you need to ask in faith! Practice this daily and you'll be blessed.

DAY 29

EDIFY

οἰκοδομέω = *'oikodomeo'*
To edify, to build a house, to cause or promote spiritual growth, to help to develop spiritual character

This word usually means *to build*, whether literally or figuratively. In 1 Peter 2:7 it is used metaphorically, in the sense of *edifying*. That is, promoting the spiritual growth and development of character in believers (by teaching or by example), suggesting that such a spiritual progress is as the result of patient labour.

Edification is said to have a serious effect upon local churches, Acts 9:31: *"So the church throughout all Judea and Galilee and Samaria enjoyed peace, being built up* (edified)*; and going on in the fear of the Lord and in the comfort of the Holy Spirit, it continued to increase."* If you want to be a real asset to your church, help people to grow spiritually. Build them up with your words. Become an essential and crucial part of people's lives by promoting their spiritual growth and the development of Christian character.

One of the greatest privileges you have as a Christian is to be able to build or *edify* those people you come into contact with daily. What an amazing opportunity for Christ to manifest His character through you! Each day, you are given a chance to improve the lives of those around you. So, don't be careless or inconsiderate, help build their lives brick by brick. To God's glory!

DAY 30

EYE

ὀφθαλμός = *'ophthalmos'*
Physical eye, sight, sharpness, mental vision, singleness of motive

Ophthalmos is similar to *sight*, and it's probably derived from a root word signifying *sharpness*. 1 Corinthians 2:9: ***But as it is written: "Eye has not seen, nor ear heard, nor have entered into the heart of man, the things which God has prepared for those who love Him."***

Here Paul writes about the truths of the Mystery that has been revealed to those who love the Lord in this dispensation of grace. "The things which God hath prepared for them that love Him" were not seen nor heard in the past, and they never "entered into the heart of man" because they were "hidden in God" (Ephesians 3:9). Hence, they were never before divulged. But Paul writes in the next verse in 1 Corinthians 2:10: ***"But God has revealed them to us by His Spirit."*** Subsequently, the Mystery has been fully revealed! You can now see and know the things God has prepared for you.

Are they truly astonishing? Yes! Are they truly overwhelming? Yes! Can you truly grasp the things that God has made ready just for you? Yes! Through prayer and meditation on God's word, you are able to see and know exactly what God has put aside for you. What's more, the Holy Spirit is fully committed to revealing these things. Hallelujah!

DAY 31

IMPOSSIBLE

ἀδύνατος = '*athunatos*'
Impossible, without strength, inability, impotent, powerless, weakness

Athunatos is used of things that are "impossible." But with God nothing will be impossible, Luke 1:36-37: *"Now indeed, Elizabeth your relative has also conceived a son in her old age; and this is now the sixth month for her who was called barren. For with God nothing will be impossible."* Let me ask you something: "How have you reacted to such an admission of God's supremacy?" That with God nothing will be impossible? If God were to supernaturally confirm this truth in your negative circumstances right now, would your reaction be to try and reason it out? The truth is, if you really believe that "with God nothing will be impossible," you will simply say, "God said it and that settles it!"

My prayer for you today is very simply, I pray that you will have such an overwhelming encounter with God "in the Spirit" that all your questions, queries, doubts and fears will be silenced; and that you will accept and be at peace with the truth which declares, "with God all things are possible!"

Abiding in this marvelous truth changes everything! If nothing is impossible with God, then nothing you are trusting Him for is impossible! So, step into the realm of the impossible today!

DAY 32

OFFSPRING

γένος = '*genos*'
Offspring, countrymen, family, race, nation, generation

Genos is akin to *ginomai*, "to become," and denotes "a family," "a race" or "an offspring." Acts 17:28: *"For in Him we live and move and exist, as even some of your own poets have said, 'For we also are His offspring'."* You are God's legitimate offspring. In 1 Peter 2:9 this word it is translated *generation*: *"But you are a chosen generation, a royal priesthood, a holy nation, a people for God's own possession."* The word "generation" in this verse of scripture is derived from the root-word "gene." A gene is the basic unit of heredity in any living organism. Genes hold the information that build and maintain an organism's cells, and pass genetic traits from parent to offspring. They determine the physical, mental, and other characteristics an individual inherits from his parents.

When God describes you as "a chosen generation," He means that you belong to a new class of conquerors – a people made up of divine genetic material. Romans 8:37 says we are "more than conquerors," meaning your lineage is one of champions and victors. No generational curse, sickness, or disease can work against you, or destroy you, because you are a new creation. You have new genes that came straight from your heavenly Father. Remind yourself of this and praise Him for the victory!

Day 33

Name

ὄνομα = '*onoma*'
Name, surname, representing authority, character, rank, majesty, power, excellence

In Philippians 2:9-11, *onoma* represents the 'dignity' and 'name' of our Lord Jesus: *"God also has highly exalted Him and given Him the name which is above every name, that at the name of Jesus every knee should bow, of those in heaven, and of those on earth, and of those under the earth, and that every tongue should confess that Jesus Christ is Lord, to the glory of God the Father."*

There is no greater name than the name of Jesus. Using the name of Jesus brings with it many blessings. When you pray in His name you can be quite sure that your heavenly Father will hear and answer you, because Jesus has asked you to pray that way. There is mighty power and great authority in the name of Jesus. It is through Him, and only through the power of His name, that you can deal with the demonic forces that confront you.

Your Saviour wants you to have His name on your lips all the time. That way, you will be able to live the super-abundant life He secured for you (John 10:10). Using the name of Jesus brings with it many victories. Speak it boldly right now, and see your wicked opponent (the devil) bow his knee!

Day 34

Only Begotten

μονογενής = '*monogenes*'
The one and only Son

Monogenes is used five times, all in the writings of the Apostle John. John 1:14, indicates that as the Son of God, Jesus was the sole representative and exact representation of the One who sent Him: *"And the Word became flesh, and dwelt among us, and we saw His glory, glory as of the only begotten from the Father, full of grace and truth."* Here, John's intention is to demonstrate what sort of *glory* it was that he and his fellow Apostles had seen. In the phrase "only begotten" it is the word *only*; expressing exclusivity, which should be emphasised. Jesus has a matchless relationship with God the Father. There is no other like Him.

The Hebrew writer distinguishes Jesus from angels and then quotes, *"But to the Son He says, 'Your throne, O God, is for ever and ever'"* (Hebrews 1:8). Notice that God Himself addresses His Son as God. No other son can ever be addressed as God. Reading on from that last quote, we come to another, along similar lines: *"You Lord, in the beginning laid the foundation of the earth."* (Hebrews 1:10). Here, God addresses His Son as Lord! The only begotten Son, *the One and only*, He is Lord and He is God!

To have an effectual relationship with Jesus Christ you must acknowledge this fact before heaven and earth.

Day 35

Need

χρεία = '*chreia*'
To have need of, to have need, to be needful,
to supply that which is needed

Chreia signifies, there is a need or to have need of. In Philippians 4:19 this word suggests 'every need of yours': *"And my God shall supply all your need according to His riches in glory by Christ Jesus."* Listen again to this incredible promise, "My God shall supply all of your need!" That includes every single essential necessity you may have need of.

Here is one of the greatest promises of God, a promise that's probably been repeated most often. Fundamentally, this covenant guarantee states that God will meet every single one of your needs. How awesome is that! It's such an *all-inclusive* pledge that every other promise of God fits under this umbrella!

If you have any need today, reach out into the supernatural and draw down on this promise. Your allocation is there! And it can never run dry. God's supernatural super-abundance is always in rich supply.

Just as a river flows into the sea, allow the unending supply of God's blessing flow into your life from day to day.

DAY 36

BEAUTIFUL

ὡραῖος = '*horaios*'

A season or time when something is at its loveliest, outside purity

Romans 10:15: *"How beautiful are the feet of those who preach the gospel of peace, who bring glad tidings of good things!"* This word describes "that which is seasonable, or produced at the right time," as of the prime of life, or the time when anything is at its loveliest and best. Likened to a flower in full bloom. In Genesis, beauty refers to all the trees in the garden of Eden, and especially to the tree of the knowledge of good and evil. Everything that God has created is in fact beautiful! Yet, the loveliest sight are the feet of those who preach the gospel of peace and spread the good news.

Every time you decide to convey the good news to someone, your feet are considered beautiful. Why is that? Feet represent that part of our anatomy which carry us to our destination. They are transporters of everything we say and do! Therefore, whenever our feet are being used to transport the good news of the gospel of our Lord Jesus Christ, in God's eyes they are beautiful.

In God's eyes, the bearers of good news are beautiful! Make sure you are as beautiful as can be - adorn yourself with the gospel.

Day 37

Accuser

διάβολος = '*diabolos*'
Someone who claims that another has committed an offence or done something wrong

Revelation 12:10: *Then I heard a loud voice saying in heaven, "Now salvation, and strength, and the kingdom of our God, and the power of His Christ have come, for the accuser of our brethren, who accused them before our God day and night, has been cast down."* The devil may be busy doing a lot of things, but he is always busy accusing the brethren. He has certainly learnt how to attack. He attacks our heart and our conscience, and he can really disturb us. That is his main intention. And his weapons are mostly accusations. Notice how He not only accuses us before man, but he accuses us before God.

A major cause of problems among believers today is unproven accusations, and people in church feeling free to make them. In fact, believers are doing the work of the devil. They have become 'comrades' of the forces of evil. If you've ever been accused of wrongdoing by a brother or sister in Christ, you will know exactly what I'm talking about. But I want to encourage you to see it as it really is. The devil is the accuser. All that has happened is he has found a voice which he can use to spread his lies. If you respond to his accusations you give them a platform and breathe life into them. Resist the devil and he will flee from you, and God will vindicate you every time.

DAY 38

AUTHOR

αἴτιος = '*aitios*'
That which causes something to come about,
the personal and definitive cause

In Hebrews 12:2, Christ is called the "Author and Perfecter of our faith." He is represented as the one who takes precedence in faith and is thus the perfect example of it: *"Looking unto Jesus, the author and finisher of our faith, who for the joy that was set before Him endured the cross, despising the shame, and has sat down at the right hand of the throne of God."* Christ is not merely the legitimate source of our faith, He is the concrete and active cause of it – the Author. He has not only caused our faith to come about, He is (as His name "Jesus" implies), our faith itself.

Jesus Christ is the Prince of life, "the life He had was not from another; the Prince or Author of life must be He who has life from Himself." But the Greek word combines the idea of the source or originating cause with that of a great leader. As the "Author and Perfecter of faith," Jesus is represented as the One who takes precedence in faith but is yet the perfect example of it. If you want to see faith, gaze upon Jesus.

When you acknowledge Jesus as the author and finisher of your faith, you acknowledge the victory He established on the cross. When you gaze upon His face, your faith increases in all areas.

DAY 39

BREAD

ἄρτος = '*artos*'
Bread of any kind, a small loaf or cake, a loaf of presentation, sustenance for life

Acts 2:42: *"And they continued steadfastly in the apostles' doctrine and fellowship, in the breaking of bread, and in prayers."* Bread represents a basic necessity for life. Throughout history people consumed it as part of a stable diet. For most it was a sustenance for life. But Jesus said that we should not live by bread alone, but by every word that proceeds out of the mouth of God (Luke 4:4). Implying that spiritual food is far more beneficial.

As a Christian, you have "bread" that will do you infinitely more good. The Word of God, and the Body of the Lord Jesus Christ are both "bread for life." Therefore, you must partake of a good measure of such bread in your daily diet. Study the Word and you will hear God's voice, and when you have heard His voice your faith surges. *"Faith comes by hearing and hearing by the word of God"* (Romans 10:17). Eat a good portion of the Word every day and you will develop enough faith to receive miracles!

I also recommend that you partake of communion as often as possible. When you remember that Christ's body was broken so that your body may be whole, healing is released, and the Lord is glorified. Consume the bread and wine today to secure your future.

DAY 40

CHEERFUL

εὐθυμέω = '*euthumeo*'
To be cheerful, to put in good spirits, to make passionately cheerful, to take heart, be merry or joyous

"For there stood by me this night an angel of the God to whom I belong and whom I serve, saying, 'Do not be afraid, Paul; you must be brought before Caesar; and indeed God has granted you all those who sail with you.' Therefore, take heart (be cheerful), *men, for I believe God that it will be just as it was told me"* (Acts 27:23-25). The apostle Paul told the sailors to cheer up!

The Greek word signifies, "to put in good spirits," "to make cheerful." Have you cheered someone up today? Have you put someone in good spirits? We need more Christians to take on this vital ministry, to take a sad heart and make it merry! This is the will of God for His people. The Gospel is good news and therefore it brings joy. Every time God communicates His plan and purposes for your life, there is good reason to be cheerful – to be in good spirits! And it's important for you to be in good spirits first, so that you can make others passionately cheerful and merry.

I pray you take on this essential service to those around you. For when you focus on bringing joy into the lives of others, your life will be flooded with joy inexpressible and boundless blessings.

DAY 41

AMAZEMENT

ἔκστασις = '*ekstasis*'
A visible standing out, a demonstration of great wonder, falling into a trance

"After three days, they found Jesus in the temple courts, sitting among the teachers, listening to them and asking them questions. Everyone who heard Him was amazed at His understanding and His answers" (Luke 2:46-47). According to this account, the boy Jesus ends up in the temple instead of heading home with his family after the Passover. Here is probably the only boyhood story about Jesus. In this snapshot of His early life we hear how the scribes, the teachers and the other people present were *amazed* at His understanding of scripture.

Whatever the truth about Jesus as a child growing up, or Him becoming a man, or the ministry He stepped into, we can't but be truly amazed! Jesus was, and is, truly amazing! Using the literal translation of the Greek word, we should be in "ecstasy" every time we encounter Him!

Stop looking elsewhere to be astounded, to become ecstatic, for the presence of Jesus will never disappoint.

Embrace Him today, worship His majesty, and behold His glory. No one can compare to Him!

Day 42

Behold

βλέπω = '*vlepo*'
To see or perceive, to observe, a mental vision, to take notice, mindfulness

"But we all, with unveiled face, beholding as in a mirror the glory of the Lord, are being transformed into the same image from glory to glory, just as by the Spirit of the Lord" (2 Corinthians 3:18). This Greek word is used both of bodily and mental vision. It can mean to gaze upon, but yet to perceive. To behold the glory of the Lord is an absolute necessity to the fulfilment of the plans and purposes of God. But more importantly, the need to continue the transformation of every Christian into the exact image of Jesus Christ.

Our verse says, "*into the same image from glory to glory.*" This is an ongoing process! And notice, you become what you behold! Literally, you become what you gaze upon. The transformation only takes place when you *see* (βλέπω) the glory. The glory represents who the Lord is and what He does. When you see His glory, you are gazing upon all His divine attributes.

The good news is this: as you observe these divine characteristics, you mature to become exactly like them, going from glory to glory. For this very reason, the veil that obstructed your development has been removed. Now, you may be more like Jesus.

DAY 43

CHERISH

θάλπω = '*thalpo*'
To cherish with tender love, to foster with tender care, to soften with heat, to keep warm

Luke 13:34: *"How often I wanted to gather your children together, as a hen gathers her brood under her wings, but you were not willing!"* '*Thalpo*' primarily means "to heat, to soften by heat" or "to keep warm," as of birds covering their young with their feathers. In Psalm 91, God the Father is likened to a hen gathering her offspring under her wings. Looking out over Jerusalem, Jesus too wanted to gather His people like a hen gathers her chicks.

If you are feeling alone, isolated or destitute, the good news is that both God the Father and Jesus Christ want to put their arms around you (with tender loving care), and keep you warm. They want to make a fuss of you because they cherish you!

So often we look in the wrong places for comfort and warmth. The tender love that only God can provide is never far away. If you are willing, He will gather you and surround you with His divine presence. It's a place of rest and peace. It's a place where no evil can come near you. It's a place where God demonstrates His great love in a practical way.

You are the apple of God's eye; you are His valued treasure!

DAY 44

ENCOURAGEMENT

παραμυθέομαι = *'paramutheomai'*
To encourage, give counsel or advice, to comfort, to reassure

1 Thessalonians 2:11: *"Just as you know how we were exhorting and encouraging and imploring each one of you as a father would his own children."* In a society that is focused on *self* it is imperative that we inspire and encourage each other daily. This, I genuinely believe, is an absolute necessity.

Barnabas was called the great encourager. If the lost are going to find us appealing, we need far more Christians to operate in the ministry of encouragement. The best way to encourage someone is to show them that you care; to be genuinely interested and take the time to learn more about them. In the world system, most people find it hard to remember anything about you after you've gone. It's the "love the one you're with" mindset. But the Bible says, *"Let this mind be in you which was in Christ Jesus"* (Philippians 2:5). The attitude that Jesus had toward others is the only attitude we should adopt. And He was always a great encouragement to others!

Our opening verse implies that you should consider others as a father would consider his own children – urging, encouraging and spurring them on to greatness. For God has planted the seed of greatness in every one of us. You are destined for greatness!

Day 45

Inheritance

κληρονομέω = '*kleronomeo*'

An inheritance, to receive as one's own, to obtain by virtue of birth right, that which is received as a gift, the reward of faith

This verb is used to describe that which you receive through faith and patience, in contrast with that which is received as your reward, Hebrews 6:11-12 ('through experiences that called for you to exercise of faith and patience'): *"And we desire that each one of you show the same diligence to the full assurance of hope until the end, that you do not become sluggish, but imitate those who through faith and patience inherit the promises."*

You inherit (receive as your own) the promises of God through faith and patience. But you are warned not to become sluggish. The Hebrews writer criticized the spiritual condition of these believers, calling them "dull of hearing." The Greek term used there, *nōthroi*, and it is exactly the same word used in this verse to warn against becoming sluggish. The same general idea applies to both, which is laziness; a lack of effort or concern.

If you are to inherit the promises of God, you must guard yourself against becoming sluggish (displaying little concern or putting in little effort). You only inherit through faith, which is active, and patience, which requires real effort. Don't fall into this trap, rather, be diligent and exercise your faith with endurance.

Day 46

Journey

ὁδός = *'hothos'*
Trip, journey, voyage, a way, path or road

Hothos means "a way, a path or road," and is used of a traveler's way, hence, "a journey." Luke 11:5-6 talks of a friend who is on a journey and visits at midnight: *And He said to them, "Which of you shall have a friend, and go to him at midnight and say to him, 'Friend, lend me three loaves; for a friend of mine has come to me on his journey, and I have nothing to set before him."* What we learn from this story is that friends' paths will cross when there is a need, and occasionally at the most inconvenient time.

But also, when we cannot supply a need, our persistence toward another friend will get us what we want. There are two ways of explaining this story... The first is that friends ought to care for each other enough to go out of their way. And second, throughout Luke 11 Jesus is revealing God as Father. Here Jesus highlights the confidence we should have within that relationship. A son would not have a problem waking his father up in the middle of the night when there is a need. What's more, he would be persistent with it!

There are times when you may feel like you've been on a long journey, and now, it's the middle of the night and you have serious needs. Well, this is the time when you should go to the Father, in the darkness of night, and persistently ask for help. Do it right now!

DAY 47

KISS

φίλημα = '*philema*'
A kiss, a kiss of love, a holy kiss, an embrace

Philema means "a kiss." In the early church, it was a token of Christian brotherhood, whether by way of welcome or farewell, "a holy kiss." Romans 16:16: *"Greet one another with a holy kiss. All the churches of Christ greet you."* 1 Peter 5:14: *"Greet one another with a kiss of love. Peace be to you all who are in Christ."* There was to be an absence of formality and hypocrisy, a freedom from prejudice arising from social distinctions, from discrimination against the poor, and from partiality towards the well-to-do. What an amazing practice! A simple kiss was able to deal with all these social discriminations.

In the churches masters and servants would salute one another without any attitude of condescension on the one part or disrespect on the other. This *greeting* also took place between persons of the same sex. In the 4th century, A.D., there was a custom whereby men sat on one side of the room where a meeting was held, and women on the other side of the room (as is frequently the case still in parts of Europe and Asia), and the men are asked to salute the men, and the women, with "the kiss of the Lord."

Why don't you try practicing it? Greet others with a *holy kiss*. Be sure it's a *holy kiss* and God will bless you every time.

Day 48

Hand

χείρ = '*cheir*'
Hand, by the action of, at the hand of

Cheiri 'the hand' is used in the biblical phrases, "by the hand of," "at the hand of," etc., to signify "by the agency of." Acts 5:12: *"At the hands of the apostles many signs and wonders were taking place among the people; and they were all with one accord in Solomon's porch."* And in Acts 14:3: *"They spent a long time there speaking boldly with reliance upon the Lord, who was testifying to the word of His grace, granting that signs and wonders be done by their hands."*

Hands are instruments through which the miracle working power of God flows. Exceptional signs and wonders are as a result of hands being used. Notice, the supernatural power of God is released through human hands. God places His hand on you, so that you can place your hand on those in need.

Today, someone you will meet has a need that only the laying on of hands will satisfy. If you are not obedient to the Spirit of God, that person may not receive their miracle. Just as miracles were done by the hands of the apostles, so too does God want to anoint your hands. He wishes to bring healing and deliverance to anyone that's oppressed by the devil. Remember, Jesus Himself went about healing all who were oppressed of the devil (Acts 10:38).

DAY 49

DESPAIR

ἐξαπορέω = '*exaporeo*'
To be completely lost and without a way out

2 Corinthians 4:8: *"We are hard-pressed on every side, yet not crushed; we are perplexed, but not in despair."* *Exaporeo* means "to be utterly without a way." That is, "to be at a loss, or without resource." I am sure we have all been in despair at some time or other. I'm sure there have been times when we have felt completely adrift, and periods when there was no understandable way out of our situation. But if God be for you, who can be against you! For greater is He who is in you than he who is in the world (the present-day circumstances).

It's interesting how the apostle Paul phrases this statement: "We are hard-pressed (struggling and stressed) on every side, yet not crushed." If you are being harassed and besieged on every side - take heart! What God said to Joshua, He is saying to you: *"Be strong and of good courage; do not be afraid, nor be dismayed, for the Lord your God is with you wherever you go"* (Joshua 1:9).

If you feel perplexed and confused, don't let your mind lead you into despair. Hold every thought captive and make it obedient to Christ (2 Corinthians 10:5). You have the victory. You have overcome. Because, everywhere you go, the Lord your God is with you.

DAY 50

ATTAIN

καταντάω = '*katantao*'
To reach or arrive at, to come opposite to, to succeed in achieving, the fulfilment of a promise

In Ephesians 4:13, it speaks of *attaining* to the unity of the faith and of the knowledge of the Son of God: *"Till we all come to (attain) the unity of the faith and of the knowledge of the Son of God, to a perfect man, to the measure of the stature of the fullness of Christ."* In its metaphorical sense of *attaining* to something, this word is used in the Book of Acts in reference to the fulfilment of the promise of God made to the ancestors of Israel - to which promise the twelve tribes "hope to attain."

As we have read, the word is used of "attaining" to the unity of the faith and of the knowledge of the Son of God. Therefore, attaining is part of the destiny of every Christian. It is the fulfilment of God's covenant promises. It is very important that you understand this principle. When you arrive at any promise of God, you come to attain (receive) that promise. The promise pertaining to your need is already active, and it belongs to you! When you choose to attain every promise that is rightfully yours everything changes for the better. It's like entering your promised land.

Until you occupy and take possession of it, it will not become yours. So, do that today, take ownership of God's promises.

Day 51

Amen

ἀμήν = '*amen*'
Let God say so, let God do so, it is and it shall be so, so let it be, so be it

2 Corinthians 1:20: *"For all the promises of God in Him are Yes, and in Him Amen, to the glory of God through us."* Amen is transliterated from Hebrew into both Greek and English. The early Christian churches followed the example of Israel in associating themselves audibly with the prayers and thanksgivings offered on their behalf, as in 1 Corinthians 14:16, where the emphasis 'the' points to a common practice. Moreover, this custom conforms to the pattern of things in the Heavenlies. An individual also said *Amen* to express his *"let it be so"* in response to the Divine *"so it shall be."* The Lord Jesus often used *Amen*, translated *verily*, to introduce new revelations of the mind of God.

Personally, I prefer the meaning, "let God say so," or "let God do so." Therefore, each time I say *Amen*, I expect God to agree with me, or to do something on my behalf. Try it! You will be amazed at the outcome. Whenever you agree with God, and He in turn agrees with you, the forces of heaven are unleashed. *Amen* should not be employed in a '*whatever will be will be*' routine. Amen is intended to agree first with God's word, and then with any request being expressed vocally. Therefore, be careful not to say Amen to anything and everything.

Say, Amen to His word!

DAY 52

CHRIST

Χριστός = '*christos*'
God's anointed, the Messiah, the anointed of the Lord

Mark 8:29: *He said to them, "But who do you say that I am?" Peter answered and said to Him "You are the Christ." Christos* translates "anointed," a term applied to the priests who were anointed with the holy oil, particularly the high priest. The prophets are called *hoi christoi Theou*, "the anointed of God." Any king of Israel was described upon occasion as *christos tou Kuriou*, "the anointed of the Lord." But Jesus was anointed beyond measure. No one has ever carried the anointing to that degree. Jesus alone is the Christ; the Messiah.

Christos is also used to signify the One who by His Holy Spirit and power dwells in believers and shapes their character in total conformity to His likeness. This is why you are called a Christian! Whenever you declare that you are a Christian, you are essentially affirming a spiritual truth. That is, the Christ in you, the hope of glory, has equipped you to do exactly what He would do if He were present. In fact, you are representing Christ (God's anointed) in the fullest and most tangible way.

Think about this... Today, the Christ has limited Himself to you. He has entrusted you with the very things He wants to do, and would do, if He was here standing beside you. So, let Christ be!

Day 53

Anointing

ἀλείφω = '*aleipho*'
A physical refreshment after washing, to pour oil on, to smear or rub with oil, to empower

Acts 10:38: *"How God anointed Jesus of Nazareth with the Holy Spirit and with power, who went about doing good and healing all who were oppressed by the devil, for God was with Him." Aleipho* is a general term used for "an anointing" of any kind, whether of physical refreshment after washing or ceremonial cleansing. The material used was either oil, or ointment. Anointing oil, is mentioned 20 times in the Old Testament, it was used for pouring on the head of the high priest and his descendants and sprinkling the tabernacle and its furnishings to mark them as holy and set apart to the Lord.

As Christians, we have the Spirit who leads us into all truth and "anoints" us continually with His grace and comfort. *"But you have an anointing from the Holy One, and all of you know the truth"* (1 John 2:20). In the New Testament, the Holy Spirit is revealed as The Anointing. He is the Person of the Anointing. When you *know* Him and have a close relationship with Him you will be able to operate in the Gifts of the Holy Spirit.

Spend quality time every day with the Holy Spirit, and ask Him to anoint you for every task you do in the service of God.

Day 54

Become

πρέπω = '*prepo*'
To be conspicuous among a number, to be eminent, distinguished or fitting, suited to a sacred character

Hebrews 7:26: *"For such a High Priest was fitting for us, who is holy, harmless, undefiled, separate from sinners, and has become higher than the heavens."* Generally, this word means being suited to a sacred character, that which is befitting in persons, and actions or things consecrated to God. Our High Priest Jesus is holy, harmless, undefiled, separate from sinners, and has become higher than the heavens. He is conspicuous among men, eminent and distinguished in all the earth. He alone is fully suited to sacred character. There is no one like Him!

What Jesus has become can never be attained by any other. Yet, what He has become, we too can become. We share in everything that Christ was given. Yes, we have become joint-heirs with Him. You need to remind yourself of the truth as often as possible. Why? Because one of the devil's primary strategies is to have you believe that you are nothing, and therefore, of no value. If you have low self-esteem, you have fallen into the devil's trap. For the truth is, what Jesus has become you have become! In Him you live, and move, and have your being (Acts 17:28). The original Greek reads: "In Him, we live, and move, and are." In Christ is who you really *are*!

Day 55

Blameless

ἄμωμος = '*amomos*'
To be without blame, to be faultless, to be without blemish, blameless in character and conduct

Philippians 2:15: *"That you may become blameless and harmless, children of God without blemish in the midst of a crooked and perverse generation, among whom you shine as lights in the world."* The will of God is that you may become blameless, so that you can shine as a light in the world. Jesus chose to be faultless and without blame before the foundations of the world. It was a choice that He made. He was blameless in character and conduct, and we all need to make the same choice every day. It is a choice that only we as individuals can make.

No one can become blameless for you. No one can develop a pure character and conduct on your behalf. Only you can make the choice to try to live a life without fault – to be more like Jesus – to let your light shine! Is it achievable? Absolutely! All you need to do is to make up your mind today that you want to live a life free of blame (without shame). Yes, you may occasionally let yourself down, but that is why we have been given 1 John 1:9: *"If you confess your sins, He is faithful to forgive you and cleanse you from all unrighteousness."*

Use this scripture like a detergent, and wash away your sins. Be blameless: without blemish or imperfection.

Day 56

Image

εἰκών = '*eikon*'
An image, exact representation, perfect likeness, complete double

Eikon denotes an *image*; the word involves the two ideas of representation and manifestation. Man was created to be a *visible* and true representation (image) of God. Romans 8:29: *"For those whom He foreknew, He also predestined to become conformed to the image of His Son, so that He would be the firstborn among many brethren."* This is a profound truth. Therefore, I pray that in every way Christ might be exalted through your conformity to Him, so you might enjoy the great assurance that because of our election and predestination everything will work together for your good.

If you are still wondering: am I among the chosen, the predestined, the called? Here's how you can fully comprehend this truth. Can you see yourself being conformed to the *image* (the perfect likeness) of our Lord Jesus? For if you can, you will fit His image perfectly. After all, that is what conformity is all about. You fitting flawlessly into the image of Christ.

The ikons we see in many Greek Orthodox churches are never the exact likeness of Jesus, however, God has predestined you to become exactly that! An image that fits Jesus' perfectly!

Day 57

Join

κολλάω = *'kollao'*
To join, glue or cement together, to unite or join firmly, to join oneself to, or be joined to

Mainly, *kollao* means "to glue or cement together." Typically, it is used to unite or join firmly, also signifying; to join oneself to or to be joined to. 1 Corinthians 1:10 says, *"Brethren, by the authority of our Lord Jesus Christ, I beg all of you to agree with each other. You should not be divided into different groups. Be completely joined together again with the same kind of thinking and the same purpose."* 1 Corinthians 6:17 states, *"But he who is joined to the Lord is one spirit with Him."*

To be joined is to be united or strengthened together. The God we serve is a God of unity who desires that His church live in unity and harmony: built on the foundation that is Jesus Christ. It is the Lord Jesus who draws us together and the power of the Holy Spirit that cements us together. The Spirit of God is the Spirit of unity. If you have the Holy Spirit in you, you are already glued or cemented to your brothers and sisters in Christ. Many may not recognize this fact, or act in a way that confirms it, but you are all *one* in Him.

Live in this reality and you will find yourself surrounded by likeminded people who have a heart to be unified to the glory of God. Such harmony is a beautiful sound in God's ears.

DAY 58

ETERNAL

αἰώνιος = *'aionios'*
Eternal, a duration without end, an undefined time, immortal

The predominant meaning of *aionios*, that setting in which it is used everywhere in the New Testament, may be seen clearly in 2 Corinthians 4:18: *"While we look not at the things which are seen, but at the things which are not seen; for the things which are seen are temporal, but the things which are not seen are eternal."* What's 'eternal' is more real than the things you see though your own eyes! You are instructed to live not by the things that are seen, but by the things that are unseen. Yet, you probably live mostly by what can be seen, what you observe day in and day out.

Some say we are the most visually overstimulated generation in history. Which may be why most of us have such difficulty with the invisible, the unseen, the intangible; as in faith. Real faith always focuses (gazes upon) that which is eternal. This is why your faith can materialise and make tangible the very things you are hoping for. True reality is located in the realm of the spirit, where things are rooted in eternal values.

Today, don't focus on the things that are decaying, rather, set your eyes upon the things that are eternal. For the things that are eternal, even though you cannot see them with your physical eyes, are real, valid and true.

Day 59

Effectual

ἐνεργέω = '*energeo*'
To work effectively, to be effectual, to put forth power, to be operative or put in effort

Energeo means "to put forth power, be operative, to work" and is rendered by the verb "to work effectually," or "to be effectual." 1 Thessalonians 2:13: *"For this reason we also thank God without ceasing, because when you received the word of God which you heard from us, you welcomed it not as the word of men, but as it is in truth, the word of God, which also effectively works in you who believe."* Notice that the word of God energizes you on the inside. So many Christians loose out because they do not understand this principle, or walk in this truth. When you welcome the word of God into your life, and believe it, effectual power begins to work in you. You can then step out in faith and do the very things that Jesus did.

Make sure you aren't just hearing the word of God, but that you are receiving it in your heart. For the word to be effectual it must be deposited in the heart. Thereafter, it needs to be acted upon. Faith without action does not benefit anyone (James 2:14). It is like a corpse, lifeless!

Make up your mind today to put your faith into action. That is, to do something good, which requires absolute trust in God.

DAY 60

BOLDNESS

παρρησιάζομαι = '*parrhesiazomai*'
To be bold, speak boldly or freely, waxing bold, to preach boldly, to speak unreservedly or confidently

Acts 4:29-30: *"Now, Lord, look on their threats, and grant to Your servants that with all boldness they may speak Your word, by stretching out Your hand to heal, and that signs and wonders may be done through the name of Your Holy Servant Jesus."* The need to speak God's word boldly is a great necessity in today's politically correct society. You have the power to change the world by using the supreme authority that God has given you through prophetic utterance. Speaking God's word boldly brings about change. His word in your mouth is as powerful as God's word in His own mouth. Why? Because God is always watching over His word to perform it; to make sure it accomplishes that for which it's intended.

The people praying this prayer in Acts 4 were in serious peril, but they realized that boldness to *speak* would usher in the overwhelming power of God. And, so it did! The building they were in was shaken and they were all filled with the Holy Spirit, and they spoke the word of God boldly. This was unreserved utterance, a freedom of speech they had not encountered before.

I encourage you to pray this prayer right now: "Pray for boldness to speak!"

Day 61

Jesus

Ἰησοῦς = '*iesous*'
Joshua, Jehovah is salvation, Jehovah is the Saviour

Matthew 1:24-25: *"Then Joseph, being aroused from sleep, did as the angel of the Lord commanded him and took to him his wife, and did not know her till she had brought forth herfirstborn Son. And he called His name Jesus."* *Iesous* is a transliteration of the Hebrew *Joshua* meaning "Jehovah is salvation." It was a common name among the Jews. Yet, it was given to the Son of God in Incarnation as His personal name. In obedience to the command of an angel, Joseph (the husband of Mary), called Him Jesus. By this name He is spoken of throughout the Gospel narratives.

To some, it's an audacious claim to say that Jesus is God, and a reprehensible blasphemy were it not true. However, Jesus can bear the name of God because He *is* God. Through the revelation of Jesus as God we come to understand the Trinity - God the Father, God the Son, and God the Holy Spirit. Three persons, but one God. The Father reveals Himself in Jesus in a way that no mind could imagine, and He is glorified as a result. It is of primary importance that you always acknowledge Jesus as God. Anything else, undermines His divine authority, and without that *authority* operating effectively you cannot live the super-abundant and victorious life Jesus came to secure for you.

Day 62

Grace

Χάρις = *'charis'*

That which causes favourable regard, or bestows pleasure, unmerited favour, getting what you don't deserve

To learn the true definition of God's grace, it's wise to understand both the Greek and Hebrew words behind this term. The prominent Old Testament word describing God's grace is *chesed.* This word speaks of deliverance from one's enemies, affliction, or adversity. It also denotes enablement, daily guidance, forgiveness, and preservation. However, *charis* the New Testament word focuses on the provision and establishment of salvation.

What is *grace*? Grace is God's love in action towards men who deserve the opposite of love. Grace means God moving heaven and earth to save sinners who could not lift a finger to save themselves. Grace may be defined as the unmerited or undeserving favour of God toward those who are under condemnation. Mercy is not getting what you deserve, grace is getting what you don't deserve.

Not understanding grace means you are not able to live in the fullness of what God has for you. Therefore, stop trying to earn God's favour, you have His favour already. Stop trying to please God through deeds designed to impress Him; He is already impressed with you. Rest in the knowledge that His grace is sufficient, and His strength is perfected in your failings (2 Corinthians 12:9).

DAY 63

BIND

δήσης = *'thisis'*
To bind, hinder, forbid or be bound

Matthew 16:19: *"I will give you the keys of the kingdom of heaven; whatever you bind on earth will be bound in heaven, and whatever you loose on earth will be loosed in heaven."* By giving you the keys of the kingdom of heaven, God has chosen to use you to bring His will to earth. He calls you to come into dialogue with Him, listen to His voice and gain prophetic revelation, so that the hope of your calling can be fulfilled. And He asks you to take that revelation into the earthly realm; using heaven as your measure.

You are to bind whatever is *bound* (forbidden) in heaven, and loose whatever is *loosed* (permitted) in heaven. Let me ask you: "Is sickness, disease, poverty, pain, suffering etc. bound (forbidden) in heaven?" Yes! Therefore, you have the legal right to bind these things in your life, and in the lives of others. What is forbidden in heaven should be outlawed on earth.

If you are willing to press toward the promises of God for your life, their fulfilment will not be prolonged. But if you allow the devil to overcome you with discouragement, hopelessness and unbelief, you too may find yourself in a prolonged season of unhappiness. God wants you to take control. He wants you to use the keys of the kingdom and set the captives free. For what you lock no one can open!

Day 64

Father

Πάτερ = *'pater'*
Father, nourisher, protector, upholder

The Lord's Prayer brings your whole life into the presence of God, and brings the whole of God into your entire life (Matthew 6:5-15). One thing you can definitely say about this prayer is that it is short. Short on flowery language and short on waffle, yet it packs such a lot into just over 50 words. Is Jesus trying to tell his disciples something here? According to Luke (Luke 11:1-4) this conversation was in response to a request to teach them a prayer as John the Baptist had done for his disciples.

One of the problems with prayer is that it can be sometimes confusing. How do you know that you're using the right form of words? How do you know that God is listening? Why would He even bother to listen to you, and how do you know that He will answer your prayer? If you still have concerns about prayer, you're probably asking yourself: "How do I deal with my uncertainties?"

Well, Jesus had a simple answer: *"Do not be like them, for your Father knows what you need before you ask him."* Instead of babbling like those religious bigots, ask the Father in full acceptance that He already knows your every need. When you do this, your prayers change, and your prayer life will become more fruitful. Try it today!

DAY 65

LORD

Κύριος = *'kirios'*
Lord, ruler, owner, master, having power

Today's politically correct *spirituality* often includes Jesus, but He is not the Jesus of Scripture. He is another Jesus who is valued by mystics, Gnostics and all the world's religions. He is accepted as a prophet, a great teacher, and even an enlightened spiritual master. It is becoming increasingly obvious that Jesus needs to be made into something everyone can accept and get along with. He needs to be *lowered* to be in reach of people in modern society. However, He is not the person modern society portrays Him as – Jesus is Lord!

Jesus is the Lord of Lords and the King of Kings! The bottom line is this: do you believe Jesus is Lord, or more so, do you believe Jesus Christ is Lord of all? Acts 10:36 states: *"The word which God sent to the children of Israel, preaching peace through Jesus Christ—He is Lord of all—that word you know."* Lordship has to do with an acknowledgement that someone has complete authority.

"Jesus Christ is Lord" is the most powerful confession in the entire universe! These words can change your life and cause you to live in victory. Speak them daily over your life, your family, your work, and anything you are involved in. Jesus is Lord of all: He has everything under His sovereign rule.

Day 66

Purpose

Πρόθεσιν = *'prothesin'*
A setting forth, a purpose, a determination

Romans 8:28: *"And we know that God causes all things to work together for good to those who love God, to those who are called according to His purpose."* All things don't just *happen* to work out for good on their own. Rather, God providentially works all things together for good for His people according to His divine purpose. But while Romans 8:28 is a source of great comfort when it is properly understood, it is often misunderstood and misapplied.

The truth revealed in this verse is foundational. If God doesn't have a purpose, then He couldn't work all things according to that purpose. But the fact is this: God has an eternal purpose for you that cannot be thwarted. Nothing can prevent God's purpose from being accomplished. Therefore, no matter what anyone does to you – suppresses you, overlooks you, denies you, rejects you, oppresses you – God has taken and factored in all those things in His plans for you already. They are not mere coincidences. So, don't let those things get you down. God has everything covered. God's plan is unchangeable and nothing and no one in this universe can stop that plan. God's blueprint for your life has a beginning, a middle and an end.

Whatever unfolds in your life is no mere chance, no random event, it's part of God's plan and purpose for today.

DAY 67

FAVOUR

Χάριν = *'charin'*

To have obtained favour, graciousness, kindness displayed

Today, I want you to change your thinking. The old mindset has said: "*I can't have it.*" But the new mindset has realized: "*God's already provided it for me.*" I want you to know that the favour of God is coming your way in spite of your past, in spite of your problems, in spite of your pain, and in spite of your negative thoughts.

God doesn't give out His favour fairly, like wages being paid to laborers. Favour is given freely. In fact, you are unable to explain the favour of God on your life because favour is not reasonable.

The favour God gave Ruth was greater than anything she had ever known. Ruth had been through extreme difficulties; she had experienced famine, destruction, poverty, and peril. But the depth of her past was an indication of the height of her future! God chose to release His powerful favour over her life. And He wants to do the same for you. Yes, He wants to pour His love and provision over your life today.

Therefore, you don't have to settle for insufficiency. God has a whole new level He wants to bring you to, and His favour will take you there. After all, He is the "All-Sufficient-One."

Day 68

Is-Able

δυναμένῳ = *'thinameno'*
Has the power, is able or capable

Do you remember the old Star Trek television series? When it first came out, it captured the imagination of an entire generation. The crew of the Starship USS Enterprise was on a five-year mission and they endeavoured "to boldly go where no man has gone before." Perhaps you've wished to live a Sci-Fi life. Seriously, have you ever longed to go beyond the natural realm and operate in the realm of the spirit? Have you ever aspired to live a supernatural life 'far-above' your present circumstances? In fact, God wants you to forget the past and keep pressing forward. He wants you to go "above" and "beyond," to where you have never gone before!

Jesus acted *above and beyond* imagination in His earthly life and ministry because He was doing what He saw His Father do. Ephesians 3:20 says, *"Now to him who is able to do immeasurably (super-abundantly) above and beyond all we ask or think or imagine, according to His mighty power that is at work within us."* I consider this to be confirmation that God is planning to take us immeasurably "above and beyond" our greatest hopes, dreams and expectations. The big questions is this: "Are you ready to let the Holy Spirit propel you forward - into the supernatural super-abundant life Jesus has already secured?" If you are, then today is your day!

DAY 69

FULLNESS

Πληρώματος = *'pliromatos'*
Fullness, that of which something is packed, filling up to the full

"I am sure that, when I come to you, I shall come in the fullness of the blessing of the gospel of Christ" (Romans 15:29). Paul wrote these words to the Christians in Rome and he was telling them: "I have no doubt that when I meet you, it will be in the fullest measure of Christ's blessing." The apostle's words imply something that every believer should fully understand. That is, there are various degrees, or measures, of Christ's blessing. Some believers obtain a full measure of this blessing, which is probably their hearts' desire. Yet, God's word tells us that we're all meant to come into a full measure of the Lord's blessing!

The previous chapter climaxes with these incredible words: *"...that you may be filled to the measure of all the fullness of God."* The word *fullness* is used in both these passages. The Greek word Paul uses here means "to complete the task of filling up to the full." This word emphasises fullness and completion. It is a state of complete superabundance. Remember, the Holy Spirit is at the centre of you living in the fullness of God. He leads you every step of the way.

The Spirit of God is the guarantee that the exceeding and abundant blessings which God has stored up for you, flood your life, from start to finish! Therefore, you can boldly declare, "I have come in the fullness of God's blessings."

Day 70

Rain

ὑετόν = *'ieton'*
Torrent, rain, flood

Hebrews 6:7: ***"For the earth which drinks in the rain that often comes upon it, and bears herbs useful for those by whom it is cultivated, receives blessing from God."*** God uses the land of Israel—its topography, its seasons, its rains—to teach us. So while the Bible may seem to be speaking of natural things like rains, harvests, or crops, there are hidden spiritual truths for us to learn.

In Egypt, the Israelites had to look down at their pedals and see their own work, but in Canaan, all they had to do was look up and see God's work. They depended on Him for rain. They depended on Him to care for their land. I encourage you today to look up and depend on God for blessings. The world can continue to look down and struggle using their own efforts; depending entirely on their own talents and strengths. But you can look up and depend on the Lord who cares for you.

The Later Rain is coming! When it comes, God will restore all the years you have lost. Many of you have lost your years to the locusts. Locusts leave fields completely empty, void of every green thing. The devil likes dry places, but when the Later Rain comes there will be no place for him to hide. The blessings of God will soon be raining down on you. Let it rain Lord – let it rain!

DAY 71

FAITH

Πίστεως = *'pisteos'*
Faith, firm persuasion or a conviction based upon hearing

If you are living by faith, your faith is likely to be tested! The faith I am referring to is not your religious beliefs, but the 'faith' described in Hebrews 11:1: *"Now faith is the substance of things hoped for, the evidence of things not seen."* James tells us quite candidly that our faith will be put to the test. I like James because he doesn't pull his punches; he says it as it is! James seems to have a knack of cutting straight through to what really matters. We are all aware that life has its tests and trials. However, in this instance it is God Himself who allows our faith to be put to the test. These are tests and trials that are divinely permitted or sent; all with a beneficial purpose or effect.

The reason why God permits trails to come upon us is this: *"Knowing that the testing of your faith produces patience. But let patience have its perfect work, that you may be perfect and complete, lacking nothing"* (James 1:3-4). I like the *"not lacking anything"* part of these verses. However, such a truly prosperous state can only be established after you have allowed *perseverance* to finish its work; and only after you have grown in faith and matured. So remember this, the reward for hanging in and exercising faith is "not lacking anything." When you keep your eyes on the reward, it's a lot easier to exercise faith, be patient, and *"consider it all joy!"*

DAY 72

BELIEF

πιστεῦσα = *'pistevsa'*

To believe, to be persuaded of, to place confidence and trust in)

What is the difference between Faith and Belief? In Mark 5, shortly after Jesus says to the woman with the issue of blood, *"Your faith has made you well"* (verse 34), He says to the ruler of the synagogue; whose daughter had just died; *"Do not be afraid; only believe"* (verse 36). Both people received the miracle they were needing, yet the Lord commended the woman for her *faith*, and He told the ruler of the synagogue to simply *believe*. This can be rather confusing if you need a miracle right now!

"*Pistevsa*" means "to be fully persuaded of," "to place complete confidence in," or "to totally trust in someone." This verb appears 99 times in the Book of John, showing us that the disciple who was most intimate with the Lord had the greatest revelation of the true meaning of the word. Confirming that belief is about relationship. Therefore, I would like to propose that you first *believe* in God, with whom you have developed a personal intimate relationship, and thereafter, place complete trust in His faithfulness.

When you have complete trust in God's faithfulness, you will find it easy to believe. That is why Jesus said, "only believe!" Simply believing in the Lord Jesus can bring about your miracle today.

Day 73

Contentment

Αυτάρκης = *'aphtarkis'*
To be satisfied in oneself, needing no assistance

To start, I would like to quote Socrates, "Whoever is not contented with what he has, would not be contented with what he would like to have." In other words, if you cannot find contentment where you are right now, you are unlikely to find it if you obtain the things you think will make you content. The apostle Paul put it this way, *"Not that I was ever in need, for I have learned how to be content with whatever I have. I know how to live on almost nothing or with everything. I have learned the secret of living in every situation, whether it is with a full stomach or empty, with plenty or little. I can do all things through Christ who strengthens me"* (Philippians 4:11-13).

"I have learned the secret," Paul says, "of being content in any and every situation." Implying that finding contentment in life is not easy. It is something you must discern and then teach yourself to do. The apostle Paul said, "I've found the secret, and I've learned it! So now I know what it means to be content." If you are struggling with being content it's mainly because of your lack of trust in God. Remember, with God everything is subject to change for the better! I'm convinced that the Lord is glorified in us *most* when we are *most* contented in Him. When you find a place of true contentment you'll be able to do all things through Christ who strengthens you.

DAY 74

AGREEMENT

συμφωνέω = *'symphoneo'*

To agree together, to come into agreement, to sound together, to be in accord - primarily of musical instruments, to be in harmony

Matthew 18:19: *"Again I say to you that if two of you agree on earth concerning anything that they ask, it will be done for them by My Father in heaven."* The word used here in the original Greek is *symphoneo,* from which comes the word symphony. It literally means "to agree in sound' or "to be in harmony," as may be heard in a symphony orchestra. Harmonic sound of two instruments is more beautiful than the sound of one. The harmonic whole becomes greater than its individual parts. In fact, by learning to blend with others, you get to understand and appreciate your own uniqueness more and more. Jesus reminds us that we do not need a crowd (verse 20). Just two or three of us harmonizing in spirit is more beautiful than the assembly of a thousand who have no bond.

Unanimity in prayer requires unity in the spirit. Merely meeting together is not enough. Our hearts need to be joined together in complete agreement. Leviticus 26:8 says, *"Five of you shall chase a hundred, and a hundred of you shall put ten thousand to flight."* Agreement is very powerful. Especially in prayer! When our hearts are joined together in faith, and our supplications are in agreement with God's, we sound like a harmonious symphony. This beautiful togetherness of hearts brings about answered prayer. Try it today.

DAY 75

JOYFULNESS

χαρᾷ - *'chara'*
Deep delight, gladness

The problem with most of us is that we are trying to sustain our own joy and not the joy we have in the Lord. Philippians 4:4 says, *"Rejoice in the Lord always."* If this is not possible we would never have been asked to do it! Therefore, maintaining joy is entirely about the Lord and has nothing to do with your own efforts. Your own joy is subject to fluctuations and variations, but the joy you experience in God's presence is totally dependable.

We are made stronger in God's presence, because that is where His joy becomes a greater reality to us. God wants us to succeed in these spiritual pilgrimages to His heart. Besides using them to display His power, He will minister to you in a way that strengthens and encourages you. The joy of the Lord is your strength!

Each spiritual journey you complete into God's presence, will enhance your joy and strengthen your understanding. Also, you must remember that it's His desire to develop and deepen the relationship you have with Him. Therefore, if ever you turn back from your spiritual journey toward His heart, you should simply start it again. God is there to help you and fill you with *joy inexpressible* (1 Peter 1:8). Psalm 84:5 declares, *"What joy for those whose strength comes from the Lord, who have set their minds on a pilgrimage."*

DAY 76

ALWAYS

Πάντα = *'panta'*
Always, continually, as a usual practice

Luke 21:1-4: *And He looked up and saw the rich putting their gifts into the treasury, and He saw also a certain poor widow putting in two mites. So He said, "Truly I say to you that this poor widow has put in more than all; for all these out of their abundance have put in offerings for God, but she out of her poverty put in all the livelihood that she had."* It is very interesting to note that the word used and translated *all* is the Greek word *πάντα*, and in the modern Greek this means *always*. This poor widow *always* put in all that she had.

It wasn't the first time Jesus had noticed her, because He would not have said always. For this woman, giving everything she had to God was a lifestyle! This should really speak to our hearts, for not many of us have the courage to always give everything to God. Notice, for her to have given everything, and then to come back and give everything again, God must have met all her needs between visits to the temple.

It should be very comforting to know that when you give sacrificially to God, He undertakes to meet your every need. Not only that, if you adopt a lifestyle of giving, Jesus will notice you every time. You will truly stand out in the crowd!

Day 77

Glory

δόξα = *'thoxa'*

To honour, praise, splendor, brightness, preeminence, majesty, absolute perfection, magnificence, excellence, dignity

2 Corinthians 3:18: *"But we all, with unveiled face, beholding as in a mirror the glory of the Lord, are being transformed into the same image from glory to glory, just as by the Spirit of the Lord."* The Greek word *thoxa* appears here, and it is used mostly to describe the nature of God in self-manifestation. That is, what He essentially is and does, as exhibited in whatever way He chooses to reveal Himself. For instance, when His grace and mighty power were evidenced, this constituted His *thoxa*.

It also denotes a supernatural demonstration of the splendour, brightness and perfection of His character, and especially His righteousness. Therefore, *thoxa* refers to the very essence of God; the divine power and substance that makes Him "God Almighty!" What God essentially is and does, in whatever and whichever may He chooses to reveal Himself, is His *glory*, and this demands your praises!

When you learn to recognise His glory, you will become a true worshipper. The reason being that no one can look at the glory of God without giving admiration. Why not start today by recognising and appreciating His divine attributes, and then responding to them with praise.

DAY 78

GOODNESS

Χρηστότητος = *'christotitos'*
Kindness of heart, expressing itself in deeds

Try not to judge God's character by your routine encounters with adverse circumstances. His goodness stands with rock-like dependability amidst the shifting fortunes of life. You must constantly remind yourself that despite the many negative things that confront you – which often make no sense at all - God is good! Yes, God is intrinsically good. Goodness is part of His divine nature; therefore, He is incapable of doing anything but good.

This is why the Bible says His goodness will follow us faithfully all the days of our lives (Psalm 23:6). Implying that, wherever you go and whatever you do, God's goodness is in hot pursuit. From the moment you awake to the time you go to bed, God's goodness is chasing you down. It never quits or backs off! It has one purpose, and that is, to overtake you and fill your life with blessings.

Remember this, God's goodness is your life jacket during the storms of life. There is no other way to make sense of it! God will not only see you through, He will undeniably use every situation for your good, but to His glory! This is His goodness chasing you down.

Stop pursuing what is actually trying to apprehend you, and allow His abundant, lavish blessings to overtake you today (Deuteronomy 28:2).

DAY 79

KNOW

γινώσκω = *'gynosko'*
To know, completely understand, perceive, feel, have knowledge of, to come to know, to become personally acquainted with

Philippians 3:10: *"That I may know Him and the power of His resurrection."* The ancient word translated *know* means to "understand completely" or "to realise fully." It frequently indicates a relationship between the person knowing and that, which is being *known*. Therefore, that which is being *known* must have real value or importance to the one who *knows'*; the one who has understood completely. Can you see? You must *know* or completely understand Christ, and *know* or completely understand the awesome power of His resurrection!

However, another aspect of knowing is 'experiencing'. Experiential knowledge is vitally important in all spiritual matters, and especially in your relationship with God. Hence, this scripture is telling you to *experience* Christ and *experience* the power of His resurrection. When was the last time you experienced Christ and experienced the power of His resurrection? Your identification with Christ in His death, burial, and resurrection is the foundation for you to experience the power of His resurrection. Furthermore, knowing Christ and His divine power gives you everything you need for life and godliness (2 Peter 1:3).

Make time to experience Christ today!

DAY 80

NEW

νέος & καινός = 'neos' & 'kainos
That which is younger and that of a different nature

Mark 2:22: *"And no one puts new (νέος) wine into old wineskins; or else the new (νέος) wine will burst the wineskins and be spilled, and the wineskins will be ruined. But new (νέος) wine must be put into new (καινός) wineskins, and both are preserved."* The new wine, that recent and energetic move or experience, cannot be poured into an old brittle vessel. The recent energetic move or experience of God's kingdom, which has evolved out of the past, can only be poured into a vessel that is completely different in essence, nature and character from that which is contrasted as old.

The word *kainos* implies something that is new in form or quality, something that has never existed before, like the new birth. Whenever God decides to do a new thing (as in Isaiah 43:18-19), He will do it through vessels that are completely new in nature and character. That is, through vessels that are totally brand new! He doesn't take what is already in use and polish it up to restore it. God creates something totally fresh that is pliable and adaptable enough to house the dynamic and effervescent *new* move of His Spirit. If you want to be used by God in this *new* move of the Spirit, be ready to step into something that has never existed before.

Yes, prepare yourself to receive a fresh anointing.

DAY 81

MIGHTY

δύναμις = *'dynamis'*
Inherent ability, intense energy or power to perform anything

2 Corinthians 12:12: *"Truly the signs of an apostle were accomplished among you with all perseverance, in signs and wonders and mighty deeds." Dynamis* is often translated power, however, when referring to the signs of an apostle it is rendered "mighty deeds." *Dynamis* refers to strength or ability and is generally used of the mighty acts of God; like the parting of the Red Sea (Exodus 14:15-31); or the violent earthquake in Philippi that loosed the chains of Paul and Silas (Acts 16:26). Jesus' own ministry was accredited by miracles, wonders and signs.

In 2 Thessalonians 1:7, Paul says, *"And to you who are troubled, rest with us, when the Lord Jesus shall be revealed from heaven with His mighty angels."* The word translated *mighty* is also the word *dynamis, which* means: "intense energy, immense ability and exceeding strength." Paul is talking about celestial beings of great might and awesome power.

The apostles were credited with the working of miraculous signs, wonders and *mighty deeds.* However, those mighty deeds were supreme acts of God. Hence, you should expect the Almighty God to exercise His power and strength in your life. Take heart, be encouraged for the same miracle-working God is with you today.

Day 82

Endure

ὑπομονῆς = *'hypomonis'*
An abiding under great stress, bearing up under pressure

Hebrews 10:36: *"For you have need of endurance, so that after you have done the will of God, you may receive the promise,"* The word translated *endurance* describes the unique capacity to continue to bear up under difficult circumstances, not with passive complacency but with hopeful fortitude that actively resists weariness and defeat. This is a steadfast and unwavering commitment to God. The verb literally means, "to remain or stay under", and is also rendered "to remain behind" in Luke 2:43 and Acts 17:14.

It is also transcribed as, "to stand one's ground; persevere; or remain steadfast," and is therefore translated *endure* in Matthew 24:13. The noun *hypomone* usually denotes courageous, steadfast, or patient endurance that does not lose hope in the face of obstacles, persecutions, trials, or temptations. Given the fallen condition of our world and its hostility to those who want to live godly lives and follow the Lord Jesus, this word is used with relative frequency in the New Testament. Therefore, the unique capacity to *endure*, to bear up under difficult circumstances, must be something you are expected to possess. And if God expects you to have this ability, He must have equipped you with the means to exercise it. You, most definitely, are able to endure under extreme difficulty. Even when you think it's not possible, God has given you the capacity to endure.

DAY 83

RECEIVE

ἀναδεξάμενος = *'anathexamenos'*
To receive, to accept, take up, take upon one's self, undertake

Hebrews 11:17: *"By faith Abraham, when he was tested, offered up Isaac, and he who had received* (accepted) *the promises, offered up his only begotten son."* Notice, Abraham had already accepted and received God's promises: "....He who had received (past tense) the promises of God offered up his son." You can never operate in faith until you have first *accepted* and then *received* God's promises. Bearing in mind that this does not have anything to do with simply accepting that the promises are true, as this is common belief. Faith has to do with intentionally accepting God at His word and receiving all His promises.

It's the process of inviting the promises of God to populate your life and making each one come alive in you. The Greek meaning is very clear. It is, "to receive by a deliberate response to what is being offered." In fact, it's exactly the same way the Lord *receives* the spirit of a departing believer (Acts 7:59). God's promises are available to be received anytime, any-place and in any circumstances. They are accessible to you right now!

Why don't you take a promise that can be applied to the very situation you find yourself in today, and then *receive* it as already fulfilled. This will activate your faith and manifest the promise.

DAY 84

STAND-FIRM

στήκετε = *'stikete'*
To stand fast, to persevere, to persist, to keep one's standing

Philippians 4:1: *"My beloved and longed-for brethren, my joy and crown, so stand fast in the Lord, beloved."* After so powerfully expressing his affection for the church, Paul asks the congregation to *stand firm.* This Greek word may also be used to describe "soldiers who are to stand at their post irrespective of the pressure to abandon it," or alternatively, "athletes who must adhere without deviation to the course marked out for them." But the primary consideration for standing fast in the Lord is one of harmony and unity with one-another. And as was usual with Paul's letters, the exhortations given here are given also to the entire Christian community.

If ever any individuals are singled out for special instruction, it is always with the understanding that they are part of the church, and that the church will be behind them primarily to support, encourage, guide, and be responsible and accountable for their well-being. You cannot stand firm in the Lord on your own, you must do it with the support of those around you.

Stop trying to stand alone during the storms of life. The people God has strategically placed around you are there for a reason. They are there to stand shoulder-to-shoulder with you during tests and trails. Standing firm is a joint effort.

Day 85

Understanding

συνιέντος = *'sunientos'*
To comprehend or assimilate, to have insight, to grasp, to set or bring together the thing perceived, to set or join together in the mind

Matthew 13:19: *"When anyone hears the word of the kingdom, and does not understand it, then the wicked one comes immediately and snatches away what was sown in the heart."* Literally, "If anyone of you has knowledge of the Word of God, and then chooses not to respond to that truth (act on it), the devil will come immediately to snatch away the seed that was sown in the heart." Notice, the devil will gladly co-operate with any person who is not willing to act on the truth.

In this Parable, we see clearly that it is very important to first "receive," and then to hear and *understand* the Word. Verse 23: *"But he who received seed on the good ground is he who hears the word and understands it, who indeed bears fruit and produces; some a hundred-fold, some sixty, some thirty."* There is a clear and distinctive relationship between; receiving, hearing or having knowledge and understanding or taking action. However, it's in the *doing*, which is the result of understanding, that you get your reward. "He wo hears the word and understands it, he indeed bears fruit!"

Make sure you bear fruit today! Put the word you've received and understood into action.

DAY 86

WALKING

περιπατο = *'peripato'*
Walking, signifying all the activities or attributes of the individual life

2 Corinthians 5:7: *"For we walk by faith and not by sight."* To *walk* in the New Testament often denotes "to live, to act, to conduct yourself in a certain way" (reference Romans 4:12; Romans 6:4). It suggests that life is a journey, or a pilgrimage, and that we are travelling from one place to another. Here, the apostle Paul is speaking to believers and he mentions a specific stance or action - walking! Walking evidences the possession of life. You can make a dead man sit or even stand in a certain position, however, to walk requires the possession of life. In this instance, Paul is referring to the inward life. Therefore, the ungodly man does not walk at all. He is like a corpse.

As a child of God, you can (and do) walk: you *walk* in newness of life! You *walk* by the Spirit and you *walk* by Faith. The sense here is, that you conduct yourself in the course of life with reference to the things that are unseen and not with reference to the things that are seen. You are openly trusting in those things you do not see.

Walking denotes progress! Therefore, your faith must keep you moving forward, making you stronger and stronger each day.

DAY 87

WISDOM

σοφία / φρόνησις = *'sophia' / 'fronisis'*
Spiritual insight into the true nature of things, understanding how to apply such wisdom

1 Corinthians 1:20 (Amp): *"Where is the wise man, the philosopher? Where is the scribe, the scholar? Where is the investigator, the logician, the debater of this present age? Has not God shown up the nonsense and the folly of this world's wisdom?* Verse 24 says, *"Christ the power of God and the wisdom of God."*

The two words that appear in the New Testament and are translated wisdom are *σοφία* and *φρόνησις*. I firmly believe that God's wisdom, or the God-kind of wisdom, must incorporate both *σοφία* and *φρόνησις*. In other words, God's wisdom; (a) gives us special insight into the true nature and state of things (*sophia*), and (b) it causes us to apply a sensible and practical approach to the hands-on use of such insight (*fronisis*).

Notice something? If you were only blessed with spiritual insight and had no practical ability to apply it in your life, it would be of no value to you, or to anyone else! God gives insight so that you can discern it correctly and apply it sensibly to impact on any situation you're confronted with. Such wisdom brings great rewards, both spiritually and materially! But it also brings happiness: *"Happy is the man who finds wisdom"* (Proverbs 3:13).

DAY 88

ANXIETY

μεριμνᾶ = *'merimna'*
To be drawn in different directions, a stressful distraction, to divide into parts

Matthew 6:25, *"Therefore, I say to you, do not worry (be anxious) about your life, what you will eat or what you will drink; not about your body, what you will put on. Is not life more than food and the body more than clothing?"* Jesus starts off by saying, "do not worry!" The Greek word used here is derived from another ancient word that means, "to divide into parts." This word implies or suggests that *worry* is a preoccupation with things that cause stress, unease, pressure and torment. Notice how the use of this word suggests that *worry* breaks up your life - it is life shattering!

Therefore, Jesus is saying that *worry* is a distraction, something that divides your focus, something that causes you to be preoccupied with things that add stress and pressure to your life. But what have you been divided or distracted from? And what have you become preoccupied with? Quite simply: you have been *distracted* from looking at your source, your Heavenly Father; and you have become *preoccupied* with worldly affairs.

Don't allow your worries and cares to break up your life. Don't allow anxiety to shatter your very existence! Remember, "the way to be anxious about nothing is to be prayerful about everything."

DAY 89

SUPER-ABOUND

ἐπερίσσευσεν = *'epepissevsen'*
To overflow, to be abundantly furnished with, to have in abundance, to exceed a fixed number of measure, to furnish one richly

Ephesians 1:7,8: *"In Him we have redemption through His blood, the forgiveness of sins, according to the riches of His grace, which He made to abound toward us in all wisdom and prudence."* Another translation says: "that He lavished on us with all wisdom." God loves to lavish things on you, because He is a very extravagant God!

The Greek word rendered *abound* (lavished) elsewhere in Scripture is also translated *abundance*, and it means to "super-abound, have in excess, great surpass, or acquire beyond measure." This word implies that there is no restraint, and whenever it is used in the context of God's Fatherly nature it serves to guarantee blessings that overtake you. These are truly abounding and astounding blessings!

The same root word appears in John 10:10: *"The thief does not come except to steal, and to kill, and to destroy. I have come that they may have life, and that they may have it more abundantly."* Literally, super-abundantly! Jesus came that you may have an *extraordinary life* where there is always a surplus, where you constantly have over and above or more than enough. Start enjoying the benefits of this "out-of-the-ordinary" life today!

DAY 90

CONFESS

ὁμολογέω = *'omologeo'*
To declare openly, admit, to say the same thing as another, to agree with, to profess, to speak out freely, to assent

Matthew 10:32: *"Therefore, whoever confesses Me before men, him I will also confess before My Father who is in heaven."* A literal translation of this verse is, "Whoever declares Me openly (unashamedly) before men, I will also declare openly (unashamedly) before My Father who is in heaven." This is a proud statement of friendship. It is like a son bringing a friend home to meet his father, after having told the friend how wonderful his father is. There is no shame of embarrassment in this action. The boy is so proud of his dad that he can't wait to introduce him to his friend! That is exactly how you are expected to act before men concerning Jesus.

When you do it, Jesus promises that He will act precisely the same way before His Father in heaven. Quite simply, when you acknowledge Christ before men, He acknowledges you before His Father in heaven. That's a good trade off! Isn't it? Suddenly your name gets heard in heaven. Yes, your name is uttered by Jesus in the throne room of grace.

So today, the question you should ask yourself is this: "Is my name known in heaven?" And the best way to make sure is to unashamedly confess Jesus to those around you.

DAY 91

RIGHTEOUSNESS

δικαιοσύνην = *'thikaiosunin'*
Purity of life, rightness, correctness of thinking feeling and acting, the condition fully acceptable to God

Matthew 5:6: *"Blessed are those who hunger and thirst for righteousness, for they shall be filled."* In the New Testament we can see the difference between producing or performing righteous acts, and being wholly and completely righteous. Notice that the word *righteous* does not focus on man, but on God, and specifically on God's divine nature. The Greek word shows "the character or quality of being right or just." It expresses a divine attribute of God and means essentially the same as His faithfulness or truthfulness. Why? Because it is totally consistent with His own nature.

Another definition which is in line with the New Testament concept of righteousness is "that which is totally compatible, and conforms perfectly, with God's life and nature." This view of righteousness will never permit man to be righteous in the sight of God on his own merits.

You need to be more righteousness conscious and less sin conscious. Your righteousness in Christ allows you access to the throne of God at any time. Making it possible to tap into heavenly wisdom, power and ability, and this in turn, makes you master over your circumstances.

DAY 92

ANSWERS

απόκρίμα = *'apokrima'*
An answer or response of God

"But the voice answered me again from heaven" (Acts 11:9). A teenager came up to me and said, "Pastor, I've tried talking to God and waited for His answer but nothing's happened. I wonder if anyone is listening." I'm sure we've all felt like that at some time or other! When needing answers from God, ask yourself this: "What kind of answers are you expecting?" Are you looking for something extraordinary or spectacular? Because if you are, it's very likely it will not happen that way. The trouble with seeking the spectacular is that you may eventually get discouraged, and as a result, you will have a hard time believing that God does answer prayer.

I'm sure you've noticed that the better you know a person, the easier it is to communicate with that person. In the same way, the better you know God, and the closer you are to Him, the more you will understand His plans and purposes for you. That's the secret to getting the right answers. Don't just sit back and think that you can't hear God. Don't shout at God from some great distance, like a stranger. Draw near to Him and He will draw near to you! Invite Him to be so close to you that you can feel His divine breath on your life. Then, and only then, you will start to hear His voice and His answers will be very personal. Remember, if God is real to you, He doesn't need to use spectacular *special effects* to communicate.

DAY 93

ACCEPTANCE

ἀπόδεκτος = *'apothektos'*
That which is regarded favourably and is well-pleasing and wholly welcome

Feelings of dissatisfaction, frustration and disengagement can have an adverse effect on your relationships and also your ability to succeed in life. Whether it's with family, friends, co-workers, or church members, we all have an inherent desire to belong. From a spiritual perspective this yearning often has to do with being connected to someone greater than ourselves - a superior power. But basically, it's about each individual developing meaningful relationships that have more substance than a simple acquaintance.

In essence, the desire to belong comes from a basic human need to give and receive *affection* from others. Therefore, for you to live a healthy and productive life, the sense of belonging needs to be satisfied on a continual basis. And this is where God comes in! In Mark 9:41 Jesus makes this statement, *"For whoever gives you a cup of water to drink in My name, because you belong to Christ, assuredly, I say to you, he will by no means lose his reward."* Because you belong to Christ, others will get a reward when caring for you. So start each day by *accepting* that you are *accepted* in the Beloved (Eph. 1:6)! Remind yourself that you belong to Christ. That way, you can have no feelings of detachment.

DAY 94

UNCHANGEABLE

ἀπαράβατον = *'aparathaton'*
Constant, unchangeable, does not pass from one to another

In my opinion, stability is absolutely necessary if you are going to achieve God's plans and purposes for your life. There should be a sense of permanence and balance when you encounter others, and they encounter you. If you were to look at the life and ministry of Jesus you would see an *unchangeable* dimension to what He represented and what He did.

Hebrews 7:24 (AMP) states: *"But He, because He continues forever, has an unchangeable (permanent) priesthood."* As Jesus had an unchangeable ministry, so does every child of God. Why? Because we have the same Spirit as Jesus; operating the very same gifts, and with the same mission on this earth. The Holy Spirit is our *anchor man* and although there are diversities and allotments of gifts, it is "the same Spirit" operating all of them (1 Corinthians 12:4).

We all have different expectations and resolutions for improving our lives and circumstances. But I would like to believe that being consistent and steadfast is high on your list. Your family and friends need you to be *unchangeable,* totally dependable, because without this quality they would find it hard to rely on you. People are looking for stability and without you manifesting this attribute of Jesus, your spirituality cannot be attractive to them. Remember, being reliable means being trustworthy.

Day 95

Rest

ἀναπαύσω = *'anapavso'*
Refreshment, to make to cease – "I will give you rest"

As a consequence of the fast-paced, technology-driven society in which we live, people find it hard to be at rest. According to a recent study, living under abnormal time pressures triggers a myriad of psychological, social and physical ailments. The result of this disconnection from God's appointed pace for life is causing people to show up in therapists' and doctors' offices every day. Disconnected from the natural rhythms of our bodies, we struggle to adapt to the strange vacuum caused by the unspiritual world we have created.

Ravi Shankar said, "Activity and rest are two vital aspects of life. To find a balance in them is a skill in itself. Wisdom is knowing when to have rest, when to have activity, and how much of each to have. People are looking, struggling, striving, fighting, rushing, and searching; all in an effort to find what only Jesus Christ can give. Many are troubled and agitated in their souls, and they try to find rest in all the wrong places. People look everywhere and try everything in the effort to find rest for their souls. Yet, the only person who can give rest is Jesus, and His invitation is simple: "Come to Me!" *"Come to Me, all you who labour and are heavy laden, and I will give you rest"* (Matthew 11:28).

Accept Jesus' invitation today and you will find rest.

Day 96

Courage

θάρσος = *'tharsos'*
To be of good courage, to be brave

In 1 Chronicles 28:20 David said to Solomon his son, *"Be strong and courageous, and do the work. Do not be afraid or discouraged, for the Lord God, my God, is with you. He will not fail you or forsake you..."* Deuteronomy 31:6 declares, *"Be strong and of good courage, do not fear nor be afraid; for the Lord your God, He is the One who goes with you. He will not leave you nor forsake you."* It's interesting that strength precedes courage. But it makes perfect sense, because how can you be courageous if you are weak? Therefore, before attempting to exercise courage you must first get strong, and the way to get strong is to *know* that God is with you.

We all want to be strong and courageous. The truth is: Do you know who the real heroes are? Who the giants of courage are? I think it is those ordinary people who face the everyday challenges of life. When you stop and think about it, courage is a greater challenge in the little things than in the major battles. Every single day you make choices that can direct you to be fearful or to be courageous. When you get into the habit of being strong and courageous in your everyday life, one day at a time, then when the bigger challenges arrive you will be *battle ready.*

Remind yourself that sometimes the biggest act of *courage* is the smallest one. Then do what you can to help.

Day 97

Suddenly

ἀφνω = *'aphno'*
Suddenly, unexpectedly, abruptly, speedily

Isaiah 48:3, *"The former things I declared of old; they went out of My mouth and I announced them; then suddenly I did them, and they came to pass."* Most of us have had a word from the Lord that has not yet come to pass. Maybe you received it by revelation or by prophecy, or maybe you are simply standing on a promise of God. But whatever it is, it just hasn't happened! If that's you, be encouraged. Often when God does something, He does it *suddenly*! So don't be surprised, if God's word *suddenly* comes to pass when you least expect it.

A wonderful example of the Holy Spirit's extraordinary power arriving suddenly is found in Acts 16:26, *"And suddenly there was a great earthquake, so that the foundations of the prison were shaken. And immediately all the doors were opened and everyone's bonds were unfastened."* In their darkest hour, while Paul and Silas were praying and singing hymns to God, the Holy Spirit inhabited their praises and His mighty power set all the prisoners free. If it feels like your darkest hour, and you can't see any way out, start singing praises to God. If you do, it is very likely that the Holy Spirit will flood your circumstances with supernatural power and *suddenly* your prison doors will open!

Your liberty is near, it's here today!

DAY 98

QUESTIONING

εκζητήσεις = *'ekzitiseis'*
Questionings, speculations, assumptions

You should never confuse healthy inquisitiveness with doubt. Curiosity has its own reason for existing, and that is, to assist you in discovering the truth. Albert Einstein said, "Learn from yesterday, live for today, hope for tomorrow. The important thing is not to stop questioning." This is definitely good advice! When you stop questioning you cease walking down the path to discovery. There are too many Christians who are afraid to question in case it causes them to doubt God, but this is a ploy of the devil. God wants you to learn and remain teachable. Therefore, He must desire for you to be curious and seek answers to any questions that will arise along your spiritual journey.

Every question you ask concerning God should lead you to a place of peace. This way you will know that the Holy Spirit has helped you to find the truth. Colossians 3:15 (AMP) confirms this, *"And let the peace from Christ rule in your hearts (deciding and settling with finality all questions that arise in your minds); this is the peaceful state to which as members of one body you were also called to live."* So, keep being curios and remain teachable; knowing that God will answer all your questions, and as a result, only good will come out of it!

You are His child, so why expect anything less?

DAY 99

WE-ARE

εσμέν = *'esmen'*
To live, exist, or remain

When my daughter Xana was younger she came up to me and said, "Dad, so many people I know are either stuck in the past or preoccupied with the future. Very few know how to live in the 'now'. Very few have mastered the art of living in the moment. Why is that?" My answer to this question is, "Most people do not know who they are." Yet, God's word gives us many clear images of who we are in Christ. "In Him" is who you really are!

On a practical level, the best way to live in the moment is to concentrate on your breathing. Yes, just take a deep breath, and then take another deep breath and you will start to appreciate the fact that God has given you life. And the life He has given you is meant to be enjoyed moment by moment (with each breath). Every breath you take should remind you that you live because He lives! *"In Him we live and move and have our being"* (Acts 17:28). The original Greek simply says, "In Him we live and move and ARE."

In Christ you are everything God has created you to be! However, you cannot grasp this truth if you do not learn the art of living in the *present*. That's right, it's the very place you are occupying right now!

DAY 100

HOPE

ἐλπίσ = *'elpis'*
A favourable and confident expectation concerning the unseen

I often hear church members say, "I hope it will be ok." Hope is the basis for all positive change. But hope expressed in this way has a sense of helplessness about it. Therefore, be careful not to weaken or undermine the power of *hope*. Hope is a very forceful entity. G. K. Chesterton put it nicely, "There is no medicine like hope, no incentive so great, and no tonic so powerful as expectation of something better tomorrow." Emily Dickinson, in one of her poems said, "Hope is a thing with feathers, that perches in the soul." Martin Luther stated, "Everything that is done in the world is done by hope."

Faith is the substance of things *hoped* for (Hebrews 11:1). That means, without *hope* faith has nothing to materialise (to put substance to). Hope is a confident expectation that something good is about to happen. Are you resting in the *sure* confidence that God will do exactly what He has promised? That is the essence of hope! It is an attribute we all need to have large quantities of.

If you are going to possess sufficient *hope* for today, you must confidently look ahead without fear or apprehension, having an absolute and complete trust in the faithfulness of God.

DAY 101

FRIENDSHIP

φιλία = *'philia'*
The idea of loving as well as being loved

Many people do not value lasting relationships, and especially between friends. Thomas Aquinas said, "Friendship is the source of the greatest pleasures, and without friends even the most agreeable pursuits become tedious." This is a wise observation and can be applied to our relationship with God as well. In John 15:15 Jesus said, *"No longer do I call you servants, for the servant does not know what his master is doing; but I have called you friends, for all that I have heard from my Father I have made known to you."*

Not many understand the true value of friendship; particularly friendship with Jesus! In Christ Jesus you have a friend who wants to take care of your every need. But have you made your needs known to Him? In John 16:24 Jesus declared, *"Until now you have asked nothing in My name. Ask, and you will receive, that your joy may be full."* Maybe you have failed in this simple practice and you have forgotten the very person who has the power, authority and ability to reach out and meet your every need. If you have, don't worry because He is a true friend who is *faithful* to do what He promised!

Ask Him today; that you may receive, and be full of joy! Jesus is a friend who sticks closer than anyone, and who cares for you more than anyone!

Day 102

Attitude

διάνοια = *'thiania'*
An attitude, mindset, temperament or disposition

Ephesians 4:23 states, *"Your attitudes and thoughts must all be constantly changing for the better"* (Living Bible). Attitudes are developed through a thought process! Proverbs 23:7 says, *"As a man thinks in his heart so is he."* Your thoughts will determine your attitude, your attitude will affect your actions, and your actions will define your character. Successes and defeats are, in large part, attributed to your thinking. When you fill your mind with unbelief and dwell on disappointment, this negative attitude will produce defeat. But a *faith-filled* attitude will cause you to be a success. Attitude is everything!

If you were to think of your life in terms of a painting, what do you envisage? Is the picture worth painting? Whether you realize it or not, your mind is an artist that paints you into whatever image you allow it to perceive. John Milton said, "The mind is its own place, and in itself can make a heaven of hell, or a hell of heaven." It may take more effort to discipline your thinking and dwell on faith-filled thoughts than to give up and accept defeat. But you can do it! Let me ask you: "How are you thinking right now?" By confessing your identity in Christ, you'll change your mind-set and affect your entire future. Start this day with thoughts of victory and enjoy a liberty that you've never known before.

Day 103

Beginnings

ἀρχή = *'arghi'*
Commencements, establishments, to begin or start again

All beginnings are hard because they require you to free yourself from the past and step into uncharted territory. You may have forgotten how stressful it is to start afresh. To learn to walk, a child must release the helping hand, and it's no different the older you get. You have to learn to "let go", no matter how unsteady you may be feeling. Observing children helps to remind us of how difficult new beginnings are. Yet, children also show us what a thrill it can be to encounter something entirely new, perhaps even unexpected!

The word of God tells us to be just like little children. Little children get excited whenever they encounter something new; they are genuinely thrilled with the unexpected; and they love to be surprised. That is the way we are told to live our lives. What a joy it is to accept change and be excited about new beginnings! When God thinks of His children He has a confident expectation about their future (Jeremiah 29:11).

Your life is not a puzzle to be figured out, rather, you should run to the Father who already knows every detail. He is the Lord of new beginnings! God is already where you need to be! With His help you can *let go* and step into what He has prepared for you. Let go today and start afresh.

DAY 104

COMFORT

παρακλήσεως = *'parakliseos'*
Comfort, 'a calling to one's side', an encouragement

Comfort is very powerful, it has the ability to restore your body, quiet your mind, and renew your soul. No matter who you are, at some point you will cry out for comfort and value it greatly when it arrives. If we weren't in need of comfort, why would Jesus have asked the Father to send us a Comforter? *"And I will ask the Father, and He will give you another Comforter, that He may remain with you forever"* (John 14:16).

The power of comfort can change your life! But you will need to stop looking for comfort in all the wrong places. Stop trying to find comfort in a change of circumstances. True comfort comes from God alone; He is called *"the God of all comfort"* (2 Corinthians 1:3). Why Him? Because the same verse tells us that God is also "the Father of mercies." The term father implies *source*, so He is the source of all kinds of goodness and mercy. Comfort is just one of His many mercies. As the God of all comfort, there is no limitation to the comfort He provides.

For you, today may be a day of sadness, a day of grief, a day of mourning, yet even in the midst of this you can be comforted and find peace. God is here - He is near! Believe in Him, trust in Him, and the God of all comfort will grant you His perfect peace.

DAY 105

PRE-DESTINATION

προορισθέντες = *'pro-oristhentes'*
Foreordained, predestined, foreknown by God

Ephesians 1:11: ***Being predestined according to the purpose of Him who works all things according to the counsel of His will.*** You are predestined (programmed) to fulfil your destiny. A God-given destiny is not a series of random events, everything He has planned for your life has been predestined and predetermined. God looked out across eternity. He saw you. He saw everything he had created and everything He would create around you. He saw the specific need on this earth that He wants you to meet. He saw the full set of traits and abilities that you require in order to complete His purpose for your life. To get started, you must live your life with a sense of destiny, and en route, never plan your future holding onto the disappointments of the past.

God wants you to become exactly who He predestined you to be. You are destined for greatness! He wants to keep developing the abilities He put inside of you. He doesn't want you to try and swap what He has given you for what He has given someone else. You are made up of a unique blend of talents and gifting and character; and you have a unique destiny upon which these are based. In God's eyes you are meant to be a success because you are very special. You one of a kind, so remind yourself of this fact on a daily basis.

DAY 106

EXPECTANCY

προσεδόκων = '*prosethokon*'
Anticipating, to be expecting, awaiting

What you confidently expect for your life, from both people and situations, will determine your attitude toward them more than any other factor. In Psalm 62:5-6 the psalmist said this, *"My soul, wait silently for God alone, for my expectation is from Him. He is my rock and my salvation; He is my defence; I shall not be moved."* Notice, if your expectations are from God you will remain steadfast. However, there is something else you must be aware of. That is, whatever you expect with confidence, becomes a self-fulfilling prophecy. This also applies to your relationship with God.

What you expect from God will determine your attitude toward Him. If you confidently expect God to be doing great things on your behalf, great things will always happen to you. However, if you expect negative things to happen, you are usually not disappointed. What you expect acts like a mirror in your life. What you see, is what you get!

Hebrews 11:1 says, *"Faith is the substance of things hoped for, the evidence of things not seen."* This could read: "Faith is the substance of things confidently expected." Your faith materialises your positive expectations. So picture yourself today with unlimited potential. After all, He has equipped you with great abilities.

Day 107

Inspiration

θεόπνευστος = *'theopnevstos'*
God-breathed, inspired by God

Human inspiration stimulates or invigorates a person with a particular emotion or to a particular action, but it has no divine influence. Consequently, any thought or emotion or action it arouses is void of God's ability to shape a person's character or positively affect their future. As a Christian, you have the greatest source of inspiration already living in you - the Holy Spirit. If you need inspiration today, simply ask Him for it! The Holy Spirit's inspiration will guide you through every dark valley and lift any cloud of confusion. He has the power to exquisitely influence your thoughts, emotions and actions for your good but to God's glory.

The Holy Spirit can inspire you to do superabundantly, far above all that you dare ask or think; and infinitely beyond your highest prayers, desires, hopes or dreams (Ephesians 3:20). Now, that is something really awesome and truly inspirational! So why settle for second best? Why allow your senses to be stimulated by the world around you when inside of you abides the source of unlimited inspiration?

What do you need from God today? It's easy to think that we should not to ask for too much, but God longs to give us the desires of our heart and pour out His favour and blessing on us. Therefore, confidently ask Him, that you may receive!

DAY 108

CONDEMNATION

κατάκριμα = ' *katakrima*'
To give judgement against, to pass sentence upon

Recently, a young lady inquired, "Pastor, I am so depressed right now because I feel that the mistakes of my past are so many that I can't have a good future. Must I suffer the rest of my life for my mistakes?" Unfortunately, such fear and condemnation is not uncommon among teenagers. Many Christians, young and old alike, think they are being punished for their mistakes. The truth is we all make mistakes. Therefore, we need to discern the difference between punishment and the consequences of our choices.

Romans 8:1 says, *"There is now no condemnation for those who are in Christ Jesus."* Hence, God does not punish you for your mistakes. If peace, joy, and fulfillment are eluding you, it's probably because you have your cup upside down, and this is preventing you from receiving the blessings that God is pouring out. He can work in any situation in your life, provided you trust Him enough to hand it over. So many precious people have missed great opportunities simply because they don't trust God enough to fix their mistakes. While things may seem hopeless and unchangeable, if you hand everything over to God, He can turn it all around and create something good from it. You're not to suffer for your mistakes, rather, to live in perfect peace.

Day 109

Miracles

σημεῖον = *'simeon'*
Miracles, signs of divine authority

How often have you prayed: "Lord, I need a miracle?" Meaning; "God, please intervene and supernaturally deal with my situation." I am sure that God wants to help every one of us, and do it in such a way that He gets all the glory, but often we ask for a miracle because it is the soft option. We take the path of least resistance. A miracle is only necessary when no person, human ability or natural occurrence has the power to accomplish what is required – only God. When something needs to be done that only God can accomplish, you need a miracle. You need Him to exercise His divine authority! Miracles are those acts that only God can perform - usually superseding natural laws.

When your heart is perfect towards Him, God watches out for an opportunity to do a great thing for you. We are all in need of miracles, and thank God, we have the God of miracles looking out for us. I sense in my spirit that you are about to receive the thing you've been waiting on. God says there's going to be an outpouring from the heavens. Everything that was bound up or held up is about to be freed. You've reached the end of your waiting season, your miracle is ready to appear.

Therefore, plan for your miracle - it's about to arrive!

Day 110

Regrets

μεταμέλομαι = *'metamelome'*
To regret, to repent, to carry sorrows

These two words, "If only," can shape your future and create an environment whereby past failures govern every decision that you make. Any regret may cause you to evaluate future things based on a negative experience, and this is not pleasing to the Lord. Having regrets implies that you have not forgiven yourself, and unforgiveness, whether it is directed towards others or yourself is a form of imprisonment (Matthew 18:21-35). Your regrets can hold you captive to the failures of the past. The fact is, we all make mistakes, have struggles, and even regret things in our past. But you are not your mistakes, you are not your struggles, and you are here now with the power to shape this day and your future.

Certainly, there is no such thing as a life lived with absolutely no regrets because we all fall short in many ways. Only Jesus truly could say, "It is finished," and know that He had perfectly completed all that God had for Him to do. The rest of us will struggle with a sense of failure, of projects uncompleted, of dreams unfulfilled, of steps not taken, or roads not travelled, or decisions made that now seem like wrong choices. There is no way of denying this! Therefore the question is, what will you do with your failures? The key is to confess: "I won't go back. I'm not going to live in the past. I won't let my yesterday's define who I am today. I am free from all regrets."

Day 111

Victorious

νίκη / νίκαω = *'niki' /'nikao'*
To overcome, overthrow, conquer, to be victorious

Throughout my ministry people have come up to me and said, "Pastor, I can't seem to get the victory!" Time and time again I have seen the desperation in their faces. So what is the answer? How can you be sure of getting the victory in every situation? The truth is, it's not an easy question to answer. You've probably heard numerous sermons about victory, or living a victorious life. Joel Osteen once said, "You cannot expect victory and plan for defeat." This immediately brings to mind 1 John 5:4, *"For whatever is born of God overcomes the world. And this is the victory that has overcome the world - our faith."*

Notice it says, "this is the victory that has (past tense) overcome – our faith." True faith has its origins in God, nowhere else, and this is what has secured the victory for us. When you have faith in the Lord Jesus and you apply God's infallible word to your situation, nothing can prevent you from being victorious! Faith is the victory! It doesn't say that your faith carries you into victory. But rather, that faith *is* the victory. Faith itself; the reality of faith in you, that is the victory! Therefore, the victory does not begin out there, in the circumstances of life. Victory begins within, between God and you. Yes, your faith has already overcome every negative situation that is confronting you. This is the victory – your *faith*!

Day 112

Accord

ὁμοθυμαδὸν = '*omothumadon*'
In one accord, gathering with passion, having one mind and purpose

Acts 5:*12, "And through the hands of the apostles many signs and wonders were done among the people. And they were all with one accord in Solomon's Porch."* The Greek word translated *with one accord* means "having one mind and purpose" and expresses "a harmony leading to action." It is derived from two other ancient Greek words. The one signifies "at the same place or time together," and the other implies, "with passion or fierce indignation." Therefore, being *of one accord* is literally, being at the same place and filled with passion. Notice how this phrase reflects a quality that is active, positive and inspiring; a passion that is missing in most of today's church services.

Whenever the Holy Spirit gathers God's people together *in one accord*, He manifests the perfect and unique features of Jesus Christ. Being *in one accord* is powerful because we collectively come under the control of the Holy Spirit. He unites us with Christ and we then have one will, one purpose and one determination. Formidable! Unity, harmony and the state of being *of one accord*, is the responsibility of every believer.

Therefore, you must earnestly pursue this condition every time you meet with other Christians. That is how signs and wonders can manifest each and every day.

DAY 113

DISCIPLE

μαθηταὶ = *'mathite'*
One who is being taught, to teach others to be teachers

Matthew 5:1, *"And seeing the multitudes, He went up on a mountain, and when He was seated His disciples came to Him."* It was the custom for rabbis to sit while teaching and Jesus did the same. When He'd found a suitable spot, His disciples gathered round. However, after a time, the *disciples* probably included a much wider audience.

The Greek word translated disciple, means a student - *'one who is being taught'*, but a better paraphrase would be *'one who is being taught to teach others to be teachers'*. A disciple teaches others, to teach others to teach! It is a recurring action brought about by a divine calling. This is a distinct process that Jesus started, having prior and full knowledge of the outcome: *"Therefore, go make disciples of all nations"* (Matthew 28:19). True disciples would impact on nations and frame the tapestry of a new society. Social and moral standards would be measured against God's word. The church and the state would become one: under One God.

You may not think that you have the ability to teach, but Jesus would not have given us the "great commission' if every believer was not equipped to *make disciples*. Inside you is a teaching gift that is aligned to the gospel (the good news). Use it and be blessed!

DAY 114

ADOPTION

υἱοθεσίας = *'iothesias'*
The placing of a son, full acceptance into a family

Romans 8:14 & 15: *"For as many as are led by the Spirit of God, these are sons of God. For you did not receive the spirit of bondage to fear, but you received the Spirit of adoption by whom we cry out 'Abba, Father'."* You have received the Holy Spirit who produces in you a consciousness and realisation of sonship whereby you cry *Abba, Father*. The word adoption is found only five times in the Bible, all in the New Testament. We notice also that it is a word used exclusively by Paul. The Greek word literally means the placing as a son, and signifies the position and condition of a son, but given to one to whom the title does not naturally apply.

Hence, a New Testament definition of *adoption* may be; that process or act by which God places and positions a repentant sinner into the divine family, in order to become a legal heir to all the rights and privileges normally only available to sons. Technically, as offspring of Adam, you are an heir to his fallen state. But now, you have been placed under the rule of the kingdom of life in Christ Jesus. The question you should be asking yourself today is this: "Do I have a conscious understanding of my sonship whereby I cry *Abba Father* (Daddy)?" For when you have a complete revelation of *adoption* you will begin to share in all the benefits of your inheritance as a joint-heir with Jesus Christ.

Day 115

Finished

τετελέσται = *'tetelestai'*
It has been finished or completed as required, it is done

John 19:30, *"So when Jesus had received the sour wine, He said, "It is finished!" And bowing His head, He gave up His spirit."* The final word spoken by Jesus and recorded by John is, *"It is finished."* The Greek word was a very common word in that society. It was used by a slave who had completed an assignment given to him by his master. He would report back and say, *"It has been finished!"* It was also used of an artist who had completed work on a painting. He would step back and say, "It's done!" It was used by a merchant who had sold merchandise on credit. When the bill had been paid in full he would write in his ledger book, *"It is finished!"* Note, this word is written in the perfect tense, which means something that took place in the past has a present abiding effect. Therefore, it could also be translated; "It stands finished and always will be finished!" In other words, Jesus is saying, "it has been done now and forevermore!"

Thank God every day that your salvation rests upon the *finished* work on the cross. It has been finished to the full, now and forevermore. When you visit the cross you are affirming your complete trust in the *forever finished* work of Jesus Christ, and nothing else. All said and done, you can live a victorious life. Jesus has established the victory by the finished work on the cross. There is nothing more that can be done!

DAY 116

GOOD

ἀγαθός / καλῆ = *'agathos' / 'kali' (kalos)*
Intrinsically good, good by nature, beneficially good

In **Luke 8:15** both *kalos* and *agathos* appear side by side in the same passage of scripture. *"But the ones that fell on the good (kali) ground are those who, having heard the word with an honest (kali) and good (agathi) heart, keep it and bear fruit with patience."* The first thing we notice is that the ground is good, yet this does not necessarily mean it is beneficial in its effect.

The fact that you have received the word in your heart makes it *good* ground, but until you have produced fruit, there cannot be any beneficial effect. Read on.... *"Having heard the word with an honest (kali) and good (agathi) heart, keep it and bear fruit with patience."* Here is my literal translation: "But the word of God that fell on right soil are those who, having heard the word with a correct attitude and an essentially good heart, take hold of the word and steadily bring forth fruit with patience and fortitude (some thirtyfold, some sixty, and some a hundred)."

If you are going to produce a good crop and prosper in life, you must hear God's word with an honest attitude and essentially good heart. Without these qualities, the soil is not good enough to bring forth fruit. But the key to producing a good crop is keeping or obeying God's word. Examine your heart and attitude today. See if your heart qualifies as *good*.

Day 117

Persecuted

Δεδιωγμένοι = *'thethiogmeni'*
To be pursued, driven away, illtreated, harassed, victimized

Matthew 5:10-11: *"Blessed are those who are persecuted from righteousness sake, for theirs is the kingdom of heaven. Blessed are you when they revile and persecute you, and say all kinds of evil falsely against you for My sake."* (Original Greek) *"Blessed are they who have been persecuted on account of righteousness."* Notice, neither translation says "on account of being righteous." Hence, the primary cause of persecution is loyalty or devotion to righteousness, and *righteousness* in this context means anything that conforms to and is consistent with the revealed will of God (as in *verse 6*). However, the revealed will of God is His Word. Therefore, whenever you align yourself to God's will for your life, or do anything that conforms to and is consistent with His Word, you attract persecution. Obedience to the Word makes you a target!

Here, we clearly see the results of spiritual maturity. As you mature, you are capable of reconciling your actions and they begin to agree with God's revealed will for you. The Greek word for means to be *pursued* or *driven away* (as an animal that is being hunted). Persecution is a direct result of your life being in complete alignment to the will of God. The good news is, the might of heaven is backing your every move. This is what the devil hates. So he tries to drive you away from the will of God. Don't let him - stand firm!

Day 118

Raise-Up

ἀναστήσας = *'anastisas'*
To raise up, having raised up, changing a physical position

Acts 13:33: *"God has fulfilled this for us their children, in that He raised up Jesus. As it is written in the second Psalm: 'You are My Son, today I have begotten You'."* In this verse the word *anastisas* appears and it can be translated "raised up" or "having raised up again." There is an argument in favour of both translations. Note, there is no mention of death; it does not say "raised up from the dead." If *anastasis* is given a meaning which indicates the "changing of one's physical position" (taking on another form), it can only mean the *new position* that Jesus was placed in when He ascended to be seated at the right hand of God. I believe this points directly to Christ's pre-eminence. His exceedingly superior position.

Ephesians 2:6 openly declares that God *"raised us up together, and made us sit together in the heavenly places in Christ Jesus."* Therefore, we have changed our physical position and have taken on another form; the very position and form that Jesus took on. Now, all our enemies are under our feet. The exceeding power and superiority given to Jesus is available to us. We have been *raised up* to rule and reign with Him!

See yourself seated with Jesus in heavenly places. You will find that everything coming against you soon disappears into obscurity.

DAY 119

WORKERS-TOGETHER

Συνεργοῦντες = *'synergountes'*
Workers together, fellow workers, collaborators, teammates, associates

In 2 Corinthians 6:1 the apostle Paul says, *"We then, as workers together with Him also plead with you not to receive the grace of God in vain."* The Greek word means to *cooperate, assist, support, collaborate* or *facilitate.* It implies a practical hands-on harmony, synergism and balance between the parties involved. There isn't any disunity, discord or incompatibility. It is exactly the way Jesus worked together with His Father.

You have the Spirit of Unity and togetherness living in you, the Holy Spirit, who helps you to keep in harmony and in perfect balance with God the Father. He is here to glorify Jesus through the work that you undertake together. However, you must first learn to *work together* and *walk together* with others as well. You are a worker who is in complete harmony with God, but you are also fully compatible with God. The interaction and cooperation between you and God produces a combined effect that is truly astounding. As a *fellow-worker*, appointed by grace, you have been given the legal right to exercise authority over every evil scheme the devil would try to implement. And when you do this, you are collaborating with the very power that defeated him in the first place. Today, as a *fellow-worker*, use the resurrection power that is at your disposal.

DAY 120

TEACH

Δίδασκο = *'thithasko'*
To teach, impart knowledge, communicate wisdom

Matthew 5:2: *"Then He opened His mouth and taught them saying..."* The Greek word for teach implies a *repetitive, ongoing process*. Notice, the scripture says Jesus opened His mouth and began to *teach* them, it does not say He began talking to them. Teaching in this context takes commitment by the teacher as it is his responsibility to see it through. Here, the new disciples were novices and therefore they needed teaching. Therefore, they could not be considered disciples until they had been fully equipped by Jesus to make teachers of others. With this in mind, Jesus starts teaching The Beatitudes for the primary benefit of His chosen few. In fact, it is not until the seventh chapter that the crowds find Him and we see a distinct change in the direction and style of His teaching.

Regarding your walk with Jesus, you must remain teachable concerning all matters of life. Proverbs 12:1 reveals how important it is to have a teachable spirit: *"Whoever loves instruction loves knowledge, But he who hates correction is stupid."* Strong words, but necessary if you are to fulfil every assignment from God. Resist the temptation to think you know enough to get along without further instruction. You always need Jesus to teach you something new, commencing immediately!

DAY 121

ANGELS

ἄγγελος = 'angelos'
A messenger (from angello, "to deliver a message"), sent whether by God or by man or by satan, guardian

Are there really angels? According to the Bible, yes! God's word speaks often of angels (about 200 times in the New Testament alone), but it explains very little about them. The most basic role that angels play is that of "delivering messages from God." Angels are mighty and very powerful beings. In God's word angels are recorded as having opened prison doors, rolled away the stone at the grave of Jesus, and even engaging in war with evil men. God grants them the ability from time to time to change the course of nature (Revelation 7:1).

Today, you should be conscious that angels are all around you, waiting for instructions that only you can give them. They *harken* (respond to and obey) the word of God (Psalm 103:20). Angels are "following the voice of His word." Now, who gives voice to God's word? You do! Each time you speak God's word, you give voice to it. And when angels hear His word, that has been vocalised, they respond! When angels hear you saying, "Thank You, Father, no evil shall befall me nor shall any plague come near my dwelling" (Psalm 91:10), they will come to your aid because you are giving *voice* to God's word. Give voice to God's Word today and see His angels respond. God's angels are activated for your benefit when you speak His Word.

DAY 122

AUTHORITY

ἐξουσία = *'exousia'*
The right to exercise power, liberty of doing as one pleases

"Behold, I give you the authority to trample on serpents and scorpions, and over all the power of the enemy, and nothing shall by any means hurt you" (Luke 10:19). So what is authority? Firstly, let us define the difference between authority and power. In the New Testament the translators have not been uniform in the rendering of many Greek words, and these two words have been especially effected. One notable instance is in our opening scripture (Luke 10:19) where *power* is frequently used twice, even though there is a different Greek word in each instance. Translating the first of these with the word *authority* gives a clearer idea of the true meaning of this passage. The Greek word *exousia* is literally "the right to exercise power", however, its root meaning is "the liberty of doing as one pleases."

Authority is delegated power. Its effectiveness depends entirely upon the force behind the user. When you are fully conscious of the divine power behind you, and of your own *authority*, you can face the enemy without fear or hesitation. So stop trying to exercise authority for the sake of it. Exercise authority because the Supreme Person (Jesus Christ), who is behind the authority you have been given, has instructed you to use it. He has given you *authority* over all the power of the devil. So don't waist it – use it!

DAY 123

PERSISTENCE

ἀναίδειαν = *'anaithian'*
Persistence, tenacity, resolve, determination

In Luke 18:1-7, Jesus gave us this parable as an example of how to pray and ask God in order to make things right. Jesus was comparing the widow to "you and me" and the judge to God the Father. He is telling us to literally *keep asking* God for what we need. To ask until He gives it to us! Many of you have probably been told at one time or other to ask God only once for what you need, for if you ask Him more than once, you are not exercising your faith correctly.

This is not true. There is a difference between babbling and believing. Jesus tells us plainly to be very persistent! Go to the Lord's prayer in Luke 11:1, then read the passage immediately after it (Luke 11:5-8). Jesus gave His listeners a parable to explain how we ought to pray. Then He gives an illustration that demonstrates persistence and insistence: *"Yet because of his persistence he will get up and give him as much as he needs."* Does it seem like God is trying to tell us something? Can we insist that He gives us what we need?

Maybe you need to change your attitude toward receiving from God. Start by acting as if you are a son or daughter in God's household, and be *persistent* when you ask! Then, if you still don't feel important enough to talk to God directly, just tell Him "Jesus sent you!" Next, keep knocking until the door opens and you get what you've been asking for.

DAY 124

DESIRE

ἐπιθυμία = *'epithymia'*
Desire, eagerness for, excessive desire, fervent longing

Psalm 37:4 says, *"Delight yourself in the Lord; and He will give you the desires of your heart."* Does this passage mean that the Father gives us whatever we want? No! Because not every *desire* is Christlike, even good aspirations can be wrong for a particular individual.

You have the Holy Spirit living in you, so ask Him to reveal which *desires* are in line with God's plan for your life. Ask yourself: "Why do I believe this desire is from God and not just from myself?" And remember, the most important thing to do is to wait. Rushing into desires can be very dangerous, and especially when your dreams have not come to fruition. Therefore, surrender the eagerness to the Lord. In other words, delight yourself in Him, commit to love and serve Him, even if your *longings* never materialise. Often, waiting prompts you to surrender a specific desire, and this may be exactly what God wants.

What if you believe that God gave you a desire but He has never granted it? There are a couple of factors here. One is the possibility that you simply need to continue waiting. Second, you may have mistaken your own desire for a God-given one. Your wishes can be so strong and enthusiastic that you think you've heard from God, when in fact, you've been misled by your own excessive longings. Most certainly, have desires today, but make sure God has put them there!

Day 125

Covet

ζηλοῦτε = *'ziloute'*
Passionate desire, crave, long for, covet

1 Corinthians 14:1: *"Covet earnestly the best gifts."* This means you should passionately desire for God's spiritual gifts to operate in you, so that others can be blessed. When the Bible uses *covet* in a negative sense, it speaks of "cravings for something inappropriate" or "something apart from God's divine will." The essence of covetousness is this... It is a selfish and greedy desire to have your own way no matter what! That means greed and covetousness are conflicting with God's will. And this type of craving never satisfies you. That's because it detracts from your affection and devotion toward God; who should be the main focus of your heartfelt desires.

The law of gravity reveals an amazing principle. It is this: "The greater an object's mass, the greater its power to attract." This explains why huge planets like Jupiter and Neptune can attract the orbit of many satellites and smaller planets like Venus and Pluto aren't large enough to attract anything. The greater the mass the greater the attraction. So what does this law of gravity teach us? It teaches us to carefully determine what enlarges our being (the human soul). Because when your life is enlarged with carnal things of the world, it will attract dark forces. However, if your life is being enlarged day-by-day with heavenly things, it will attract divine forces. It's your life, it's your choice!

DAY 126

DESTROY

λύση = *'lusi'*

To destroy, to loose, to release, to dissolve, to set at naught

1 John 3:8: *"For this purpose the Son of God was manifested, that He might destroy the works of the devil."* God has purposed that every atom of the terrible work of the devil upon the earth shall be destroyed! Yes, mark that word, *destroyed*. Not limited, nor alleviated, nor neutralised, but totally destroyed! If this is the Divine decree, then the devil trembles at the very thought of it. For there shall come an end, all his evil works.

The image of God in us has been marred by the work of satan. Could we restore that image? That which has been done by the powers of darkness must be undone by the Eternal Light. It is God's purpose to win such a victory over the Prince of Darkness, so that every work of his shall be destroyed! Jesus our Champion has come out with a shout of victory to divide the spoils with us. Our arch-enemy has been vanquished and his works are destroyed.

Are you living your life in the reality that *all* the works of the devil have been destroyed? You may be thinking, "What proof do I have." Well, if Jesus came, then the obliteration has already happened. Our opening scripture states, "For this purpose Jesus was manifested!" His prior determination was to call on this earth and destroy all the works of the devil. Now, it important for you to live like that's a reality.

DAY 127

HOME

οικος = '*oikos*' .

A house, dwelling, to home, to a house, to (their) home

When we welcome Jesus into our lives we find ourselves at *home* as children in His household. If someone were to ask you where home is, what would you tell them? Home in a sense is to where you return - perhaps literally or mentally - certainly relationally. Many of us still think of *home* as the place where we grew up. Others, the place where we raised our children. But as a child of God, you must consider having a permanent place (a spiritual home) where you can return each day and spend time with your heavenly Father.

In Mark 8, before Jesus feeds the multitudes, He said this, *"And if I send them away hungry to their own homes, they will faint on the way; for some of them have come from afar"* (verse 3). This raises a question: "If Jesus would not send anyone home hungry, would He have anyone in His own house be hungry?" Definitely not! Therefore, every time you visit God's household, you can expect Him to meet your basic necessities (Matthew 7:11).

A home is a place of refuge, a place of peace, a sanctuary where you feel protected and loved. And this is what you will discover when you develop an intimate relationship with your heavenly Father. It reminds me of Psalm 91: *"He who dwells in the secret place of the Most High, shall abide under the shadow of the Almighty."* Make your home today, "in the secret place of the Most High!"

Day 128

Jealousy

ζῆλος = *'zelos'*
Envy, zeal, jealousy, greed, resentment

Romans 13:13 (NIV): *"Let us behave decently, as in the daytime, not in carousing and drunkenness, not in sexual immorality and debauchery, and not in dissension and jealousy."* Benjamin Franklin said, "It is the eyes of other people that ruin us. If all but myself were blind, I should want neither a fine house nor fine furniture." This quote is an example of defective assumptions that too many of us are guilty of. We all need to find the root causes of jealousy. The Greeks get very concerned about the *evil eye*, so they pin a porcelain eye on the vest of a child to ward of the curse of jealousy. A bit extreme, but there is an element of truth in it. Sinful actions can start with what the eye perceives!

There's a distinction between jealousy and envy. To envy is to want something which belongs to another person. In contrast, jealousy is the fear that something which you possess will be taken away by another person. Although jealousy can apply to your job, your possessions, or your reputation, the word more often refers to anxiety that comes when you are afraid that the affections of a loved one might be lost to a rival. You can counteract jealousy with God's help. So, ask the Lord to help you replace any jealous feelings with a trust in His ability to do what is best for you today. He will do this in His own sovereign way.

DAY 129

POSSESS

κτᾶσθαι = *'ktasthe'*
To possess, to procure for oneself, to acquire or obtain

When defining his ministry the apostle Paul said this: *"As poor, yet making many rich; as having nothing and yet possessing all things"* (2 Corinthians 6:10). He was letting others know that possessions do not matter. He could be poor and yet be rich, he might have nothing and yet possess all things. What a great attitude to have. Most people would not be content with having nothing. But it must be made clear, God wants you to possess the things He has put aside for you.

So what are we to possess? We're to possess the promises of God. But be warned, it may not always be that easy! When God told the Israelites to go in and possess the Promised Land, it appeared as though the Jordan River was an impenetrable barrier between them and the land of promise. You see, the river was at flood stage, and there was no way to cross it. Has a river at flood stage come into your life, causing you a lot of problems? Instead of taking a step of faith, are you standing at the bank crying, "Lord, will You do something about the river"? Possessing what God has for you takes faith. Standing on the edge of obedience with wishful thinking won't get you across your river and into your promised land. It's time that you begin to speak the Word with authority over your situation. Then, move out in the power of the Holy Spirit to receive what already belongs to you. Today is your day to begin possessing the promise.

DAY 130

TRIUMPH

θριαμβεύω = 'thriambeuo'
To lead in triumph, used of a conqueror with reference to the vanquished

2 Corinthians 2:14: *"Now thanks be to God who always leads us in triumph in Christ, and through us diffuses the fragrance of His knowledge in every place."* Paraphrased it reads, "He leads us about here and there and displays us to all the world." Those who are led are not captives exposed to humiliation, but are displayed as the devoted subjects of Him who leads (*as with a Roman procession*). On such occasions the general's sons, with various officers, rode behind his chariot. The main thought is that of the pageant *in Christ* which displays conquest. And it is exactly what we all share in.

In Colossians 2:15 the circumstances and subjects are quite different, and relate to Christ's victory over spiritual foes at the time of His death; accordingly that reference may also be the triumphant display of a defeated foe. *"Having disarmed principalities and powers, He made a public spectacle of them, triumphing over them in it."* In what? In the work of the cross! Because of the Cross, and the victory it established over the enemy, you are able to live your life as if you are constantly on parade (behind Jesus) flaunting His conquest. You're more than a conqueror! Let your life be a triumphant procession displaying victory after victory. Starting today!

Day 131

Reaping

θερίζω = *'therizo'*
To reap, harvest, gain, procure

"Do not be deceived: God cannot be mocked. A man reaps what he sows." (Galatians 6:7). Here Paul is thinking about the pathway of God's blessing for believers so he uses the illustration of sowing and reaping to drive the point home. The explanation goes like this: Since you always reap whatever you sow, generous giving results in generous blessing. The principle itself is easy to understand. If you plant apple seeds, apple trees are what you get. You can't plant carrots and expect to harvest corn and you can't plant wheat and expect to harvest rice. You reap only what you sow. That is true in the spiritual realm as well.

Picture a country estate with two large fields. One is labeled Flesh, the other is labeled Spirit. Every day you have hundreds of chances to sow in one field or the other. In fact, everything you do is either sowing to the flesh or sowing to the Spirit. There is no third alternative. Every word you speak, every step you take, every chance conversation, even the tiniest decision leads you in one direction or the other. This includes what you read, how you dress, and who you are associating with. Life is a series of choices every day, and every choice is sowing a seed into the *flesh* field or sowing a seed into the *spirit* field. So, if you want to reap a harvest of God's blessings, make sure you are sowing your seeds in the right field.

DAY 132

LIGHT

φῶς = *'phos'*

To give light, light as seen by the eye, light as reaching the mind

John 1:4: *"In Him was life, and the life was the light of men. And the light shines in the darkness, and the darkness did not comprehend it."* People often follow the counterfeit light of the world system. It may be bright and very enticing; and it appeals to the basic human need to live in the light. However, it's not the True Light! Be careful for the Bible tells us that the devil comes as an angel of light to deceive many. All that shines brightly is not all that it seems! True light always leads you to Christ - to a place of worship.

What's more, the true Light (Jesus) will lead you into fellowship with God, and with others. This is the ministry of reconciliation! God's glorious light shines brightly into your life: lighting up your path and directing your ways. Without God's light you would be in darkness; lost and confused.

Without the Light of Life reconciliation could not be made between God and you. Hence, without the Light you would not be able to experience the "peace of God which surpasses all understanding" (Philippians 4:7). If you want to fill your life with happiness, you must first fill your life with Light. So make sure Christ is the only Star you are following today. His light is His presence, and in His presence is fullness of joy.

DAY 133

LION

λέων = 'leon'

Lion, majesty and strength, indicative of royalty, courage

"Then one of the elders said to me, "Do not weep! See, the Lion of the tribe of Judah, the Root of David, has triumphed. He is able to open the scroll and its seven seals" (Revelation 5:5). The lion, in relation to the Lord, is an image of the absolute fearlessness and invincible strength with which He stands by us, to teach the truth and to protect us from evil. We have only to trust Him, and we will be safe.

In Psalm 104:21 it says, *"The young lions roar after their prey, and seek their food from God."* The lions are meant to be the angels of heaven; and their roaring after their prey, is described as the desire of the angels for renewed love and wisdom from the Lord. The angels are called young lions, and the Lord a Lion. The angels, like young lions, constantly seek food. So they look to the Lord for nourishment.

Notice how young lions are fierce, they roar loudly, and are characterised by their hunger! They seek food all the time - not milk, but meat! Together with the angels in heaven, we should be like young lions, ever hungry for the Lord. We must move away from desiring milk, to strong meat for spiritual food. We should have tasted of the Lord, and as a result, desire nothing else. Are you as hungry as a young lion today? Have you savoured the Lord Jesus today? For if you have, you will yearn for nothing else.

DAY 134

BREAKTHROUGH

διορύσσω = *'thiorysso'*
To breakthrough, to dig through, to break in

The battle is the Lord's, however, you have a part to play, and that is, to trust and believe His promises in the face of impossibilities and what seems at times to be unbearable. Faith demands that you turn over all your problems; all your critical situations, all your fears, all your anxieties; into the capable hand of the Lord. When you have done all you can, and you know that your battle is beyond any human abilities, you must then surrender everything to the Lord and expect a break-through (like a raging flood). Live in anticipation of a break-through! He will move heaven and earth to deliver you and make a way for total victory. The way out today is simply to trust! *"God makes wars to cease"* (Psalm 46:9).

In what areas of your life are you wanting God to *break-through*? God is the Master Breaker and He will bring *break-through* into your life. All you need to do is ask Him! God is true to His word, so He will break through in any situation, no matter what you are going through. Speak to God from your heart and ask Him for a *breakthrough*. Proclaim Him to be *Baal-Perazim* "the God who breaks through like a raging river."

Even when the odds are stacked against you, He is still the Lord who breaks through. He is the Master Breaker! Nothing can resist His power and might.

DAY 135

WINGS

πτέρυξ = *'pterux'*
Wings of a bird, wings of the great eagle

Revelation 12:14: *"The two wings of the great eagle."* Have you ever thought about the wings of God? When I was young I kept pigeons. I remember the mother bird laying her eggs and guarding those eggs by sitting on them and watching over them. When those eggs hatched these tiny, helpless little birds appeared. They had no feathers, their eyes were shut, and they looked very vulnerable. However, the mother was there, and with her instinct to provide protection and care, she kept her young chicks under her wings and provided a place of protection and security. Those wings were a refuge for her offspring.

Looking into the psalms, there are a number of verses which talk about how the "wings of God" provide a place of safety, security and refuge for us. The first thing we will notice is that the "wings of God" are a place of refreshment; Psalm 63 is a psalm that was written by David when he was out in the wilderness of Judah; he was in a dry, parched place. Yet in the midst of that dry place, he found the "wings of God" - a place of satisfaction and a place of refreshing. I would like to remind you today that you have a safe place, a refuge, a shelter in the midst of any hardship you may be experiencing. Approach the Lord right now and say, "Lord, I come to find refuge under Your wings. You are more than enough; You are sufficient; You are my hiding place; and in You I am completely safe."

DAY 136

BOATS

πλοιάριον = *'plyarion'*
A small boat, a fishing vessel

Jesus always meets you where you are! Three times in the Gospels we find Jesus meeting people in situations that involve boats, and each time we see different reactions from those involved. We can all learn something from their responses to the storms of life.

(1) "The boat of your fears" (Mark 4:35-41). The Lord chose to exercise His authority over the wind and the waves, but those on board became fearful. In what areas of your life are you tempted to respond with fear rather than faith? It may seem like you have been forsaken, left exposed to the elements, but you need to rest in faith during every storm.
(2) "The boat of your disappointments" (Matthew 14:25-32). Each time that Peter failed he managed to gather himself. He never failed, despite his disappointments. You too must have this sort of determination and drive to ensure that you also come through.
(3) "The boat of your lack" (John 21:3-8). If you've been fishing all night and haven't caught a thing, don't be discouraged. All you need to do is listen. When you hear His voice, simply cast out your net in the exact location He tells you. Yes, obey His voice, there's a miracle catch awaiting you!

DAY 137

ENTHUSIASM

ζέω = *'zeo'*

To be hot, to boil, to be fervent, enthusiastic, to have zeal

If you are anything like me, you are probably living in your enthusiasm or 'passions'. I've never been ashamed of being a wholehearted person. There is a line in a well-known hymn that says, *"Love with every passion blending"*. This states that love (and it is speaking of our human love) is foundational; all other passions must be submitted to and blended with the grand passion of love. But we don't love alone, God loves too! And God is zealous; impassioned and enthusiastic.

A major study was done to find the one single trait that great leaders all possess, and it was *enthusiasm*. Colossians 4:12 tells us of a man who prayed enthusiastically for others, *"Epaphras, who is one of you, a bondservant of Christ, greets you, always labouring fervently for you in prayers, that you may stand perfect and complete in all the will of God."* How enthusiastic are you for God? You can't love God and be indifferent! Elie Wiesel, the most articulate Jewish survivor of the Holocaust, repeats in all his books that the contradiction of love is not hatred; the contradiction of love is indifference. If Jesus was indifferent He couldn't love you the way He does. In response, you need to display the same enthusiasm, the same *passion* He has for you; first, toward God and then toward others.

DAY 138

TOGETHERNESS

συμβιβάζω = *'sumbivazo'*
To cause to unite, to join or knit together

Ephesians 4:16: *"From whom the whole body, joined and knit together by what every joint supplies, according to the effective working by which every part does its share, causes growth of the body for the edifying of itself in love."* Togetherness is a very powerful action! According to this verse, when we all work diligently together and do our share, it causes growth and improvement. That is a very good reason to be in unity.

If you have ever been to a symphony, then you can appreciate the importance of togetherness. At the beginning of the performance, the orchestra warms up, and this is when everyone plays on their own without considering others. The noise is atrocious, however, when the conductor lifts the baton, the racket stops and all eyes are on him. With a gentle wave of the baton the orchestra begins to play an incredible melody. Heavenly sounds are produced because there is harmony and synchronisation. What makes the difference? Togetherness! No one is doing their own thing! And when they all do their part the music is pleasing to the ear. On their own, the music doesn't amount to much but together they are breathtaking. You too, need to harmonise and synchronise your plans and purposes. First, with God and then with others. Do that today and you'll discover the power of togetherness.

DAY 139

PRAYER

εὔχομαι = *'euchomai'*
To pray to God

James 5:15, *"And the prayer offered in faith will make the sick person well; the Lord will raise him up. If he has sinned, he will be forgiven."* Notice that it is the "prayer of faith" which gets a positive outcome. Many kinds of prayers may be used at various times and under differing demands. There are prayers of "thanksgiving," when you thank God for His goodness and mercy. There are prayers of "praise" when you tell God how good He is. There are prayers of "petition and supplication" in which you will make a special request to God. There are scripted prayers, spontaneous prayers, and ceremonial prayers. However, there is only one kind of prayer that brings results - the prayer of faith.

The *prayer of faith* is a prayer that changes things, yet, it changes things and not people. People do not change against their will. Anything that can be physically seen is subject to change and can be affected by a *prayer of faith.* ***"For the things which are seen are temporal; but the things which are not seen are eternal"*** (2 Corinthians 4:18). God's will is for you to prosper in all matters of life and be in good health, even as your soul prospers (3 John 1:2). Also, God wants to reward those who diligently seek Him, therefore, when you stand praying and dare to believe that you've *received* whatever you've asked for; you will have exactly what you've requested (Mark 11:24). Praise God!

DAY 140

LAND

γῆ = *'gi'*
Physical land, ground, earth

"The righteous will inherit the land and dwell in it forever" (Psalm 37:29). In the Old Testament few issues are as important as that of the promise of the *land* to the patriarchs and the nation of Israel. In fact, *land* is the fourth most frequent topic with regards 'rights and duties' in the Hebrew Torah. The Old Testament is most insistent on the fact that *land* was promised to the patriarchs as a "gift" by God Himself - a place where their descendants would reside and rule as a nation. It's an important part of the Abrahamic covenant, which applies to you as well.

Your inheritance remains as a "gift" even when the actual possession of the *land* is lagging behind the promise of God. So what is the key to receiving your inheritance? Faith! The "*gift of land*" that God has provided may be lagging behind His promises, but your *faith* will ensure that you take full possession of it. Therefore you need to have the same faith the Abraham had, *"he did not waver at the promise of God through unbelief, but was strengthened in faith, giving glory to God"* (Romans 4:20). Receiving God's promise of land will take faith even though it's your rightful inheritance! You are just about to cross over and possess the *land* which the Lord has given you. As with Joshua, God is wanting you to focus on the victory. When you take possession you will begin to have dominion. So why not *believe* God for some land today?

DAY 141

SURRENDER

Παρέδωκεν = *'parethoken'*
To surrender, to hand over, to deliver into

What does the word surrender tell you? In literal terms, it means "to give up something to another person." It also means to *hand over* something granted to you. This may include your goals, possessions, power or even your life. Christians today often hear about the surrendered life, but what does it mean exactly? The surrendered life is the act of giving back to Jesus the life He graciously granted you. It's relinquishing control, rights, power, direction, all the things you do and say. It's totally resigning your life over to His hands to do with it as He pleases.

Jesus himself lived a surrendered life: *"I came down from heaven, not to do Mine own will, but the will of Him that sent Me"* (John 6:38). *"I seek not Mine own glory"* (John 8:50). Jesus never did anything on His own, He took no action and spoke no word without being instructed by His Father. Jesus' full surrender to the Father is an example of how we all should live. When you stand before God at the judgment, you won't be judged by your ministry achievements. There will be but one measure of success on that day: "was your heart fully and completely surrendered to God?" The truth is, you can have as much of Christ as you want, or you can continue to do your own thing, it's entirely up to you! God will never force the *surrendered life* upon you.

Day 142

Tree

Δένδρον = *'thendron'*
A tree, a shrub, a bush

If we were to trace the use of the word *tree* through the Scriptures we would find two main images and both these images explain the significance of the Cross. The first tree is the *Tree of Life*; this was placed in the Garden of Eden together with the "*Tree of the Knowledge of Good and Evil*" from which Adam and Eve ate the forbidden fruit. God gave Adam and Eve (mankind) permission to eat from every tree. So we have no reason to believe that they did not eat of the *Tree of Life* prior to the fall; God intended us to live forever.

The second tree is the *Cross of Jesus Christ*. The New Testament often uses tree rather than *cross*. Acts 10:39 says, *"They put Him to death by hanging Him on a tree."* The apostle Paul reminds us that the ancient Jewish law openly declared: *"Cursed be anyone who is hanged upon a tree"* (Galatians 3:13). Yet, Peter explains more clearly what was involved: *"For He Himself bore our sins in His body on the tree, that we might die to sin and live to righteousness"* (1 Peter 2:24). Jesus accepted the curse you should have received and underwent death in your place so that you might not die but live. The triumph of the Cross is the expulsion from Eden reversed, therefore, spiritually, we're back! Today, remind yourself that the *tree* was where all your sins and curses were hung. That means you can now live the abundant life that's full of liberty and victory.

DAY 143

FIRE

Πυρός = *'pyros'*
Fire, blaze, intensity

As Spirit-filled believers we should place more emphasis upon Pentecost than any other Christian festival. For many, the Day of Pentecost is correctly understood to signify the *turning point* of all human history. It was when the "*resurrection power of God*" came to equip His Church. Note, power can be used in at least two ways: (1) it can be unleashed, or (2) it can be harnessed. For instance, the energy in ten gallons of petrol can be released explosively by dropping a lighted match into the container; or it can be channeled through the engine of a motor car (in a controlled burn) and used to transport people for hundreds of miles. Explosions are spectacular, but controlled burns have lasting effect (staying power). The *fire* of the Holy Spirit is meant to have a lasting effect on your life.

The Holy Spirit can work both ways. At Pentecost, He exploded on the scene; His presence was like *"tongues of fire"* (Acts 2:3). Thousands were affected by one burst of God's power. However. He also works through the Church - the institution God poured His Holy Spirit's power into for the long haul. Subsequently through service, worship and fellowship, you are now provided with *staying power*. Don't underestimate the power you've received that's at work in you right now. If you feel like giving up today, remind yourself that you have *staying power* already in you.

Day 144

Waiting

ἐκδεχόμενος = *'ekthechomenos'*
To be waiting, awaiting or expecting

It is always hard to wait, especially when you're waiting on God. We all want God to give us everything right now, but we need to make ourselves comfortable in the waiting room. God gives specific instructions and directions for being in the waiting room; firstly, you need to trust the One in charge and stay close to Him. Psalm 46:1 says, *"God is our refuge and strength, a very present help in trouble."* God is ever present! So, don't desert the waiting room because that is where you are most likely to meet with and hear from God.

You also need to be still, Psalm 46:10; *"Be still, and know that I am God."* Literally, "Let your hands hang down." You may want to do something but God plans to do something *in* you. Before God can do anything special for you, or through you, you must be *still* (quiet, silent). Being *still* expresses your confidence in Him, and Him alone.

Remember, God doesn't do His deepest work in the shallowest part of your life. Be alone with God for a time of reflection, evaluation, correction and dedication. Get ready for some of the most awesome discoveries and experiences, because they are sure to happen while you are in the *waiting room.*

The waiting room is your dwelling place before take-off!

Day 145

Timing

Πληρόω = *'pleroho'*

To fully come, to complete, to be fully developed

Timing is everything! *"But when the time had fully come, God sent His Son, born of a woman, born under law"* (Galatians 4:4). The phrase "had fully come" is a very graphic Greek expression. It speaks of something that is complete and fully developed, like a ripe apple ready to be picked. It describes the time in history when all things were in place, when all the pieces were laid out correctly; that one moment when the stage was perfectly set. At that instant, God sent forth His Son Jesus to be born of a virgin. He came *at the appointed time* - not a moment too late, not a second too early.

Most people struggle with God's timing. Often, you can easily become frustrated, even doubting Him, however, be reassured that God works all things together for good in His time and in His way. I love the way Charles Spurgeon put it; "There are no loose threads in the providence of God ... The great clock of the universe keeps good time." Some of us need to hear this because we secretly fear that God has forgotten us. Perhaps you've ended up with a deep sense of disappointment or a sense of dread about what tomorrow will bring. But fear not, God's timing is perfect.

Don't forget, you're never far from your miracle. God who is faithful cannot deny Himself.

DAY 146

WARFARE

στρατείαν = *'stratian'*
Warfare, a campaign, expedition, military offensive

When the apostle Paul wrote to young Timothy, he said, *"This charge I commit to you, son Timothy, according to the prophecies previously made concerning you, that by them you may wage the good warfare"* (1 Timothy 1:18). What he was saying was, "Son, you are in a battle, in warfare, and it is not going to be easy." Paul also wrote this, *"Endure hardness, as a good soldier of Jesus Christ"* (2 Timothy 2:3). What do soldiers do? They do not spend all their time on the parade ground, no, they engage in warfare! What's more, they are expected to be tough and resilient because they must endure hardship, both in training and on the battlefield.

Do you live in this reality? Or, are you acting like nothing is going on in the spirit realm? Don't bury your head in the sand and think that you can sit on the side-lines and watch the battle from a safe place. God is with you and He will protect you; no weapon formed against you will prosper. So put on the whole armour of God, and pick up the shield which extinguishes all the fiery darts of the devil, and then use your sword. The word of God is the most effect weapon against the enemy. Jesus used it (Luke 4:4)! Therefore, so must you. You are equipped to outlast every battle and collect the spoils of war, for you are more than conqueror through Christ who loves you.

DAY 147

GIFTED

δωρεά = *'thorea'*
A gift, a free gift without repayment

You are all *gifted* whether we like it or not! God the Father, in His supreme wisdom, has distributed unique gifts to all His children. Right now, you have a divine gift (a special grace) in you that God prepared before time began. He knew exactly what you would need in order to be effective in His Kingdom. However, in troubled times it's so easy to lose sight of the fact that God has given each of us a unique gift, and this gift not only brings fulfilment to our lives but great blessing to others. We are all gifted, and when we use our gifts as God intended they demonstrate the glorious riches of His grace.

Romans 12:6: *"Having then gifts differing according to the grace that is given to us, let us use them."* We must use the gifts that God has placed in us. You may be thinking, "How do I find my gift?" Gifts are found as you humble yourself before God to do what He wants you to do. As you do this, He will uncover your gifts, and you can then trust Him to open the door to use those gifts. As you obediently follow God's leading, He will prepare you (grace you with His gifts), and give you many opportunities to use them. Your *gift* discovery will take care of itself as you walk with God and serve Him. In the meantime serve Him with what you have in your hand and He will give you what you have in your heart!

Day 148

Waters

ὕδατι = *'hydati'*
Water, waters, seawaters

You may remember the song by Simon & Garfunkel called "Bridge Over Troubled Waters?" Well, from time to time, we all have troubled waters to cross. However, when God is involved there is no need to build a bridge, only men build bridges, God creates "a pathway through" troubled waters. There is no need to go over your troubles or around them for God simply makes a way. Therefore, if you are facing troubled waters today, I have good news for you, a miraculous path is about to appear; a path that will get you to the other side. Troubled waters can no longer hold you back. You are going to cross over into your promised land. Yes, that is God's pledge to you today.

Luke 8:22; *Now it happened, on a certain day, that He got into a boat with His disciples. And He said to them, "Let us cross over to the other side of the lake." And they launched out.* Jesus is saying to you, "We are going to the other side!" Even if a storm should come, He will silence the wind and carry you across. Jesus doesn't need to build a bridge as all the elements obey His command. He has already worked out a plan for you and He has made a path through your raging waters. There is a place of success awaiting you on the other side, a place where you can "shout for joy" in spite of your troubles. Start to thank Him for His mercies and His faithfulness, and give praise right now!

DAY 149

HELP

βοήθειαν = *'boētheian'*
Help, assistance, aid, benefit, support

"I will lift up my eyes to the hills - from whence comes my help? My help comes from the Lord, Who made heaven and earth" (Psalm 121:1-2). In this Psalm we find the pilgrim still some way from Jerusalem and considering the journey ahead of him. So he "lifts up his eyes to the hills." Perhaps the hills remind him of the goal of his journey, but they most certainly also remind him of the dangers of his journey as well. The dangers of the climb; the danger of bandits; the danger of heatstroke and exhaustion in the fierce summer heat; the danger of wild animals at night.

As with all journeys toward a God given destination, there will be some opposition and risks. Therefore, on the journey toward your destiny you too will need to adopt the same attitude as this pilgrim. It doesn't matter how daunting the mountain ahead of you may seem, your God is *greater*! Why? Simply because God cares for you. With the psalmist this prompted the question, "Where does my help come from?" The answer was immediate, and emphatic, "My help comes from the Lord." Never forget where your help comes from. You can boldly approach God at any time and in any place. *"Let us therefore come boldly to the throne of grace, that we may obtain mercy and find grace to help in time of need"* (Hebrews 4:16). Lift up your eyes today – raise them high toward the throne of grace!

DAY 150

VALUE

διαφέρω = *'thiaphero'*
To differ, to excel, to be of more value

In Matthew 6:26 Jesus said, *"Look at the birds of the air, for they neither sow nor reap nor gather into barns; yet your heavenly Father feeds them. Are you not of more value than they?"* Jesus did not say that He doesn't value the birds of the air. After all, He cares for them by making sure they are well fed. However, He places greater value on you. In this passage, you can see clearly that your Heavenly Father's priority is to provide your basic necessities. And the reason for that is: He values you greatly!

If you cannot comprehend the great value God places on you, you can never strengthen your faith. Therefore, it is so important that you do not get God's priorities mixed up. No matter what's troubling right now your Heavenly Father has a list of promises He wants to fulfil in order for you to live a super-abundant life. That's top of His priority list and nothing can change it! If you are unable to comprehend how valuable you are in God's sight you will always end up worrying about every little thing and living in unbelief. However, I want to encourage you to stop looking for value in the wrong places; you will never be satisfied.

You have however a Heavenly Father who has made you His first priority, and in His divine value-system you are already number one.

DAY 151

PROSPER

εὐοδόω = *'euothoó'*

To prosper, to help on one's way, to have a prosperous journey

"Beloved, I pray that you may prosper in all things and be in health, just as your soul prospers" (3 John 1:2). God wants you to prosper in all matters of life. Prosperity pleases God, He delights in the prosperity of His children (Psalm 35:27). Did you know that? Do you believe it? If you are struggling to accept God's provision, or if you doubt that God wants you to prosper in every area of life, then you need to adjust your thinking, and change your confession. When you start confessing in line with God's word you will start to prosper. Ask the Holy Spirit to reveal the truth to you concerning prosperity and show you how that reality applies to every area of your life. Then begin to confess those realities over yourself and over your family.

Prosperity is real! It is not an empty hope, a pipedream or something reserved for a chosen few. The Lord wants you to enjoy your life and be a blessing to others. Proverbs 10:22: *"The blessing of the Lord makes a person rich, and He adds no sorrow with it."* The prosperity that God has put aside for you will bring you happiness. So many people are trying to find the secret to happiness and contentment when they can only be found in "the blessings of the Lord." There can be no satisfaction in your life until you recognize your need to prosper. Approach God today *in faith* and ask Him to prosper you in all matters of life.

Day 152

Unfailing

οὐδέποτε-πίπτει = *'outhepote-piptei'*
Unfailing, never changing, enduring, unshakable, steadfast

"Let the morning bring me word of your unfailing love, for I have put my trust in you. Show me the way I should go, for to you I entrust my life" (Psalm 143:8). I have a saying: "Unfailing love, unfailing life!" 1 Corinthians 13:8 tells us that "love never fails," therefore, God's love must be the most effective power in the universe. It is unfailing, never changing and completely dependable. Governments can fail but God's love will last; crowns are temporary but love is eternal; things may run out but His love never will.

How could God have a love like this? No one has *unfailing* love. No person can love with perfection. But God can! Unlike our love, His love never fails. The love of God is born from within Him not from what He finds in you and His love is unconditional, spontaneous and intentional. *"This is love: not that we loved God, but that He loved us"* (1 John 4:10).

Here is another powerful truth: "Nothing can separate you from His love" (Romans 8:37-39). Think about that! Whatever happens in your life, you will always be connected to the Father's love. When you truly grasp the magnitude of God's love, your life will not be marked by failure but abundant success. Thank God today for His unfailing love, from which you cannot be separated.

Day 153

Wilderness

ἐρημία = *'eremia'*
Wilderness, an uninhabitable place, a desert

You may find yourself having a wilderness experience. But be encouraged, it's only for a season (Luke 4:13). Jesus has entered into the wasteland of your *wilderness* and has found you, His lost sheep, and He has provided everything you need and more. Jesus himself is your provision. When you find yourself in the *wilderness*, realise that though you may not feel like it at present, you are in the very place where the Bible reveals that true worship can occur.

In the wilderness you will probably find that you have nothing to much to say. You can find no words to articulate the complexity and the dimensions of your disappointments, hunger, thirst, frustrations, or anger. If this is where you find yourself, then I would like to suggest that you are poised on the edge of a favourable situation. You need only to push on toward the discovery of what God expects of you, of what He anticipates as the proper response to that which you find unbearable. That is, worship - worship in the wilderness!

When you see clearly how the Good Shepherd feeds you, how He leads you and protects you, your response ought to be *worship*; a recognition of all that He is. The wilderness is not a place of mourning but a place of thanksgiving! It's a place where you can build a perfect future with Jesus.

Day 154

Covenant

διαθήκη = *'diatheki'*
Covenant, promise, agreement, to cut or divide, pledge

A *divine covenant* implies much more than a contract, pledge or simple agreement. All of human covenants have an end date while a divine covenant is a permanent perpetual arrangement. A general contract usually involves only one part of a person, such as a skill or ability, while a *divine covenant* covers a person's total being. Also, a contract of law never extends to an unconditional *sharing* of what one has and what one intrinsically is. In the covenant God has made with you, He guarantees to share everything, and it's not dependent on you honouring your part of the arrangement. What's more, He pledges to honour His part for eternity.

The Bible tells us that we have a new and better covenant (2 Corinthians 5:15-17). What the First covenant failed to achieve, the new covenant accomplished when Jesus said, "It is finished." We now have a sovereign irrevocable promise written in the shed blood of Jesus Christ. The blood-bought ratification of the earlier covenants were a shadow of the "new covenant in Jesus' blood" (Luke 22:20). Christ's blood was shed as the sign and the seal of our redemption; once for all, and for all time (Hebrews 10:5-19).

Today, fully acknowledge the eternal truth that God can never revoke the covenant He has made with you. That means, all His promises are permanently "Yes and Amen!"

Day 155

Harvest

θερισμός = *'therismos'*
To harvest, the act of harvesting, to reap

"Let us not become weary in doing good, for at the proper time we will reap a harvest if we do not give up" (Galatians 6:9). Anyone who has ever farmed for a living knows exactly what this verse means. It's one thing to plant a few tomatoes in your back yard; it's something else to plant 5,000 acres of wheat. Full-time farming is a year-round task. You start early and you work late, 52 weeks a year.

There is no end of tasks to be completed. Even during the winter there is equipment to maintain and preparation to be made for the upcoming planting season. You don't get a harvest by accident and you can't treat it as a weekend hobby. If you want the harvest, you've got to work even when you feel like giving up. Persistence, determination are supreme, and this is especially true in the spirit realm. Because we live in a fallen world and deal constantly with fallen people, it's easy to grow weary and say, "What's the use?" You must keep on sowing, even through your tears and with a weary heart. Yes, keep on sowing, even in famine. In the end you will rejoice; when your harvest finally comes in. This is all God asks of you: "Don't give up! Don't stop! Don't grow weary! Keep on going!" For if you do, there will be a wonderful and bountiful harvest to come. Open your eyes, your field is ready for the harvest!

Day 156

Blood

αἷμα = *'aima'*
Blood, lifeblood, essence

Pleading the *blood* of Jesus is the greatest testimony any child of God can have. Testifying to what the blood of Jesus has done for you will release the *life-force* of God into your natural life. You cannot truly testify without pleading the blood. John 6:53 says, *"Except you eat of the flesh of the Son of Man and partake of His blood, you have no life in you."* As a believer you have partaken of Christ's blood, and therefore, you have His all-conquering *life-force* in you. You have partaken of the divine substance that brings forth *divine life*. The scripture we've just read says, "Unless you consume the blood of Jesus, you have no life (zoe) in you."

What is it about the blood that causes the devil to run in fear? Quite simply, it represents the *life-force* of God. This *life-force* is the divine substance that contains the very essence of God. Nothing can penetrate the blood; no sin is too great to resist the cleansing power of the blood. Satan and all his demons are terrified of the blood because it was the blood that brought about their defeat. And today, it is the blood that enforces their defeat. *Divine life* is in the blood, and the blood is still alive today! It represents the *life-force* of the Godhead. The Blood of Jesus has no boundaries, it has no limitations, it has no restrictions; it is all-powerful, all-encompassing, all-conquering. Plead the blood of Jesus over your loved ones today and expect His life-force to manifest.

Day 157

Shield

θυρεός = *'thureos'*
Shield, protection, armour, a stone for closing the entrance of a cave

Ephesians 6:16: *"Above all, taking the shield of faith with which you will be able to quench all the fiery darts of the wicked one."* The shield of faith is an integral part of your spiritual body armour. Not only does it protect you, it also extinguishes all the fiery darts of the enemy, however, there is something else that the *shield* represents, which brings about many blessings: Psalm 5:12 states, *"For You, O Lord will bless the righteous, with favour. You will surround him as with a shield."* This verse declares that you have a promise from God concerning His *shield of favour,* and it is surrounding you right now.

Note, you cannot earn the favour of God, it is a free gift that came when you gave your heart to Christ and received His righteousness (2 Corinthians 5:21). Remember this, you cannot enjoy the benefits of any promise of God which you do not know about, or understand, or have claimed for your own life. It is similar to having an insurance policy, you can only take advantage of the benefits listed in the terms. God wants to *favour* you today - right now! But you must put in a *claim* for this precious promise. If you believe His word, then declare it (in faith) expecting to see it come to pass. That way, you draw down on the promise. God's *favour* is for you, it surrounds you like a shield. So step into it right now, and experience all its benefits.

DAY 158

HEARING

ἀκοή = *'akoi' / 'akouo'*
To hear, the word of hearing, the sense of hearing, the faith of hearing

Romans 10:17 says, *"So then faith comes by hearing and hearing by the word of God."* Faith comes by hearing and hearing by the word (*rhema*) of God. Hence, true faith will spring forth when you have *heard* a *spoken word* concerning your situation and then acted upon it. It's the revealed word that you *hear* which produces faith.

This is a personal word from God, which the Spirit uses to awaken a response of faith within you. For that reason, it is the reliability of the word of God you've *heard* on which your faith should rest. But hearing with the ears is not enough, you must hear with an open heart and mind, willing to be presented with the truth. When you do, you will find that the word (*rhema*) always has the ring of truth, and that the truth is self-authenticating. But the *hearing* referred to in this verse doesn't necessarily involve the ears exclusively; the message you have received might have come through a Bible verse you've read. So, to *hear* means to receive or have knowledge of the word of God by whatever means, as long as it's Holy Spirit inspired – God breathed.

Maybe you are trying too hard to walk in faith. Real faith is a product of the *hearing* and the *doing* of the word of God. It takes no effort whatsoever on the part of your intellect or human will to obtain faith. Simply act on what you've *heard*!

DAY 159

DARKNESS

σκότος = *'skotos'*
Darkness, evil powers, spiritual darkness, satan's domain

Acts 26:18, *"Open their eyes in order to turn them from darkness to light, and from the power of satan to God."* Ephesians 2:2 says, *"In which you once walked according to the course of this world, according to the prince of the power of the air, the spirit who now works in the sons of disobedience."* To see all things as relative we can say God represents *light* (life), and the satan represents *darkness* (death). Satan has no power to bring death but his power over us is death - the *fear of death.* Christ became flesh and in the flesh He died in order to offer us life, thus removing the *fear of death* from us. Snatching satan's own sword right out of his hand! If you do not fear death, then satan has no power, no leverage, over you. Satan's purpose is to stop life; to frustrate it, to block it wherever he can to keep our souls from Heaven. But the Prince of Peace is the Victor.

Ephesians 2:4, begins with two of the greatest words in the Bible. *"But God..."* Carry in your heart these two words today. You were dead in trespasses and sins; *"But God..."* You walked according to the course of this world; *"But God..."* You walked according to the prince of the power of the air; *"But God..."* You were raised from the lowest depths to the highest heights, because as helpless and hopeless as your situation was, God intervened. Allow Him today to continue intervening; interrupting your life to deliver you.

Day 160

Breathe

Θευ-πνεύματος = *'theo-pnevmatos'*
God-breathed, to breathe upon, breathe on

"All Scripture is breathed out by God and profitable for teaching, for reproof, for correction, and for training in righteousness" (2 Timothy 6:16 ESV). Other translations say, "God-breathed." The word translated God-breathed or God-inspired is *theo-pnevmatos* and it contains *pnev* which is the root of *pnevma* spirit. Primarily, this word denotes the wind; also breath. Hence its application when referring to the Holy Spirit *Agios Pnevmas*. God's Spirit is like the wind - invisible, immaterial and powerful! This is the only verse in the whole Bible that speaks of the *inspiration* or *illumination* of Scripture. Therefore, if we were to misunderstand it we could easily misinterpret *illumination* and *inspiration* in the context of God's infallible word and consequently misread how we should use it.

Therefore, the way this verse is interpreted can have a significant effect of the way you hear from God and apply His word in your life. The original Greek reads: "Everything written is breathed out by God and of assistance for...." Notice, the paradox? That which is written is being *breathed-out*, and only then can it be of any benefit! God never stops *breathing-out* His word. Why? Because His word is Spirit and Life. Without His breath on it there can be no *inspiration* or *illumination*. Therefore, every time we fellowship around God's word we feel His divine breath on it.

DAY 161

CALLING

κλήσεως = *'kliseos'*

A calling, an invitation, a divine mission

"I, therefore, the prisoner of the Lord, beseech you to walk worthy of the calling with which you were called" (Ephesians 4:1). I suggest you remove the thought from your mind of expecting God to come and force you to fulfil His plans and purposes. When the Lord Jesus called His disciples, He did it without overwhelming pressure from the outside. The quiet, yet passionate insistence of His "follow Me" was spoken to men whose very senses were already receptive (Matthew 4:19). Remember, to be *called* of God is to receive a personal and exclusive appointment or invitation from Him to serve Him in a particular way. But it's then left up to you to respond to that calling.

Isaiah 43:1 reflects the intimacy God shares with you, *"Thus says the Lord, who created you: 'Fear not, for I have redeemed you; I have called you by your name; you are Mine'."* What an awesome statement! When God looked down the corridors of time and *called* you by your name, He was in fact beckoning His own family. You belong to Him and that is why your *calling* is so personal. God called you with something distinct and unique in mind, therefore, the matter in question is not whether you are *called*, rather, whether you respond to that *calling*. Never be afraid to chase after your calling for He who has *called* you is faithful and He will equip you and work with you until it is realised.

DAY 162

PURITY

ἁγνότητος = *'ahgnotetos'*
Purity in devotion, chastity, consecration, devoutness

In 2 Corinthians 11:3 the apostle Paul writes,*"But I am afraid that just as Eve was deceived by the serpent's cunning, your minds may somehow be led astray from your sincere and pure devotion to Christ."* You are told to maintain a sincere and pure devotion to Christ. As a Christian, you must develop the habit of private devotions, and in order to do this, the time and place may have to be the same, and the act of devotion must never supersede the devotion you have in your heart toward Christ in everything. Mother Teresa said, "There is always the danger that we may just do the work for the sake of work. This is where the respect and the love and the devotion come in – that we do it to Christ - that's why we try to do it as beautifully as possible." When your heart is fully devoted to God it will be obvious.

If Jesus, the Son of God, found it needful to spend time alone with the Father, how much more should you! The Psalmist said, *"I rise before the dawning of the morning, and cry for help; I hope in Your word. My eyes are awake through the night watches, that I may meditate on Your word"* (Psalm 119:147-148). You too, may be fearful and stressed and cannot find inner peace, so I encourage you to lay everything aside and make an effort to draw near to God. That is where you will find shelter and tranquility. Drawing nearer and walking closer should be a way of life... Try it!

DAY 163

FEAR

Φόβος = *'phovos'*
Panic flight, fear, the causing of fear, terror

Is it possible for you to live without fear? Well, according to God's infallible word - it is! You can live a life that's free from fear and anxiety. *"There is no fear in love"* (1 John 4:18). Have you noticed, the world system is programmed to promote fear. Wherever you turn, you will probably find good reason to become stressed or anxious, and out there, fear is common place in most people's psyche. The Greek word has very negative connotations, namely, "a fearful harassing care which causes unreasonable, out of proportion stress." But, it may also be used to describe someone who is "attempting to carry the burden of the future, the unknown, all on their own" or having "unreasonable concern especially about things over which no one has any control."

Philippians 4:6-7 speaks of *imaginary* troubles or *phantom* anxieties. Paul tells his readers to stop worrying, and not to be overtly anxious or fearful over anything. Leaving them no exceptions! Anxiety, is an emotional state in which you feel uneasy, apprehensive, stressed or fearful. You experience anxiety about events you cannot control or predict, or about matters in life that seem threatening or dangerous. Today you can do something about it. I love what the psalmist said in Psalm 34:4, *"I sought the Lord, and he heard me, and delivered me from all my fears."* Seek the Lord and He will hear you and deliver you from all your fears. Peace to you this day!

Day 164

Guidance

ὁδηγέω = *'othigeo'*
Guidance, to lead the way, to direct

"This also comes from the Lord of hosts, Who is wonderful in counsel and excellent in guidance" (Isaiah 28:29). Supernatural guidance only *comes from the Lord,* and *by His Spirit* (John 16:13). *"The spirit of man is the candle of the Lord, searching all the inward parts of the heart"* (Proverbs 20:27). If God wants to reveal anything to you He will speak to your heart and not your mind. Psalm 119:130 confirms this, *"The entrance of Your words gives light; it gives understanding to the simple."* From these two verses we can see a definite process; as the word of God enters the human spirit it brings forth *revelation* and this *light* searches your innermost parts in order to bring about change. If you want to change the way you think, you must allow the *light* of God's word to first enter your heart and thereafter shine onto your mind. Until the *light* of God's word has radiated new thoughts onto the mind it will remain in darkness.

If you require supernatural guidance, you must learn to hear God's voice. Yes, you need to know what God is saying to your spirit throughout the day. Every revelation from God will guide you toward your destiny. Psalm 119:105, *"Your word is a lamp to my feet and a light to my path."* Whenever God speaks to your heart He is shining a light onto His chosen path of your life. Revelation from God is not like an atomic bomb inside of you, but rather a candle that lights up your heart and transforms your mind. Be truly *guided* today.

Day 165

Peace

ειρήνη = *'eirini'*

To bring rest and contentment, harmonious relationships

Luke 2:14: *"Glory to God in the highest, And on earth peace, goodwill toward men!"* The meaning of *peace* in the English language conjures up a passive picture, one showing an absence of civil disturbance or hostilities, or a behaviour free from internal and external strife. The biblical concept of *peace* is larger than that and rests heavily on the Hebrew, even in the Greek, which means to be *complete* or to be *sound*. This verb conveys both a dynamic and a static meaning to be complete, whole or to live well. Perfect peace is something God premeditated when He sent Jesus to earth. It was His main consideration when planning reconciliation.

Jesus came to give us His *peace*. *"Peace I leave with you, My peace I give to you; not as the world gives do I give to you. Let not your heart be troubled neither let it be afraid"* (John 14:27). This is a supernatural peace that transcends all our understanding: *"And the peace of God, which surpasses all understanding, will guard your hearts and minds through Christ Jesus"* (Philippians 4:7). Because mankind is so deeply flawed and because we are people who hurt one another, God sent us His son, Jesus, the Prince of peace to impart a spirit of peace. Jesus says: "I have come to bring you peace, to teach you to walk in the paths of peace. I have come to teach you what you need to learn most...to be a person of peace." Be a peacemaker today and you will attract God's blessings.

DAY 166

STORMS

λαῖλαψ = *'lelaps'*
Storm, torrent, tempest, hurricane, whirlwind

The primary reason God allows storms to come is because He wants you to have revelation concerning the foundations your life is being built on. Is your life built on sinking sand or on the Rock of Ages? The only way to find out is by examining what is left after the wind and the rain have subsided. *"He is like a man building a house, who dug deep and laid the foundation on the rock. And when the flood arose, the stream beat vehemently against that house, and could not shake it, for it was founded on the rock"* (Luke 6:48). To the onlooker both houses looked the same; until after the storm. Your life may appear to be secure but unless the foundations are right, a collapse will surely happen. So, make sure your life is built on the word of God.

If you are currently being tossed around in a storm, you will find the most likely cause is simply that you are at the helm, and not Jesus. You ceased to trust and have decided to take hold of the wheel and steer the vessel yourself. Check to see whose fingerprints are on the wheel and then hand it back immediately! Any storm you may be encountering is an unexpected disturbance that is trying to overwhelmed you. This is often violent and relentless in nature, but don't be dismayed, Jesus is right there in the eye of the storm with you. He is still on the boat, even if He appears to be asleep. Jesus promised to get you to the other side and that's exactly where you're going!

DAY 167

ZEAL

ζῆλος = *'zylos'*

Zeal, fervor, enthusiasm, eagerness

Then His disciples remembered that it was written, "Zeal for Your house has eaten Mẹ up" (John 2:17). The original Greek says they were consumed with a *zeal* for God's house. We need more believers with a *zeal* for God's house. Far too many churches are struggling because their members have lost their zeal, have you lost your zeal?

In 1 Kings 19:14 Elijah states, *"I have been very zealous for the Lord."* A key to the extraordinary life of Elijah may very well be found in this simple statement, and these two words probably explain Elijah's behavior; *very zealous*. We all need to aspire to this. Elijah's zealousness is related to the Lord being given His rightful place, that is what Elijah typified and undoubtedly it's what is meant by the "zeal of the Lord." When people ask me what it is to be very zealous for God, I immediately think of how passionate for the Lord Elijah was. This remarkable man was totally disconnected from his own interests; from any personal agenda. He had completely surrendered to God's will for his life; this was an utter attachment to the Lord, not for personal interests but for God's interests alone.

If you want to experience the miraculous and see the supernatural power of God at work in your life you too must be consumed with *zeal* for God.

Day 168

Influence

ἀπαγόμενοι = *'apagomeni'*
To be carried away, influenced, led astray

"You know that when you were pagans, somehow or other you were influenced and led astray to mute idols" (1 Corinthians 12:2 NIV). You can be *influenced* by the world or be *influenced* by the Holy Spirit! If you are *influenced* by God's Spirit, you will become influential. The dictionary says, "influence is the power or ability to effect a person's character, beliefs or actions." God is strategically placing His children in positions of notable *influence*. He is giving birth to influential individuals; people who'll have a significant effect on the character, beliefs and actions of others. These believers have been supernaturally equipped to represent God in every aspect of today's society.

We have entered an era where the Church will display one of its primary functions, *"To the intent that now the manifold wisdom of God might be made known by the church to the principalities and powers in heavenly places"* (Ephesians 3:10). God intends to display His Church as the instrument He uses to dispense what has already been secured in Christ Jesus. It's the wisdom of God that defeated the devil (1 Corinthians 2:7,8), but notice, the wisdom of God has many shades and colourful expressions. Therefore, whatever He does through you should reflect the same diverse expression. Allow His wisdom to express itself through you today and you will become very influential.

Day 169

Strength

ἰσχύος = *'isghus'*
strength (absolutely), power, might, force, ability

God is in the supply business! He supplies *strength* and *ability* in measures that cause the miraculous to manifest. The word translated *supply* is a very interesting one. Among the ancient Greeks it meant "to lead a stage chorus or dance troop;" implying harmony, orchestration or synchronisation. Then later it's meaning became "to provide the money to pay the expenses of a chorus." With this in mind let's read 1 Peter 4:11: *"If anyone speaks, let him speak as the oracles of God. If anyone ministers, let him do it as with the* (ability) *strength which God supplies."* There was a price to be paid so that your gift could operate correctly and that cost was covered by God through Jesus Christ. Hence, because the cost was fully covered, your gift carries supernatural strength and ability.

Peter declares that you have been given a special gift. Your *gift* represents a service that God calls you to perform. Therefore, it's only as you actively *employ* your gift that you become a "good steward of the manifold grace of God." Are you using our gift? Are you performing the ministry that God has called you to? You will be judged by how faithful you were when using your gift. There's a direct correlation between faithfulness and God's *strength* and *ability*. God's Spirit empowers people who are faithful with unique gifts; gifts He has entrusted them with. Why don't you allow Him empower you today?

Day 170

Beatitudes

Μακαριώτατοι = *'makariotatoi"*
Blessedness, bliss, blissfulness

The Beatitudes describe the blessedness of those who have certain qualities or experiences peculiar to those belonging to the Kingdom of Heaven. The Beatitudes tell us what our *attitudes* should become and admonish us to be lights in the world. They tells us how to pray, fast, do charitable deeds, layup treasure in heaven, be single minded, exercise our faith in trusting God, seek Him before all other things in life, and much more. The point is clear. These are all things the converted must actively do to witness for God, and bring Him glory. They are not intended to be the limit, but merely a summary of the views, thoughts and works of anyone striving to extend the Kingdom of God on the earth.

What application does this passage have for you today? There is hardly a verse in the entire Sermon where Jesus is not contrasting what He wants you to be with the way the world was in His day. This is its underlying theme. Human nature never changes, so the same challenges placed before His disciples face you also. The contrasts are drawn to leave you without excuse about knowing what is expected of you. Therefore, the Sermon on the Mount communicates that you are to be different; different from both the religious and the ungodly secular world.

Be different and be blessed today!

Day 171

Communion

κοινωνία = *'kinonia'*

A having in common, intimacy, fellowship, drawing near

The most important thing about coming into God's presence is not essentially getting your needs met: it is *communing* or connecting with Him for who He is. Being close and intimate with your Creator is what brings God pleasure, it is your act of worship, and the very least that you can do. Therefore, there is no need to fret, just *draw near* and know that He can be trusted to keep His promises. There's a confidence and assurance in this knowledge that comes only through faith. Faith in the Person you've had communion with: the Person with whom you've been intimate.

This *communion* or *drawing near* is not a physical act: it is an invisible act of the heart. You can do it while standing absolutely still or lying in bed, or while sitting in church listening to a sermon. Being in *communion* is a directing of the heart into the presence of God. Here is a paradox; God is as distant as the "Holy of Holies" in heaven, and yet He is as near as you want Him to be. The truth is, God is the One inviting you to come; to approach Him, to *draw near* to Him, to *commune* with Him. In fact, this is the very heart of the Gospel, isn't it? That Christ came into the world to make a way for you to come into the presence of God without any guilt and condemnation. So, don't allow yourself to be side-tracked today. Draw near to Him and He will draw near to you. Commune with Him and He will connect with you!

DAY 172

FAITHFUL

πιστός = *'pistos'*

Trustworthy, faithful, reliable, believing

Luke 16:10 says, *"He who is faithful in what is least is faithful also in much."* Matthew 25:21 says, *"His lord said to him, 'Well done, good and faithful servant: you have been faithful over a few things, I will make you ruler over many things; enter into the joy of thy lord'."* Success in God is a result of both *divine activity* and *human effort*. The Lord promises to do what you cannot do for yourself, but expects you to do that which He will not do for you.

Jesus lays out a principle for life that is simple: whoever is *faithful* with the small things will be a candidate for expanded responsibility in His kingdom. It's not about how much you get; it is all about what you do with what you have. You were not created to be average or mediocre, or to merely exist. God created you to be unique. Being human was not intended to be a curse, but a *gift*. While you may dream of a better life or the better person you could become, only God knows the person you were intended to be. Only He knows the full measure of your potential. Conversely, only God knows the full measure of what has been neglected or lost when you do nothing.

Being *faithful* with what He has given you is something Jesus cannot do for you. So be faithful in everything!

DAY 173

FAMILY

πατριὰ = *'patria'*
Family, lineage, ancestry, tribe

"For this reason I bow my knees to the Father of our Lord Jesus Christ, from whom the whole family in heaven and earth is named" (Ephesians 3:2). God the Father is building a permanent family here on earth. He offers us a family of friends - friends who are family - His church. *"Having predestined us to adoption as sons by Jesus Christ to Himself, according to the good pleasure of His will"* (Ephesians 1:5). The word *family* far exceeds any other biblical term to describe the Church. The words *brothers* and *sisters*, and their variations, appear 148 times between the Book of Acts and Revelation. Family is important to God.

The Father is great: He makes no mistakes. You can be truly thankful for His plans and purposes for you. He has a sovereign plan for your long-term well-being. God doesn't just place you in a certain family setting and then disappear from the scene. He does not wait until you have grown up before He interacts with you; He wants to engage with you intimately every day. God has no favourites, but He does have many *intimates*. Are you one of them?

Do you have an intimate relationship with your Heavenly Father – whom the whole *family* in heaven and earth is named? Today, make sure you act as if you really *belong* to the most important family in the universe.

DAY 174

INSTRUMENTS

ὅπλα = *'opla'*
An instrument, implement, a tool, a weapon

"And do not present your members as instruments of unrighteousness to sin, but present yourselves to God as being alive from the dead, and your members as instruments of righteousness to God" (Romans 6:13). This means choosing to step out in faith and acting in ways that are consistent with your new identity. This is the step that makes what you have learned a living truth. Presenting, usually involves both a negative and positive step. It is necessary to choose to turn away from immoral habits, but It is also necessary to turn to God in ways that expose you to His alternatives. Real change always involves the willingness to say "No!" However, this is ultimately futile unless you also say "Yes!" to the ways which expose you to God's life-changing power. This is the "Resist and Replace" principle.

The point here is that God alone meets your deepest desires and human necessities through your new identity in Christ. To the extent that you are ignorant of and/or don't apply this truth, you will go on suffering needlessly, trying to get other people or materials things to meet your needs and being disappointed by them when they don't. Remember, it is "God who supplies all your need according to His riches in glory by Christ Jesus." Keep your eyes on Him! You can become an *instrument* of His glory by stepping into your new identity in Christ today.

Day 175

Diligence

σπούδασον = *'spoudason'*
To make haste, to give diligence, to hasten

"Be diligent to present yourself approved to God, a worker who does not need to be ashamed, rightly dividing the word of truth" (2 Timothy 2:15). In order to be diligent and show yourself approved you must be teachable. When you truly seek God and spend time studying His word, you develop a spirit of confidence. You can be taught and led! You have a secure, assured spirit because you know who you are in Christ. You know that He loves you; you know that He has called you; you know that constructive criticism will help you grow more into His likeness. Therefore, God can truly touch you. Further, if you make yourself accessible, He can teach you all things; and if He can teach you, you will have a *teachable* spirit. The result being, you'll be able to be taught by others.

You can never know fully God's will for your life unless you are both *diligent* and *teachable.* Discerning God's will requires you to keep taking instructions directly from Him. It is therefore imperative that you have a *teachable* spirit in all spiritual matters. A man called Charles Simpson once said, "I'd rather teach a man how to learn than to teach him all I know." It is of immeasurable importance for you to have a heart that is willing to be taught and receive instruction. *"Give instruction to a wise man, and he will be still wiser; Teach a just man, and he will increase in learning"* (Proverbs 9:9). You can choose to *increase in learning* and become wiser, or you can remain where you are. So make a positive choice!

Day 176

Holiness

ἁγιασμός = *'agiasmos'*
The process of becoming holy, set apart, sanctification, consecration

"Pursue peace with all people, and holiness, without which no one will see the Lord." Unless you pursue peace and *holiness* you shall not see the works of God – the awesome deeds of power that only He can do. Therefore, holiness precedes power! Stop looking for a shortcut to the supernatural life; to *see* the power of God in operation. The truth is, God's mighty power is available to you, but not without *holiness.* God empowers that which He has first made *holy* (set apart for His own use). Do you want your life to be really effective? Then pursue Jesus Christ as your source and your standard of *holiness.* Do you want to *see* the power of God operating in your circumstances? Seek Christ's purity of heart! Remember, as a mature believer you should be both holy and influential.

The work of making you holy is the work of the *Spirit of holiness.* God's goal is that you should become more like Christ every day. He places in your heart a hunger and thirst for the righteousness of God. God, the Holy Spirit dwells within the temple of a believer's body (*1 Corinthians 3:16; 6:19; 2 Corinthians 6:16*). Since He dwells within you, you can be clothed with the presence and power of the Holy Spirit. His indwelling presence empowers you, and as a result, you shall be both *holy* and *powerful.* Don't forget, *holiness* will always precede power! God is saying to you today: "Be holy, for I am holy!"

Day 177

Assurance

ὑπόστασις = *'hypostasis'*
Assurance, a giving substance (or reality) to, or a guaranteeing

"Now faith is the substance (assurance) *of things hoped for, the evidence of things not seen"* (Hebrews 11:1). This verse gives us a description of what faith is. Your faith makes you absolutely sure of the things you are hoping for, and that *assurance* is in itself proof of these things. Suppose you go to a car dealership and buy a car. The car is exactly what you want, however, something needs to be done to it, so you can't drive it home that day. You will have to wait a couple of days before taking possession. However, you have the "Bill of Sale," therefore, you have proof (*evidence*) that you bought the car and that it is yours. If anyone asks you whether you really bought the car, you can pull out that paper and say, "See, I own that car." That paper *assures* you that you own the car; it *assures* you that in a couple of days, what you hope for will become real. That's what faith is: faith is the Bill of Sale. It makes you absolutely sure of what you hope for, and it is actual proof that what you hope for is actually yours.

To make it simpler: "What is faith?" Faith is translated from the Greek word *pistis*: it basically means "confident belief" or "assured belief." However, this *assured belief* is only there because you know that God is faithful; and because of this reality, anything you hope for (even the things you cannot yet see) are yours. How awesome is that! Today, be *self-assured* of the things you are hoping for.

DAY 178

HEALING

ιώμενος = *'iomenos'*

To heal, generally of the physical, sometimes of spiritual, disease

"How God anointed Jesus of Nazareth with the Holy Spirit and with power, who went about doing good and healing all who were oppressed by the devil, for God was with Him" (Acts 10:38). The Holy Spirit in Jesus was a *healing Spirit*, and He is the *same* Spirit that was in the disciples after Pentecost. For that reason, signs and wonders was a continuous experience of the early Church (Acts 3:7; 4:30; 5:12). The abundant and continuous outpouring of the Spirit produced abundant and continuous healings. What a lesson for us today! The early Church wasn't politically correct: it did not have Christian television or hold seminars; but what it did have made all the difference. The church had a special measure of the Holy Spirit – the Anointing!

Healing is the work of God's Spirit. Christ's redemption has extended its powerful working to your physical body, and the Holy Spirit is responsible both to transmit it to and maintain it in you. Your body shares in all the benefits of the redemptive work of the Cross, and even now it can receive the promise of divine *healing*. It is Jesus Christ who heals, and Jesus who anoints with the Holy Spirit. Yes, Jesus, has sent you God's Spirit; either to keep sickness away from you, or to restore you to health when sickness has taken hold of you. "Receive your healing right now - in Jesus Name!"

DAY 179

COMPASSION

σπλαγχνίζομαι = *'splagchnizomai'*
To be moved in the inward parts, to feel compassion

"But when He saw the multitudes, He was moved with compassion for them, because they were weary and scattered, like sheep having no shepherd" (Matthew 9:36). What is the principal evidence that *compassion* has been extended? What does *compassion* leave in its wake? The most significant consequence of *compassion* is, it alleviates suffering. It lifts people's burdens and makes their lives more bearable. And that's what the Lord Jesus was all about! Christ has often been called, "The Man of Compassion." That's because He entered the arena of human suffering and lifted their burdens - portraying true mercy. Mercy is more than an emotional experience of feeling someone's pain, it's doing whatever's possible to alleviate it. Compassion is *action*! The action of *compassion* always confirms a genuine feeling of love: love that one has for another!

Jesus was moved with *compassion* because He loved the people who had genuine needs. Jesus couldn't look at people without being *stirred in His inwards parts* to intervene. He was specially moved when people were experiencing pain, sickness, distress and sorrow; He was moved when people were hungry or lonely or confused. Today, He is moved when He sees you in a similar situation. Be encouraged because the God of all comfort, the Lord of all *compassion*, is watching over you looking for an opportunity to take action!

Day 180

Solitary

μόνος = *'monos'*
Alone, only, solitary, desolate

"And He who sent Me is with Me. The Father has not left Me alone, for I always do those things that please Him" (John 8:29). The Father never left Jesus alone; not for a second! And it is the same with you. Through good times and bad times, there is a truth you must always hold on to, and that is, you are not alone! One of the biggest temptations in life is to "go it alone." If you choose to do so, God will let you, but this is not His desire for you. From the beginning, God looked down the corridors of time and called you by your name. In Isaiah 43:1 it states, *"Thus says the Lord, who created you, O Jacob, And He who formed you, O Israel: 'Fear not, for I have redeemed you; I have called you by your name; you are Mine'."* God always intended for you to be in an cherished ongoing relationship with Him. Listen to how deeply personal He makes it... "You are Mine!"

God doesn't want you to be alone. As a Father, He wants to fulfil His parental responsibility. Many of you do not have any children, yet you still care for those around you. You look after your parents or your brothers and sisters, and you are probably that way with good friends as well. The bottom-line is; if the people that you love the most are *alone*, will you not reach out and comfort them? Your Heavenly Father wants to reach out to you today. He wants to fill that void in your life; He wants you to know that you are not alone!

DAY 181

SERVANT

διάκονος = *'thiakonos'*
A servant, minister, a waiter; then of any one who performs any service

"Yet it shall not be so among you; but whoever desires to become great among you, let him be your servant" (Matthew 20:26). You cannot get anywhere in the Kingdom of God unless you have a servant's heart. So what exactly is that? The English Dictionary says a servant is "a person who performs duties for others," or is "a devoted and helpful follower of another." In the context of God's Kingdom, a *servant* is "a devoted and helpful follower of Jesus; who performs duties toward others on His behalf." Therefore, you cannot have a *servant's* heart unless you are devoted to Jesus and you are prepared to serve others on His behalf.

All of us have the ability to *serve* three parties: (1) God, (2) others and (3) self. Yet, it is possible to serve them all, provided you serve God first. Through God, you can serve others and self. The problem is, most people get this process wrong, they *serve* God and others through *self*. Jesus was lifted up because of His servant-heart, and He expects the same of you. When God removed your heart of stone, He replaced it with a *servant's heart* – a heart just like Jesus had when He walked the earth.

Why not make up your mind today to be the person God created you to be? For as you *serve* others you will find fulfilment and true happiness.

Day 182

Chains

δεσμοῖς = *'thesmois'*
A chain, bond, imprisonment; a ligament, an impediment

"And because of my chains, most of the brothers and sisters have become confident in the Lord and dare all the more to proclaim the gospel without fear" (Philippians 1:14). The apostle Paul demonstrated how you can be in chains yet still live in complete freedom. Through Christ's work on the cross, you have received your freedom, but maybe you are still living in chains. Therefore, it would be interesting to know why some can experience true freedom and others are always imprisoned by their circumstances. All of us have probably experienced an enslaved soul or have known loved ones who have struggled to break free from wicked chains. Nonetheless, in whatever category you classify your slavery, the result is the same, you fail to experience the abundant life Jesus promised.

Your freedom is not reliant on the physical circumstances that may have led or contributed to your bondage. True freedom is not about changing your outward circumstances. This is a significant concept because it reveals that Jesus can free you wherever you are because your freedom is spiritual! Therefore, since your freedom is *spiritual* you can only practise freedom in the natural if you are free in your soul. Paul and Silas were in chains (*Acts 16:24-25*), yet they were able to sing praises to the Lord due to their spiritual state. Start praising the Lord and your chains will be broken today!

Day 183

Heavenlies

ἐπουράνιος = *'epouravios'*
Heavenlies, in the heavenly sphere, the sphere of spiritual activities

"For we do not wrestle against flesh and blood, but against principalities, against powers, against the rulers of the darkness of this age, against spiritual hosts of wickedness in the heavenlies" (Ephesians 6:12). The battleground is the *heavenly places*, therefore, whoever controls the heavenlies wins! Every challenge you face today is, in essence, a spiritual problem that has a natural manifestation. This is why it is so essential to understand the reality of the *heavenly places*, because that is where those challenges must be met and overcome.

Likewise, the most pressing social problems we face today are spiritual in nature. Abortion, violence, bigotry, corruption and systemic poverty are spiritual problems with a human covering. Let us meet the enemy, the real enemy the devil, in the *heavenlies* and let's defeat him by using the divinely powerful weapons available to us: *"For the weapons of our warfare are not carnal, but mighty through God to the pulling down of strongholds"* (2 Corinthians 10:4). The battle must be won in the heavenlies!

The strongholds you face today are all situated in the heavenlies, however, you have the authority in Jesus Christ to pull them down – to destroy them! Use that authority and see the spiritual atmosphere around you quickly change.

Day 184

Charity

ἐλεημοσύνη = *'elehemosuni'*
Charity, giving alms, showing mercy

"And a certain man lame from his mother's womb was carried, whom they laid daily at the gate of the temple which is called Beautiful, to ask alms from those who entered the temple; who, seeing Peter and John about to go into the temple, asked for charity" (Acts 3:2-3). The healing of this lame man is a very familiar story. It's very *indicative* in terms of our modern society. This is a story of humanity's helplessness and her willingness to settle for infinitely less than the best. Here is a lesson for you to be the liberating force in your community, and not to concede to humanity's transient aspirations under the pressure of unbelievers who long for the secular and are indifferent or antagonistic to the eternal.

The man being carried, was lame from birth (his problem was inherited), and he was laid daily at the gate. He was totally helpless, so much so, that he could not even help himself to a position where others could help him: "To ask for charity!" What a pitiful resignation to poverty! His highest hope was to be successful at begging. This is all he expected from life – handouts! Thank God there was infinitely more prepared for him; an answer which exceeded his wildest dreams; an answer he had long ceased to hope for. It's the same for you. God wants to exceed your wildest dreams, for He has infinitely more prepared for you today.

DAY 185

WEAKNESS

ἀσθενείᾳ = *'astheneia'*
Weakness, frailty, feebleness

"Most gladly I will rather boast in my weaknesses, that the power of Christ may rest upon me. Therefore I take pleasure in weaknesses, in reproaches, in needs, in persecutions, in distresses, for Christ's sake. For when I am weak, then I am strong" (2 Corinthians 12:10). Instead of bragging about your personal experiences, triumphs and achievements, may you follow Paul's example to accept your *weaknesses*. That way, you will be able to reach more people and do more good: "Whenever I am weak, then I am strong." Accepting your limitations and trusting that God's power is sufficient to conquer all that comes against you requires believing and then confessing... "Nothing, no matter how severe, can happen for which God does not also provide a way out - because God's grace will always prevail over life's challenges."

It is my hope that the anyone battling relentless struggles will recover to go from "glory to glory." I pray that the boundless and unconditional love of God shall be present with you in everything. Paul prayed in such a way for the church in Corinth; that they might realise God's grace was sufficient for them (even in the midst of their turmoil). The fact that he wrote such a letter at all, in the midst of his own emotional pain, reveals his desire for that congregation to accept their weaknesses and to make place for Christ to dwell within them. May it be so for you this day!

DAY 186

FEELINGS

ὁμοιοπαθής = *'homoiopathés'*
Like feelings, like nature, similar passion

James 5:17: *"Elijah was a man with like feelings just like ours"* (*Literal translation*). When you read that Elijah was just like you; with like feelings and a like nature; be honest, it's hard to admit. When you look at your life and then at the things Elijah did you'll probably think: "I'm nothing like Elijah."

Elijah prayed, and a young boy who was dead came back to life! If any of you were like that the whole world would want to know you. 1 Kings 17:22: *"The Lord heard Elijah's prayer, and the life of the child returned, and he came back to life!"* On another occasion, Elijah prays that it will not rain, so it doesn't rain for over three years. Then Elijah prays again that it would rain and it rains! Next, Elijah challenges the political and religious powers of his day to follow God or to follow Baal. What an audacious move!

Yet, in 1 Kings 19:9 we find this great man of God hiding in a cave, and God says to him,*"What are you doing here, Elijah?"* In other words, "What are you doing being a slave to fear and negative thoughts?" "What are you doing trying to fill a hole in you that only God can fill?" I believe that if you listen intently God is speaking to you today, and He is saying, "What are you doing here? Step out of your cave; step out of your hiding place; step out now, for I am all you need!

Day 187

Circumstances

πεϱὶ = *'peri'*
Regarding or concerning something

"Whom I did send unto you for this very thing, that he might know the things concerning you, and might comfort your hearts" (Colossians 4:8 – literal translation). God often sends someone who will get to know your circumstances, things regarding you, that your heart may be comforted. The NKJ says, *"...that he may know your circumstances and comfort your hearts."* When others get to know your circumstances, they are moved to act and this brings you comfort. However, God's word encourages you not to be dependent on your circumstances!

Martha Washington, the wife of America's first president, made a surprising observation, she said: "The greatest part of our happiness depends on our disposition, not our circumstances." Are you allowing your circumstances to determine your attitude? Enjoying life only when you don't have any problems is wasting a very large portion of your life. The truth is, when everything is rosy and you are facing no challenges, it's for a season only. The same applies to negative circumstances. Therefore, you must learn not to be dependent on any situation, whether good or bad, life is full of surprises; sometimes they are wonderful and other times they are very unpleasant. Remember, being able to decide *how* you will behave apart from *how* you feel is one of the greatest privileges God has given you.

Day 188

Command

ἔπω = *'epo'*
Say, command, answer, bring a word

"Now when they bring you to the synagogues and magistrates and authorities, do not worry about how or what you should answer, or what you should say. For the Holy Spirit will teach you in that very hour what you ought to say" (Luke 12:11-12). Do you know, God wants to put His words in your mouth today! In that very hour He will impart what you ought to *say* or command. According to these two verses; during every trial, you should never be without something to *say*. In fact, God's Spirit wishes to give you words to *command* in every challenging circumstance.

Therefore, how much more may you depend on Him in less threatening situations. One of the reasons I want you to enjoy this particular work of the Holy Spirit is that I have found it so true, amazing and precious in my own life. With the Holy Spirit's inspiration and guidance in this area, you will always have something to say. Yes, God is going to do the work for you! If you think you know the Word of God and know the enemy well enough to take away your anxiety, you invalidate this promise; for the point is, what's really needed in any such predicament is beyond you. You need the Holy Spirit! Jesus promises He will always be there for you, therefore, choose to live close to Him daily. So when the trials of life come, He will be there to give you the words you need to command. Yes, the exact words to say!

DAY 189

SLEEPING

Καθεύδει = *'katheudei'*
Sleeping, asleep

In Mark 5:39 when Jesus entered the house of the ruler of the synagogue He said to them, *"Why make this commotion and weep? The child is not dead, but sleeping."* Mourners were literally paid to wail, and in the death of a child of a prominent citizen, there were probably many funeral-goers present. Only a few, like the girl's mother, were genuinely grieved. She was dead and in a state from which only Jesus could wake her. If the funeral-goers were genuinely grieving they might have heard His faith-filled words, but since they were paid to look grieved, they reacted instead with scornful laughter. Hence, Jesus sends them all out before He goes into the child's room. What the mourners didn't know is that Jesus never attended a funeral He didn't disrupt!

When it comes to death many people still have questions. Sure, Jesus can calm storms and drive out demons, but where is He when the real tragedies strike? Where is He when sickness won't let go? Where is He when death takes hold? The underlying question is this: "Does Jesus really care? And if He does, can He do anything about it?" And the answer is simply; "You have never met anyone who cares as much as Jesus." At some time you will face death or serious loss in your life, but Jesus cares enough to take you by the hand and awaken you from your tragedy. Today, He wants to breathe life into your heartbreaking situation.

DAY 190

YES

Ναί = *'nai'*

Yes (indeed), certainly, even so

And when He had come into the house, the blind men came to Him. And Jesus said to them, "Do you believe that I am able to do this?" They said to Him, "Yes, Lord" (Matthew 9:28). Jesus asked a simple question, "Do you believe that I am able to do this?" When was the last time you said, "Yes Lord, I believe?" As you know, there are many great ways to say "*yes*" to the Lord; no matter what your age, your gender, your situation or your particular talents. But it will take faith.

God will not ask you to do anything that you are not capable of doing. So how does He ask you? Probably not by letter, text, telephone call or e-mail; not even via Twitter. In the Bible He appeared as a burning bush or as a voice out of a thundercloud, but I wouldn't count on that. He certainly has other ways to connect. It may be a gentle stirring of the soul, a twinge of conscience, or a feeling of elation. God will ask you to do things, or not to do things, in subtle ways. But it's your response that sets the stage for a miracle!

When God asks you something, you have the right to say "no!" You can say, "let me think about it and get back to you" or "I'd rather serve you in some other way" or any number of self-serving answers. But the answer most pleasing to God today, and the answer that will open the door to a miracle is simply "Yes."

Day 191

Winning

καταλαμβάνω = *'katalambano'*
To lay hold of, obtain, seize, to win, arrest or capture

1 Corinthians 9:24-27, ***"Do you not know that those who run in a race all run, but one receives the prize? Run in such a way that you may obtain it."*** Another translation simply says, ***"Run in such a way as to win!"*** The apostle Paul is calling on a basic human desire *to win* and directs it toward obtaining an eternal prize from God. He compares the Christian life to a competitive race, and says that we should *run to win.* He wants to keep us from abandoning our faith in Christ, and to help us train to run our own race. So he says, *"I run with purpose,"* and, *"I discipline my body... So I am not disqualified."* For you to *win* you too must train hard!

In this passage, Paul mentions three things, (1) *focus*, (2) *discipline*, and (3) *endurance*. In your own race, you must train yourself to *keep focused, be disciplined* and *build stamina*. If you get caught up in the mundane affairs of life, and quit focusing on Jesus, and the rewards He has for you, you will lose your position in the race and end up settling for second best. That's not what the Lord wants for you. He want you to run the race marked out for you with a single-minded focus on pleasing Him. Therefore, you must live a life that is free from those things that hold you back in your spiritual development, and experience the joy of *winning*! The Lord wants you to win the race set before you – and collect the prize!

Day 192

Nevertheless

μέντοι = *"mentoi'*
Nevertheless, indeed, however

"Nevertheless the solid foundation of God stands, having this seal: 'The Lord knows those who are His'." (2 Timothy 2:19). Indeed, no matter what happens in life, this solid foundation of God stands (and is sealed): *"The Lord knows you because you are His!"* Nevertheless! What an incredible word! It is the *nevertheless* of grace, the great *surprise* God has for you. No matter what sin you may have committed, you are declared righteous by God Almighty: clean and innocent, the moment you place our faith and trust in Jesus.

It was once said: "Faith triumphs over our failures as long as we know the *nevertheless* of justification by faith in Christ. Everyone who humbles himself and cries 'God, have mercy on me' will go home justified." This is the *nevertheless* of the gospel of grace, so remember it. Repeat it to yourself over and over again. Shout it out aloud whenever satan attacks you. Declare: "Nevertheless, I am declared righteous; I am justified freely by His grace through the redemption that came by Christ."

Nevertheless, because you believe in Jesus Christ! Once you start declaring your righteousness in Him, that's when things start to change. Your success is set before you and nothing more needs to done. Nothing less will do; nothing else is necessary. Hallelujah!

Day 193

Intercession

ὑπερεντυγχάνει = *'huperentigchanei'*
To intercede, to make petition for, to arbitrate

"Likewise the Spirit also helps in our weaknesses. For we do not know what we should pray for as we ought, but the Spirit Himself makes intercession for us with groanings which cannot be uttered" (Romans 8:26). God's word has much to say about intercession. In 1 Timothy 2:1 it says we should have *intercession* and *thanksgiving* for all men. In Romans 8 it says we should make intercession for all the saints according to the will of God. However, in our opening verse we see that someone else is interceding on our behalf – the Holy Spirit! The Holy Spirit dwelling inside us gives us direction; searching our hearts, moving us and revealing the will of God. *"Now He who searches the hearts knows what the mind of the Spirit is, because He makes intercession for the saints according to the will of God"* (verse 27).

Since the Bible is the *word* of God, and the *word* of God is called the 'sword of the Spirit' (*Ephesians 6:17*), you have a weapon to wage war in the spiritual realm. Because the Holy Spirit dwells in you, the *words* in the Bible become your way of understanding the will of God. The Spirit uses the *word* for you to know God's will, and by knowing the will of God, you can stay in harmony with God; always seeing the victory! It's comforting to know that when you are praying and are not sure what to pray for, or how to pray, the Holy Spirit is praying the perfect prayer in agreement to the will of God.

Day 194

Resurrection

ἀνάστασις = *'anastsis'*
Resurrection, a raising again, a standing up

Philippians 3:10 declares, *"That I may know Him and the power of His resurrection."* This should be the cry of every heart! There is power and authority in the *resurrection* of Jesus Christ. The King rules and reigns, and He is seated at the right hand of God with His enemies under His feet. He is alive; so we, as joint-heirs have the very same privileges. If Jesus never rose from the dead there would be no victory to enjoy, His resurrection has caused us to be more than conquerors. This verse implores us to become familiar with the *power* and *resurrection* of Jesus. The same power that resurrected Him from the dead now exists in you and me.

For Jesus Christ to rule and reign over everything His death had already purchased, He needed to be *resurrected* to new life! It took *resurrection power* to bring this about. Note, if Jesus died a spotless and sinless man, and nothing else, the price for our sins would have been paid and we would have been redeemed. However, there would be no one watching over our souls; there would be no *authority* to enforce the devil's defeat; there would be no King on the throne of the kingdom of God. It would be like a person securing an empire and not being around to rule over it. Nonetheless the *resurrection* is a fact, and that means you can have all the benefits it has secured. As with the early church, you can give witness to the *resurrection* with *great power* (Acts 4:33).

DAY 195

TRANSFORMATION

μεταμορφούμεθα = *'metamorphoometha'*
To transform, to transfigure, to transmute

"But we all, with unveiled face, beholding as in a mirror the glory of the Lord, are being transformed into the same image from glory to glory, just as by the Spirit of the Lord" (2 Corinthians 3:18). The Greek for translated *transformed* is where we get the English word *metamorphosis* which is to dramatically change through growth and differentiation. As you *'see'* the glory of the Lord, you are dramatically changed into His exact likeness!

The *same image* is the image of the Lord Jesus Christ. By nature you are not at all like Christ, but you are to strive to become more like Him day by day. If you make this effort, the result is "an ever increasing reflection of glory", and those who see you grow in grace will have to conclude that the cause of this miraculous transformation must be "from the Spirit of the Lord."

However, to genuinely reflect God's glory you must do it His way. The true power source for transformation must be the Holy Spirit, not our own human efforts. The more you seek to meddle, by placing yourself into the picture, the more others will see only your face. When those around you look into the mirror of your life they should only see a clear reflection of the Lord Jesus Christ. His glory shining on you!

Arise, shine for the glory of the Lord has risen upon you.

Day 196

Recommendation

συστατικῶν = *'sustatikon'*
Recommendation, commendation, introduction

2 Corinthians 3:1 states, *"Are we beginning to commend ourselves again? Or do we need, like some people, letters of recommendation to you or from you? You yourselves are our letter, written on our hearts, known and read by everyone."* The best recommendation you can have is the lives of the people you have influenced! Paul knew that God's way was to "make known" His message through the lives of the Corinthians themselves. Their lives were legitimate and sincere "letters of recommendation," demonstrating the true effect of his ministry. People were to look at his followers, look at their spiritual growth and service, and conclude; "truly, this must be the work of God we are seeing."

How do you glorify God? You allow Him to reveal Himself through you. If you continue to follow Him, continue to grow spiritually, continue to bear up under pressure; His power, His love and His glory will indeed be reproduced in your life. Paul's words here do not mean that you should seek to glorify God merely by saying, "I am a Christian." No, you can only echo His glory by living your life so that others will say, "this must be the power of God we see." Notice, if you shine His glory on others, they will see exactly what you are reflecting, and as a result, God is glorified! Do that today. Shine like a bright star into the lives of those around you.

DAY 197

APPREHEND

κατειληφέναι = *'katalyphenai'*

To apprehend, seize tight hold of, arrest, catch, capture, appropriate

"...I press on that I may lay hold of that for which Christ Jesus has also apprehended me. I do not consider myself to have apprehended, but one thing I do, forgetting those things which are behind and reaching forward to those things which are ahead" (Philippians 3:12-13). The apostle Paul *seized a tight hold* of that which Christ had *seized* a tight hold of him. That was why he was able to make progress in his pursuit of the fulfilment of His calling. According to this scripture progress was his primary goal for life. He knew that completion will not come without progress and destination will not come without the journey.

Progress is *advancement* and it is a necessity when fulfilling God's plans and purposes. Therefore, progress should be the underlying objective for achieving all your goals. To step into the abundant life that God intended for you there needs to be an earnest commitment to advancement. As with Paul, not just the desire to start, but the gutsy determination to finish strong. The condition of your life today is a true reflection of the effort you made up to this point. Effort is what drives you forward, no effort no progress - it's that simple! Today, co-operate with the process that accompanies real growth. Keep advancing "step by step" toward your destination and you will *apprehend* all the wonderful things God has put aside for you.

DAY 198

DELIGHT

συνήδομαι = *'synithomai'*
To delight inwardly in, rejoice together, congratulate

The apostle Paul made this statement in Romans 7:22: *"For I delight in the law of God according to the inward man."* He *delighted* in God's word according to his inward man (the new creation). The only way to *delight* yourself in the Lord is to follow the promptings of your inner man. Your inner man is in complete agreement with God's Spirit, Who is leading and guiding you every step of the way. Whenever you do that, many blessings shall follow.

Psalm 37:4 says: "***Delight yourself also in the Lord, and [then] He will give you the desires and secret petitions of your heart***" (Amplified). If you get pleasure purely by serving God, then your priorities are wrong. What's likely to then happen is that your life will become stressful. Why? Because you are expecting God to grant you the desires of your heart through *good works* instead of adoration, worship and intimacy. Serving God with zeal is definitely a good pursuit, and it should be one of your major goals, but I don't believe it should be at the top of your priority list. *Delighting* yourself "*in Him*" by seeking Him alone; being worshipful, intimate and loving toward Him; should be your highest priority and your most direct pursuit. Only then, can God give you the *desires* of your heart! As you give Him devotion, as you delight yourself in Him alone, I pray He blesses you abundantly.

DAY 199

PICTURES

ὀπτασίας = *'optasias'*
A vision, supernatural appearance, a picture

Talking about Pictures of Paradise, in 2 Corinthians 12:1 Paul says, *"It is doubtless not profitable for me to boast. I will come to visions and revelations of the Lord."* No doubt there are people who have been able to see into heaven. But that should not be your focus in life. Yet, there are times when God will draw a picture on your heart to enlighten you. After teaching on Colossians 1:27, *"Christ in you, the hope of glory."* I was in a room with one of our pastors and suddenly the Lord prompted me to lay my hands on her. She was sitting down at the time so I stood in front of her and extended my right hand. As I did that, the Lord manifested Himself in me in a profound way. The Lord's divine "*Person*" had unexpectedly inhabited every aspect of my being! Then I saw (in my spirit) a picture of her as a young girl, even though she was probably the oldest person in our church. When I told her what I had seen she started to weep. That very morning she was thinking of the time she started her walk with Jesus as a young girl. The *picture* God fashioned on my spirit blessed this pastor and touched her heart deeply.

My prayer today is that God's portraits become vividly painted on the inside of you, and as a result, they truly capture your imagination and make His divine thoughts so memorable that your life will be transformed. His *pictures* on your heart will make you see the world differently!

Day 200

Paths

τροχιὰς = *'trochias'*
A path, a trail, the track of a wheel

"Therefore strengthen the hands which hang down, and the feeble knees, and make straight paths for your feet, so that what is lame may not be dislocated, but rather be healed" (Hebrews 12:12-13). To strengthen and renew your spiritual vitality you are told to make straight *paths* for your feet. In other words, to have your steps well-organized! In Robert Frost's poem, "The Road Less Traveled", he comes to a crossroad in the woods. He studies the two paths carefully, and one of the two roads has signs of travel: the grass was worn by the steps before so it was the safe path; it was the secure path.

Yet, there was another path as well. Few had walked that path because the grass was not bent by many footsteps; the way was not as known. Adventure beckoned from that path with possible wonder. You could take that path with a sense of expectation, but you had to choose which path to walk. Choosing one path would mean not choosing the other, for coming back was not an option. Choosing the path as the poem says, *makes all the difference*. So, what path will you choose to take? If you follow Christ, you cannot choose the safe path. You must take up your cross and walk the very path He walked. The greatest blessings and opportunities, and the greatest miracles are found down that path. Don't choose the path of *least resistance*, choose to walk with Jesus!

Day 201

Come

δεῦτε = *'thefte'*
To come, approach, to come hither

In Matthew 11:28 Jesus sends out an invitation, He says, *"Come to Me, all you who labour and are heavy laden, and I will give you rest."* That one phrase "*Come to Me*" says it all! Love personified is beckoning you to come and receive rest and refreshment for your soul. How comforting it is to know that there is someone you can go to whenever you feel things are overwhelming you; when you are so overloaded and over-burdened that you cannot cope anymore. I love the promise of God mentioned in Isaiah 43:2, *"When you pass through the waters, I will be with you; And through the rivers, they shall not overflow you. When you walk through the fire, you shall not be burned, Nor shall the flame scorch you."*

With this awesome promise, and such an irresistible invitation from Jesus, how can you ever feel overwhelmed or heavy-burdened? Whether you are feeling overawed, troubled, or oppressed, the remedy is still the same: Jesus said, "Come to Me." Accept this invitation and draw near to Him today. If you do, anything that has been harassing you will flee in every direction. In the company of the Lord of Lords and the King of Kings there can stand no evil. For, "He has set a table before you in the presence of your enemies" (Psalm 23:5)!

DAY 202

KINGDOM

βασιλεία = *'basiliah'*
Kingdom, sovereignty, royal power

When Jesus sent out the seventy, He gave them this instruction, *"Whatever city you enter, and they receive you, eat such things as are set before you. And heal the sick there, and say to them, 'The kingdom of God has come near to you'."* Paraphrased: "Whenever you enter a town and you are accepted, heal the sick of that town and tell everyone that the kingdom of God is here!" The Lord gave the very same instructions when He sent out the twelve: *"And as you go, preach (make a declaration), saying, 'The kingdom of Heaven is at hand'. Heal the sick, cleanse the lepers, raise the dead, and cast out demons"* (Matthew 10:7,8).

Notice something, the coming of God's *kingdom* and the ministry of healing cannot be separated. The ministry of healing cannot be separated from the complete declaration of the *kingdom's* abiding presence. The Holy Spirit delights in confirming the presence of God's *kingdom* by operating through the ministry of healing, together with other supernatural signs and wonders. God's *kingdom* is constantly demonstrating God's rule in the lives of men and women because that's there you will find His kingdom. When you arrive on the scene, so too does the kingdom of God! The kingdom of God accompanies you everywhere you go. Most importantly, the Kingdom of God is now, this very moment!

Day 203

Dominion

κράτος = *'kratos'*
Dominion, power, authority and strength

"If anyone ministers, let him do it as with the ability which God supplies, that in all things God may be glorified through Jesus Christ, to whom belong the glory and the dominion forever and ever. Amen" (1 Peter 4:11). The glory and *dominion* belong to Jesus Christ forever and ever! Dominion is comprised of both power and authority, hence, all those who are seated with Him in heavenly places share in Christ's dominion (Ephesians 2:6).

As identified in the word of God, you have been given a realm of great authority in Jesus Christ. This delegated authority is grounded in the original creative order which God established for man. God, in His wisdom, intended it to be a re-established and reinstated order through the saving work of Jesus Christ. Therefore, true dominion has to do with the privilege you have as a believer to resist those things that disrupt God's proper and ordained purposes for your life. What He intended is so often encroached upon by the rule of modern society. God said, "nothing in this earth is outside of His control." That is; dominion, authority and power over all the works of the devil. God left nothing outside of His control and in turn, your control. You may not have stopped distressing things from happening in your life because you've not fully understood the rights that come with having dominion in Christ, on this earth.

DAY 204

ABUNDANTLY

περισσὸν = *'perisson'*
Abundantly, more, greater, excessive, exceedingly

John 10:10 is one of my favourite verses in the Bible: *"The thief does not come except to steal, and to kill, and to destroy. I have come that they may have life, and that they may have it more abundantly."* The *abundant* life, or the rich and satisfying life that the Lord is referring to is not established through what you get from God, but rather, by what you receive from Him. If you are not constantly living in *receiving* mode, you will never be able to enjoy life in *abundance*. Let me explain:

When you are in *get* mode, you are attempting to get hold of something through your own strength and efforts, that's always a struggle. As a result, anything you've obtained through this practice is going to be unenjoyable. If life is always strenuous and requires serious effort, it becomes challenging and exhausting and that's not the *abundant* life Jesus came to give you. No, God wants you to live a life of righteous *ease*; a life that's full of grace and inner peace. This will help to keep you from striving and struggling, so as a result, you will be able to experience true happiness. If you are to enjoy life to the full you must first understand that God loves you unconditionally and that He desires to be *with you* to bless you super-abundantly. In this kind of reality there are never any struggles. Purpose to pursue a stress-free, super-abundant life and nothing else!

DAY 205

LAUGHTER

γελάω = *'gelao'*
To laugh, smile, or rejoice

"Blessed are you who hunger now, For you shall be filled. Blessed are you who weep now, For you shall laugh" (Luke 6:21). We all need to laugh more; we need to have a happy heart. Throughout the Bible we are encouraged to "*rejoice*" to "*be joyful*" and to "*be glad.*" There are over 50 direct references to happiness. Being happy has great benefits; not only does it strengthen you, it can completely change your attitude and outlook on life. Someone once said, "What everyone wants from life is continuous and genuine happiness."

The truth is: if you're happy, you will know it! And if you *know it* you will show it! Research has revealed that *laughter* actually releases tension, anxiety, anger, fear, shame and guilt. Laughter also increases antibodies and is believed to have a protective capacity against viruses, bacteria and other micro-organisms. Both science and the Bible agree that *laughter* is like a medicine. Proverbs 17:22 says, *"A happy heart is good medicine"* (Amp). Studies have shown that laughter discharges endorphins into the body. They reduce stress, enhance circulation, boost the immune system and strengthen the heart. Like a good massage, a hearty laugh can stimulate all the major organs in your body. Some say it's like an internal aerobic exercise! So why don't you have a good healthy laugh today and feel the benefits?

Day 206

I-Am

εἰμι / εἰμὲ = *'eimi' / 'eime'*
I am, I am he, I exist, me

In John 14:6 Jesus said, *"I am the way, and the truth, and the life; no one comes to the Father, but through Me."* In John 15:1 He declares, *"I am the true vine, and My Father is the vine-dresser.... I am the vine, and you are the branches."* Nothing can describe Jesus better than His *own* words. By listening to what He says about Himself we can get the most accurate image of who He really is. I am referring to the "I am" statements of Jesus and the absolute truth that they unveil. What Jesus said about Himself is paramount to our faith. Every word documented concerning who Jesus said He was, is deliberate, but especially the declaration "I am!"

What Jesus declared is true, as it is in line with the statement God made to Moses in Exodus 3:14: *"I am Who I am!"* That means, as God, Jesus is entitled to the devotion, worship and obedience reserved for the Godhead. And He is worthy of being called "the great I am." The great "I am" is with you right now! Ready and willing to do what only He can do. Are you willing to let Him be what only He can be? Jesus wants to be your *healer*; He wants to be your *deliverer*; He wants to be your *peace*; He wants to be your *strength*; He wants to be your *prosperity*; and He wants to be your *great reward.* More than any of these things, He wants to be the lover of your soul. Love Him for who "He is" and allow Him to be who He wants to be in your life!

Day 207

Resist

ἀντίστητε = *"antistite'*
Resist, set against, withstand, oppose

"Therefore submit to God. Resist the devil and he will flee from you. Draw near to God and He will draw near to you" (James 4:7-8). You resist the devil by consistently drawing near and remaining close to God. The first step is to allow God to remove the devil's influence over your mind, and this is achieved by confessing any sin you may have committed. God's word likens this to you coming back to life!

When you genuinely repent and wholeheartedly submit to God, you become truly blessed. Why? Because the devil has run away from you. Literally, the devil has bolted in every direction! No longer do you have to deal with the tests and trials he brought your way; no longer do you have to fight the temptations he placed before you; no longer do you have to avoid the traps he set for you. He is not present in your company any longer!

The most important aspect of drawing near to God is this: "You must initiate it." When you draw near, He draws near! It's His presence that has replaced the devil's presence in your life, which brings about triumph. Go through this process today: (1) *Submit to God*, (2) *Resist the devil*, and (3) *Draw near to God*. Be rest assured, you will have a great time of freedom and conquest!

DAY 208

TOUCH

ἥψατο = *'ipsato'*
To touch, lay hold of, fasten to

Then Jesus, moved with compassion, stretched out His hand and touched him, and said to him, "I am willing; be cleansed" (Mark 1:41). Lepers were untouchable, yet Jesus dared to touch the untouchable. Can you imagine how wonderful it must have been for the poor leper to feel the touch of another person? Jesus said, *"I am willing, be clean"* and instantly the leprosy left the man. He was completely healed by the words uttered by Jesus.

Jesus didn't have to touch him, but he did anyway because he knew how much it would mean to the leper. This not only strengthened the faith of the leper, but was also a witness to all who came into contact with him. The man was so excited about being healed that he quickly spread the news in the surrounding area. He was happy to tell others how much Jesus had done for him. The question is, "Are you? Do you let everyone know when Jesus blesses you?"

If ever you get sick, remember that Jesus can heal any disease. Remember to thank Jesus for healing you; just as the leper was excited about his healing, you should be excited to tell others about the great things God has done for you. Jesus wants to *touch* you today, no matter what you've done or where you've come from, Jesus cares enough to extend a loving tender touch.

Day 209

Greater

μείζων = *'meizon'*
Great, boundless, large, in the widest sense

1 John 4:4 declares, *"You are of God, little children, and have overcome them, because He who is in you is greater than he who is in the world."* To hear some people talk, you would think the one who is "less" lives on the inside of them. No, the One who is "more," the greater One is on the inside of you! This should be the heart cry of every believer: "The greater One lives within me, and He who dwells within me causes me to triumph in every circumstance of life." It is because of the *greater* One who lives within you that you are victorious. It is because of the greater One who lives within you that you are successful. Some people would say this is bragging. This certainly isn't bragging on yourself, it is bragging on God and His ability. You're not saying what you can do but what the Almighty God in you can do.

You should make it a habit to continually declare that the Greater One in you makes you victorious. Whenever you proclaim this, you are lining your words up with God's words. When you boldly speak His words, you are giving God a place to work in your life. This is not presumption it's obedience. Presumption is to assume something, but that is not the case, for you are acting on what you know to be true and declaring it to be so. Today, start to declare openly - in obedience to God's word - that the Greater One "in you" will cause you to overcome.

DAY 210

GRATITUDE

εὐχαριστέω = *'eucharisteo'*
To be grateful, thankful, appreciative

"With gratitude and prayer, I thank my God upon every remembrance of you" (Philippians 1:3). Real gratitude was expressed by the various women who supported Jesus's ministry. Namely, Mary Magdalene, Joanna, Susanna (Luke 8:1-3). These women were helping to support Jesus out of their own means. One translation says, *"Who ministered to and provided for Him out of their own property and personal belongings."* What's quite obvious is that these women were women of substance, but they were full of *gratitude* for what Jesus has done for them. Are you truly grateful for what the Lord Jesus has done for you?

Being grateful is not only one of God's essential and vital requirements for you, it is also for your own good, your own benefit. You will never be dissatisfied with your lot in life if you are grateful for all you already have. And I'm sure you can find many things to be grateful for. Gratitude unlocks the fullness of life; it turns what you have into enough and more. It can turn a meal into a feast, a house into a home, and a stranger into a friend. Gratitude makes sense of your past, brings peace for today and creates a vision for tomorrow. Therefore, in all things be grateful! Developing an "attitude of gratitude" for your current blessings will unleash the power of God for you to receive many more!

DAY 211

EMMANUEL

Ἐμμανουήλ = *'Emmanouel'*
A Messianic title derived from Isaiah 7:14 = God with us

Behold, the virgin shall be with child, and bear a Son, and they shall call His name Immanuel," which is translated, "God with us" (Matthew 1:23). The theme of God being *with us* runs through the entire Bible, and it's also quite striking how frequently the idea appears. In Matthew's Gospel, the name to be given to Jesus is *Emmanuel*, and the risen Jesus ends the gospel by promising His disciples that He will be "with them to the end of time" (Matthew 28:20). In Luke, the angel addressing Mary assures her that "the Lord is with you" (Luke 1:28). Indeed, in John's Gospel we find Jesus Himself describing His Father as being *with* Him. Therefore, what are we to make of all these references to God being with various people? There is mention of this from Moses through to John the Baptist, Paul and Jesus Himself!

When studying the Bible, see how many times you can find references to God being *with* you. For God promises to be with you regardless of your inadequacies or deficiencies. The main reason for God's *presence* being with you is so that He may perform His promises in your life. God said to Jeremiah: *"Don't be afraid of them for I am with you to deliver you"* (Jeremiah 1:8). Today, God is saying the same to you. Therefore, you should not be afraid or dismayed, for His *presence* is with you, and it's crucial for your protection and security.

DAY 212

REIGN

βασιλεύω = *'basilevo'*

To reign, to rule as a king, to lord over

"For if by the one man's offense death reigned through the one, much more those who receive abundance of grace and of the gift of righteousness will reign in life through the One, Jesus Christ" (Romans 5:17). You have received the gift of righteousness and an abundance of grace; you reign as a king in the realm of life. Yes, this life! God never intended that you should be a servant or have a subservient spirit. His love has taken you out of the slave-realm and into the Son-realm. His love has taken you away from the sense of inferiority and given you the sense of our *oneness* with Christ. The old inferiority complex that comes from sin-consciousness has been abolished, instead love-consciousness and son-consciousness have taken its place.

This places a different emphasis on how you now live your life. You must stop waiting for something to be found, created or established; in its place, start to release what you already have on the inside of you. For instance, stop looking for prosperity and start living prosperity! Wherever you go and whatever you do, you have the power to release God's ability. In fact, in every situation you bring success and prosperity along with you, so stop waiting for success to happen; rather, expect success to come about because you are present. Don't forget, the success you are looking for is already manifested in you!

Day 213

Sovereignty

βασιλείαν = *'basileian'*
Sovereignty, royal power, kingdom

There is nothing which happens in your life that is out of God's influence. Being the King or Kings and the Lord of Lords, God has no limitations. God is the Alpha and Omega, He is above all things and before all things. He created all things and holds all things together by the word of His power. He knows all things past, present and future; God can do all things and accomplish all things; He is in control of all things, and rules over all things. That's what being sovereign means!

God's sovereignty is exercised in His kingdom: *"But seek first the kingdom of God and His righteous-ness, and all these things shall be added to you"* (Matthew 6:33). This is a verse which you should commit to memory. It provides you with the key to acquiring *all things*. Before you misunderstand what I am saying, the all things are the "good things that come down from the Father of lights" (James 1:17). You are instructed to seek first the kingdom of God. The Greek word for *first* means "to place in front of other priorities." Notice, it doesn't say you shouldn't seek anything else, it says to seek the kingdom of God first! Once you get the order of your priorities right God promises to add all the *good* things you are in need of. Today, why don't you become kingdom minded and allow the *sovereignty* of God to inspire and direct you. You'll be truly amazed!

DAY 214

HAPPY

μακάριος = *'makarios'*
Happy, blessed, to be envied

Romans 14:22 says, *"Do you have faith? Have it to yourself before God. Happy is he who does not condemn himself in what he approves."* This verse is telling us to be honest with ourselves concerning what we believe, and if we do not condemn ourselves we will be happy. Happiness in the New Testament is often translated "blessed," though happiness also suggests being free from the burden of not being blessed. We should possess both! Psalm 144:15 states: *"Happy are the people whose God is the Lord."* We are happy only because we have a God who is Ruler and Master of everything and everyone on our side!

Most of us don't know how to be happy or how to stay happy; we think that more money will make us happy, or more possessions will make us happy. Yet, we have probably all found this to be a complete fallacy. Just think about the last thing that you really wanted and then acquired; whether it was shoes or clothes, a boat or a TV, a house or a car. It may have brought you temporary pleasure but it didn't bring lasting happiness. Things cannot make you happy; because there will always be something else, something bigger or better to tempt you to want even more. However, knowing that God is your Lord, and that He has full control over your life, brings lasting happiness. Today, take your eyes of *things* and place them of God, for He can supply your every need!

Day 215

Fortress

ὀχύρωμα = *'ochuroma'*
A fortress, strong defense, stronghold

2 Corinthians 10:4 mentions the spiritual weapons we can use to destroy the enemy's fortresses: *"For the weapons of our warfare are not carnal but mighty in God for pulling down strongholds (fortresses)."* No fortification that the devil builds can withstand the weapons God has given you. Your enemy is defenceless against them!

In contrast, God Himself is also a *mighty fortress* (Psalm 46), and that is where you can take refuge in troubled times. Verse 1 says, *"God is our refuge and strength, an ever present help in trouble."* God is *ever-present* and that is why you can take shelter and find protection in Him - anytime and anywhere! To know that no matter what kind of trouble you face today God is present and available; He is never too busy or too far off. The first line is like the thesis for the whole Psalm: our God is a *refuge*, a *strength*, a *fortress*, and therefore, when trouble comes your way you can find Him easily and quickly and go to Him for shelter.

God is very aware that the world today is full of anguish. You may experience some seriously violent storms. Still, the claim of this Psalm is that there is always a place to run to where you can find shelter. God: He is your fortress! A fortress is a place that you can visit to escape from harm; a safe haven, a place of sanctuary, and a *strong tower*!

DAY 216

TOMORROW

αὔριον = *"avrion'*
Tomorrow, the next day

"Therefore do not worry about tomorrow, for tomorrow will worry about its own things. Sufficient for the day is its own trouble" (Matthew 6:34). Don't focus on the worries and troubles of tomorrow, the future. The truth is, no one knows the future except God. He keeps the times and seasons under His own authority (Acts 1:7), and this includes the times and seasons concerning your personal life. With regards the future, or things to come, God's knowledge is called *"foreknowledge"* (1 Peter 1:2), and the excellency of God's knowledge involves "all things knowable." Our God is infinite; He knows it all because He created it all. People are always bewildered or confused by what they don't know, but James 4:14 says, *"Why, you do not even know what will happen tomorrow!"*

What should all this mean to you? It should create an absolute trust in God; who does know the future and who works all things for your benefit, but to His glory. The question is: "Are you able to entrust all our tomorrows to Him?" Never be afraid to entrust an unknown future to a known God. You may not know what tomorrow holds but you do know the One who holds tomorrow. Your heavenly Father has a perfect plan for your life, so commit this day to God the Father; you will be so glad you did!

Day 217

Fasting

νηστεία = *'nisteiah'*
A fasting, a voluntary absence of food

If you are under satanic oppression, or attack, then it's time to fast and pray! The devil doesn't want you to do this because it's so powerful. Jesus said to His disciples in Mark 9:29, *"This kind can come out by nothing but prayer and fasting."* How powerful is that? Prayer and fasting increase the faith and the anointing in your life. When the enemy comes like a flood, the Spirit of the Lord lifts up the standard against him (Isaiah 59:19), so you need to prepare yourself when there are stronger evil forces around.

The disciples were trying to cast out the demons in a young man's life but they couldn't (Mark 9:17-18). Religious lives and shallow commitments to Jesus will not stand when certain demons are active. Jesus rebuked His disciples for being faithless and perverse; that's why they couldn't cast out the demons. These are the words of Jesus: *"This kind can come out by nothing but prayer and fasting!"* There is nothing else you can do about particular evil spirits but to be on guard. Some versions of the Bible have removed "*fasting*" from any verses, even though prayer alone is not sufficient.

Fasting will empower your prayers. Everyone can pray but not everyone can fast. Fasting is humbling one's self before God: this is denying yourself in order to let the Holy Spirit lead you. You can't truly "die to self" without fasting.

Day 218

Prepare

ἑτοιμάζω = *'etimazo'*
To prepare, make ready, to prepare beforehand

2 Timothy 2:21 talks about you being "made ready" or "prepared" for every good work. ***"If anyone cleanses himself from the latter, he will be a vessel for honour, sanctified and useful for the Master, prepared for every good work."*** The first part of this passage says there are vessels of honour and dishonour, which means that some of us may be vessels of dishonour. Nevertheless, if you read next the part of the verse you will see clearly that it is entirely your choice which vessel you become.

Therefore, if there is any predetermination in your life it should be a good one. You don't have to do much to damage your good future; it's enough if you do nothing! Not putting your faith to action will hinder what God has in store for you. The truth is, God has prepared everything beforehand: He knew you intimately before time began. God called you by name, He knew about your needs and about your desires, and since He has created you, He also knows about your gifts and talents. He has prepared a way for you based on foreknowledge of who you are and who you will become. Note, both the practical and the spiritual are needed to achieve the right results. So prepare yourself for a great future! Make yourself ready to receive all that God has predestined for you, that is, what He has prepared beforehand!

Day 219

Hesitate

διακρίνω = *'thiakrino'*
To waver, hesitate, doubt

"He did not hesitate at the promise of God through unbelief, but was strengthened in faith, giving glory to God" (Romans 4:20). There are times in your life when you *hesitate.* Paul brought out the nature of Abraham's faith in this verse: he did not *hesitate* or waver at the promise of God through unbelief. There is a double contrast in Abraham's faith: (1) He did not doubt God's promise, and (2) God strengthened his faith. The word *waver* or *hesitate* means being divided. Sometimes this word can mean *doubt* (James 1:6). Doubt is a divided mind, a mind that vacillates between faith and uncertainty. Abraham did not doubt God's promise; he did not waver at the seeming impossibility of having a child by Sarah in his old age; he did not permit unbelief to judge God's promise. The nature of faith is to have complete trust in the faithfulness of God.

Abraham was empowered by faith in God's words. His faith originated in God; it was not Abraham's faith that gave him strength, it was the God of his faith that gave him strength. You need to adopt the same attitude, have the same spirit of faith. *"For He who has promised is faithful"* (Hebrews 10:23). Today, do not hesitate, do not waver at the promise of God; be strengthened in your faith! Since God can never change His mind you can always count on Him. Right now, count on Him *completely*!

Day 220

Armour

πανοπλία = *'panoplia'*
The complete armour, full armour

"Put on the whole armour of God, that you may be able to stand against the wiles of the devil" (Ephesians 6:11). If you do what this verse says you will be dressed for victory. Like it or not, there is a *spiritual battle* that every one of us is involved in. The battleground for this intense spiritual struggle is not some earthy territory; it is the human heart. Both Jesus and the devil are supremely interested in taking possession of minds and hearts, for this reason, you are called to be more than a peaceful spectator or mediator in this violent conflict. You must be a committed front-line commando, ready to do what your Commander in Chief tells you. But remember, your weapons and armour are mighty *"through God."* Therefore, they belong to Him and not you!

This verse tells you to put on the *whole* or *complete* armour of God. The Greek word used is one word, implying that God's armour does not come incomplete or in sections. Therefore, putting on part of the armour is not an option because you are told to do this for your own protection. God has paid the cost for your entire arsenal. All that you need was purchased at Calvary by the blood of His own dear Son. Just as Jonathan so loved David that he gave him his armour, sword, robe, and indeed his very throne (1 Samuel 18:3-4), so Jesus has given you all you will need in this spiritual battle. You are dressed for victory, so today, act like it.

Day 221

Drink

πotίζω = *'potizo'*
Made to drink, to give to drink

1 Corinthians 12:13 states, *"For by one Spirit we were all baptized into one body - whether Jews or Greeks, whether slaves or free - and have all been made to drink into one Spirit."* It is important to understand the meaning of the two Greek words that are used in this verse of scripture. The first word *baptizo* means *to immerse*: "to draw water by dipping a vessel into another" or, "to dye a garment by dipping it into a liquid." On a cold day you may relax in a bath and let the water warm you; in this instance, you have chosen to be immersed into something pleasant. Therefore, baptism is more to do with *immersion* than *infilling*; it is the act of dipping a vessel into another!

On the other hand, the second word *potizo* literally means to "make to drink" and it has to do with infilling. It's used for pouring liquid into another vessel, or pouring fluid onto another object; it has to do with *being made full* or *fully absorbing* that which is being poured out. Drinking the Holy Spirit is like deliberately opening your mouth to have a drink. It is the intentional act of receiving that which the Spirit is pouring out. In order to live the super-abundant life Jesus came to secure for you, you must be *"continually filled with the Holy Spirit"* (Ephesians 5:18). For this to happen, you should intentionally accept and receive what He is pouring out, because that which He is pouring out today is for today!

Day 222

Fellowship

κοινωνία = *'koinonia'*
Fellowship, communion, partnership

In his closing prayer from his prison in Rome, the apostle Paul said, *"The grace of the Lord Jesus Christ, and the love of God, and the communion of the Holy Spirit be with you all. Amen"* (2 Corinthians 13:14). Your relationship with the Holy Spirit is both wonderful and incredible, but as with all relationships it can either be developed or neglected. If you are feeling spiritually dry, you have probably neglected this relationship. The remedy is to give yourself sufficient time to reconnect with the Spirit through *fellowship* with Him.

You experience the grace of the Lord and the love of God through the fellowship of the Spirit. For the relationship to grow and be established fellowship involves companionship and communication. You have to spend time interacting with the Holy Spirit and listening to His voice. This requires some discipline otherwise the relationship will be neglected and you will disconnect. In Psalm 131:2, David says *"I have stilled and quietened my soul."* The Holy Spirit communicates with you in a "*gentle whisper*" (1 Kings 19:12); so you have to learn to still your soul in order to hear His voice. Picture a lake: when the lake is still and calm, any small pebble that is thrown into it will be seen and recognised, but when it is stormy you could throw a large boulder into it and it would not be noticed. With practice, you should be able to still your mind and make way for true *fellowship* with the Spirit.

Day 223

Spiritual

πνευματικῇ = *'pneumatiki'*
Spiritual, realm of the spirit

"Blessed be the God and Father of our Lord Jesus Christ, who has blessed us with every spiritual blessing in heavenly places in Christ" (Ephesians 1:3). In Christ, God has (*past tense*) blessed you with every spiritual blessing! Too many of God's children are more comfortable facing their circumstances than facing their God: "the source of all blessings." You need to acknowledge who is the *source* of all true blessings in your life. *"Blessed be God, even the Father of our Lord Jesus Christ, the Father of mercies, and the God of all comfort"* (2 Corinthians 1:3). In his time of great need Hezekiah turned his face to the Father of mercies and the God of all comfort (2 Kings 20:4-7), and his request was granted.

In response to Hezekiah's prayer, God gave him fifteen years more. Now, because Hezekiah recovered, was God's word proven to be false: "...you shall die and not live"? No! God was simply stating a fact concerning the king's poor health as it was at the time; if Hezekiah had not turned his face to his *source*, the Father of mercies, he would have died. After God had answered his prayer, Hezekiah suddenly found himself a uniquely wealthy man. None of us have this guarantee, and that is why we should live each day at a time. Each day you must make a *conscious* effort to turn your back on the past and face your source. To be truly spiritual you must fix your eyes on the *"Author and finisher of your faith."*

Day 224

First

πρῶτος = *'protos'*
First, chief, most important

In Revelation 2:4 we hear a warning from Jesus that we should all be very mindful of. *"Nevertheless I have this against you, that you have left your first love."* Forgetting your first love is a common practice today. The word *left* can mean: "to let go," "to neglect," "forsake," "leave alone" or "abandon." But what does it mean to have *left* or *abandoned* your first love? Notice, it's identified as something that calls for repentance and this repentance must include doing the good deeds you did at first.

The "deeds of love" you did when you were first saved, when your faith was young, when you were supernaturally grounded in selflessness; watching out for the interests of others instead of your own and giving till you had nothing left to give. In my opinion this was the *"first love"* that the church in Ephesus had neglected - the selfless love for others. The remedy that God provides is simple: repent and start doing again what you did at first.

More importantly, put first things first! Rekindle your *first love* for Jesus. The Lord's amazing love for you never diminishes or grows cold, but because of your human frailties your love will grow cold if you do nothing to sustain or restore it. Don't abandon your first love! Each day, make a determined effort to kindle the flame of love for Christ.

DAY 225

THIEF

κλέπτης = *'kleptis'*
The thief, robber, bandit

In John 10:10 we find a clear mandate from our Lord Jesus and at the same time He identifies the devil's strategy. *"The thief does not come except to steal, and to kill, and to destroy. I have come that they may have life, and that they may have it more abundantly."* The contrast could not be more striking! Jesus mentions "the thief," but He is speaking about a larger grouping of thieves, robbers, wolves and strangers who come to harm the sheep. Such people tried to approach the sheep without going through the shepherd. This was because they wanted to exploit the sheep, whereas Jesus was prepared to die defending His sheep from these thieves, robbers and wolves.

We often quote this verse and miss its direct application. That said, satan has a mandate to steal, kill and destroy; he is "the chief thief." But remember, Jesus always addressed the spirit that's behind such things and not necessarily the people doing them. You must fully comprehend the words of Jesus in John 10:10: He said, *"The thief comes 'only' to steal and kill and destroy."* That's the only thing on his mind! But Jesus has triumphed over the devil making an open show of Him; displaying His victory through His church! Now, you can demand that everything that's been stolen be returned! God ordains restitution *in the spirit*, so whatever the thief has stolen from you he must give back sevenfold. Amen to that!

Day 226

Fallen

ἔπεσεν = *'epesen'*
Fallen, to fall under, to fall prostrate

In Revelation 18 the apostle John saw an angel coming down from heaven declaring: *"Babylon the great is fallen..."* (verse 2). Then verse 4 says, "*And I heard another voice from heaven saying, 'Come out of her, my people, lest you share in her sins'.*" Babylon represents a decadent, evil world. For us it represents a life of spiritual indifference and compromise; a religion that believes in God but denies His power to radically change lives. God is raising up a new generation, a growing remnant of holy, set-apart believers whose hearts have been stirred. Is that you?

These believers are tired of the compromise of today's communities. They hear the Holy Spirit calling them to a life of holiness and separation from the world. They have come out of Babylon, out of the deadness and corruption of apostasy, and they refuse to bow to the idols of materialism and popularity. They are a holy people, truly separated; they are hungry for the word and are consumed with declaring the wonders of God and making His name great.

Don't you want to be one of those people? If you do, join me in this prayer: "*God please help me listen. Do whatever you have to do to keep my eyes on You. Train my ears to hear Your voice. Help me to walk in Your peace. Lord, reassure me today, as only You can. Equip me to help restore a fallen world!*"

DAY 227

SINCERE

ἀνυποκρίτου = *'anupokritou'*
Sincere, genuine, without hypocrisy

When writing to his protégé Timothy, the apostle Paul commented on his grandmother's *sincere* faith: *"I call to remembrance the genuine faith that is in you, which dwelt first in your grandmother Lois and your mother Eunice, and I am persuaded is in you also"* (2 Timothy 1:5). Sincere faith is generational! It can be passed on to your children's children; as with Timothy's mother and grandmother. This you can do not only by your instruction, but also by your lifestyle and the good use of your resources.

You equip the next generation by example, or you make the means available for others to continue impacting on their lives. This is very crucial as you need to leave a true legacy. Consider the old cartoon which showed two men discussing a third man who had just died. One asked, "how much did he leave?" The other replied, "everything!" Are you going to leave everything? You probably are! The question is, where? It is your personal responsibility to pass on your *sincere* faith to the next generation. Therefore, you need to consciously give glory to God for His mighty works and deeds of power; in the heart of the next generation.

Like Lois and Eunice, you must tell everyone about your great and awesome God. Just like these two women, your *sincere faith* should be conspicuous to those around you.

DAY 228

SONG

ᾠδὴν = *'othin'*
Song, ode, hymn,

We are encouraged to be filled with the Spirit, *"speaking to one another in psalms and hymns and spiritual songs"* (Ephesians 5:18-19). Therefore, one of the manifestations of being filled with the Spirit of God is having a *spiritual song*! The question is: "How do you make a song visible for everyone to see it? Do you have to show everyone the music notes and the lyrics of the song so they can see the song?" The answer is no. All you need is a *new song* in your heart. Quite simply, God wants you to live your life as a *new song* so that others will see Christ shining through. It's surprising how many times in the Bible it says, *"Sing a new song unto the Lord."* Implying that the *song* in your heart is always fresh!

Is the *song* in your heart fresh today? Maybe your heart has lost its enthusiasm for singing? Have you lost your joy for living? There are too many believers who have simply lost their song! Have you ever considered what causes you to lose your *song* and how you can get it back? What are the *song-stealers*; and what are the *song-makers*? Complaining and self-pity will steal your song. The only way to make a melody in your heart and sing a new *song* is to be *"filled with the Spirit!"* If you've lost your *song*, ask Him to fill you with a fresh anointing. Purpose today to get back the song in your heart so that others can enjoy it. Don't lose your song!

Day 229

Praise

αἴνεσις = *'ainesis'*
Praise, a thank-offering, commendation

Praise is an effective weapon you can use against the evil schemes of the devil. When you start to *praise* God, despite your circumstances, you gain ascendance over every satanic power coming against you. This is because you have brought the Almighty onto the scene: *"But You are holy, You who inhabit the praises of Your people"* (Psalm 22:3). Another translation says, *"enthroned on the praises of Your people."* As the Lord is "*hallowed*" by your praises, He "*hallows*" you with His presence! What a wonderful synergy of love and unity.

Most would agree that the Lord is the One we love and value most. Why then is it so difficult for so many believers to *praise* Him? In *Reflections on the Psalms*, C.S. Lewis writes that praise is; "inner health made audible." Isn't that utterly beautiful? For those with a healthy spiritual life, praise is natural; it easily flows from the heart of one who has an intimate relationship with God the Father. However, the power generated within a relationship centres around *praise* and should never be underestimated. In the Old Testament, the praisers were placed in front of the army (2 Chronicles 20:21). Before you go into battle make sure your *praises* have gone before you! Today, why don't you offer up the *"sacrifice of praise to God continually, that is, the fruit of your lips giving thanks to His name"* (Hebrews 13:15).

Day 230

Shepherd

ποιμήν = *'poimin'*
Shepherd, protector, guardian

Jesus referred to Himself as the "*Good Shepherd*" who would lay down His life for the sheep (John 10:11). What other intrinsic qualities does the Good Shepherd possess? I would like to highlight three: (1) The Good Shepherd is concerned and interested in you; you really matter to Him. (2) The Good Shepherd knows everything about you; He even knows your voice. (3) The Good Shepherd laid down His life for you; He was not only prepared to die for you, actually did!

I'm sure you will agree that there is no one else who could have done what Jesus did for you. Listen to His own words once more, *"I am the good shepherd. The good shepherd gives His life for the sheep."* Jesus sacrificed His life in order that you might be redeemed; He willingly gave His life for your life; He became the sacrificial shepherd for you.

When you think of these characteristics of the Good Shepherd you should simply be amazed! Jesus is the Good Shepherd; a caring Shepherd, an understanding Shepherd, a sacrificial Shepherd and a living Shepherd. Because He gave His life for you doesn't mean Jesus is dead. In fact, He is watching over you right now! You are a sheep in His pasture and nothing can come against you, today, or any other day!

Day 231

Magnify

μεγαλύνω = *'megaluno'*
Magnify, to enlarge, to declare great

The Song of Mary, "the Magnificat," starts off with this tender statement: *"My soul magnifies the Lord"* (Luke 1:46). It's an expression gushing forth from a heart filled to overflowing with gratitude. Mary could have responded in some other negative way, but thankfully she didn't. She knew intuitively that a life of jealousy, complaining, dissatisfaction, resentment, grumbling and grieving never brings happiness. But neither does indifference. Happiness does not come because we have reluctantly accepted a new situation; a challenging or difficult responsibility; but rather, when we embrace it and *thank God* for the opportunity to grow.

Mary did not simply resign herself to her fate; she saw God acting, God loving, God offering; she wholeheartedly embraced the new reality and burst into a song of praise and thanksgiving. She found true happiness in a life filled with appreciation. Often, when you are in negative situations it is easy to see God in the context of your personal difficulties. Yet God is infinitely greater than your circumstances! So in order to get the victory you must change your view of God. He is a magnificent God! Today and every day, and in all humility, remind your soul to *magnify* the Lord. God must increase in your life in every way!

DAY 232

READY

ἕτοιμος = *'etoimos'*
Ready, prepared, willing, set

In Luke 22:33 we find that Peter had forgotten the "never say never" principle in life. *"But Peter said to Him, 'Lord, I am ready to go with You, both to prison and to death'."* No one is above falling into the very same snare of the enemy. Only when you are being sifted like wheat can you know exactly what you will do in such circumstances. It is a dangerous thing to rely upon yourself and your ability to withstand temptation and testing. We've all seen someone act in certain ways and we've said, "I would never do that!" But be very careful, "never say never!"

Often, you are weakest in the area of your greatest strength. That may sound like a contradiction or a paradox, but it is true nonetheless. When you think you have an area of your life absolutely conquered, you will tend to let your guard down and that's when the enemy could target you for sifting. Therefore, when you state that you are ready, be on the lookout, for you may have to adjust your plans. Never say never to God! God is not finished with you and He definitely isn't finished with your situation. Never give up on God because He will never give up on you. No matter what you've done, or what your circumstances are, never say never to God. Be ready for a breakthrough; be ready for great and exceeding blessings. Today, be ready for change! Don't forget, your *readiness* is putting your faith into action!

DAY 233

BROTHER

ἀδελφός = *'athelphos'*
Brother, member of the same family

Losing a brother must be one of the most distressing incidents in any family, but this is exactly what Mary and her sister Martha went through when Lazarus got sick and died. In John 11:21, Martha said to Jesus, *"Lord, if you had been here my brother would not have died."* Later when Mary came to where Jesus was, she repeated the exact same words. Martha and Mary's despair over Jesus not coming sooner confirms that they both thought: "It's too late." Yes, they repeated the same message of hopelessness and anguish: "It's too late!" What this awesome miracle emphatically confirms is; "with Jesus it's never too late!"

Be rest assured, before the final resurrection comes, God has some resurrections to perform in your life. It's not too late for your marriage; it's not too late for your healing; it's not too late for your career or your finances; it's never too late with Jesus! Despite the long delays, the Lord wants to say to you, "Don't despair. For that which you thought was dead will be resurrected!" Doctors may have said it is *too late*; all of the studies and statistics may have indicated that it is *too late*; your family may have taken a view that it is *too late*; even you, may have thought of conceding defeat because everyone told you that it's *too late*. But today, I want to assure you; with Jesus it's never too late and it's never over when He is in control.

DAY 234

LITTLE-FAITH

ὀλιγόπιστος = *'oligopistos'*
Little faith - little in number and low in quality

Jesus spoke one word to Peter "*come*," and hearing that one word, Peter was able to step out of the boat and walk on water. You'd think that Jesus would have commended him for that alone, but instead, in Matthew 14:31, Peter was told, *"O you of little faith!"* Little-faith is a single Greek word and it implies "little in number" and "low in quality." The Lord can easily identify and measure your faith. We've heard Him use the terms; *great-faith*, *little-faith* and *no-faith*. If you were to take a snapshot of your faith today what would it look like? Would it be little in number and low in quality?

The reason why Jesus did not praise Peter for his efforts is found in the next phrase in the same verse: *"Why did you doubt?"* Unbelief impedes your faith as it nullifies everything you have just achieved. If Peter had not doubted Jesus' word he would have kept walking on the water and completed his miraculous assignment. Once Peter heard his Master's voice he had to take a step that goes contrary to all the laws of nature; he had to act on the *word* he had just heard! Remember, miracles do not happen until you begin to take Jesus at His *word*, therefore, when you ask the Lord for instructions, be prepared to act on them immediately.

Yes, you can walk on water today, provided you do not doubt!

Day 235

Created

γίνομαι = *'ginomai'*
To create, to come into being, to make happen

John 1:3 clearly reveals the role of the Creator: *"All things were made* (created) *through Him, and without Him nothing was made* (created) *that was made* (created)." Therefore, in terms of creativity, the Lord's power is immeasurable. The Creator of heaven and earth is the most *creative* Person in the entire universe. If you don't understand this truth you will never acknowledge where your creativity stems from.

We are all creative, whether we recognise this gift or not, therefore, never allow your skills, abilities and capabilities to ever cause you to forget who it was who gave you them in the first place. What's more, it is by His grace that you were empowered anyway! If you are an artistic person, don't you just love the moments when the creative flow is going at full speed and things are coming together effortlessly? I love the quote from Eric Liddell (*the Scottish runner who was depicted in the film Chariots of Fire*); he said that when he ran he felt *God's* pleasure. In other words, Eric Liddell was only doing what God had gifted him to do!

You too should have moments when you feel the *pleasure* of God, for in those moments it's the Holy Spirit perfecting God's will for you and bringing glory to Christ. But it's also when you have truly plugged in to His supreme creativeness. Earnestly think about using your gift of creativity today.

Day 236

Signs

σημεῖα = *'simeia'*
A sign, a miracle, a mark, a token

"And truly Jesus did many other signs in the presence of His disciples, which are not written in this book" (John 20:30). Someone once said, "You will never understand the Gospel of John unless you too have placed your head on the Lord's chest." God's word tells us that the number of miracles performed by Jesus would fill the libraries of the world; if they were to be fully documented. John is not promoting signs and wonders but the Miracle Worker Himself - Jesus Christ! Maybe this is where the modern church has missed it? Have we placed more emphasis on the "*signs*" than on God's Anointed One?

Are you looking for the supernatural power of God to manifest instead of looking to find Jesus in the midst of your circumstances? Miracles for miracles sake is a futile exercise. John makes it clear that *signs* were documented to cause us to believe in the Christ, and as a result of us believing, obtain the very life He came to secure for us. I'm convinced that signs and wonders reveal the Lord's heart. In fact, they point to Him like a road-sign points to a destination! Today, why don't you join John by putting your head on the Lord's chest to listen to His heartbeat. That way, you will feel His life-giving breath on your brow and come to experience His miraculous deeds of power. To God be the glory for the signs and wonders only He can perform!

DAY 237

POSSIBLE

δυνατός = *'thinatos'*
Strong, mighty, possible

"With God all things are possible!" It's interesting that the word in Matthew 19:26 translated *possible* is a "power" word. It literally means "strong and mighty." All things are possible because of God's awesome strength and mighty power. This verse tells us of the divine *power* that only God possesses, and it confirms that He performs what is not humanly possible. If God did only what was humanly possible He wouldn't be God; for He is a God of the impossible! Yet, the majority of people choose to live by their own limited resources and abilities because they would rather not have to depend on a supernatural all-powerful God. It doesn't make sense, but it's true! For us, as believers, the moment we receive Christ we were called to live in the unseen realm where "all things are possible."

When you stepped out of the kingdom of darkness and into the kingdom of His dear Son, you stepped out of the "impossible with man" realm and into the "possible with God" realm: the supernatural, superabundant realm of the Spirit. God's power is limitless, however, if you are not prepared to approach Him, He will simply pass you by. Why not call out to Him right now! Yes, don't let Jesus pass you by today, for He never walks past anyone who's heart is crying out for a response.

DAY 238

SEEING

ὁράω = *'orao'*
To see, look upon, perceive, discern

We've all heard the term "seeing is believing!" Yet, this is not scriptural, Jesus said*: "Blessed are they who have not seen and yet have believed!"* However, there is another important principle revealed in God's word, and that is, "what you see, you must act upon." When God asked the prophet Jeremiah "what did he see," He followed with this statement: *"You have seen well, for I am ready to perform My word "* (Jeremiah 1:12). When you see human need, or suffering, God wants to perform His word. In fact, He watches over His word to perform it! God is always ready to act on what you see.

What you *see* decides whether you live the victorious life here on earth, or not. But not only you, those around you as well; for if you are blind to the needs of others, God is not able to *perform* His word and bless them. It takes courage to face the reality of the world around you and see what is actually going on. But then it takes faith to do something about it! There is no point in seeing issues that need to be addressed and not doing something about them.

Remember, God has promised to watch over His word, therefore, if you deal with matters in accordance with His word He will do what is necessary to perform every task - to His glory but to your benefit.

DAY 239

TREASURE

θησαυρῶν = *'thysauron'*
Treasure, store house, precious things

Concerning the faith of Moses and his willingness to suffer affliction, Hebrews 11:26 says, *"Esteeming the reproach of Christ of greater value than the treasures in Egypt; for he looked to the reward."* The level to which you truly value something will determine the level to which you are prepared to wait for it. God's desire is that through your struggles you will allow Him to turn you into a useful vessel that is ready for His service. This doesn't mean you have to see yourself as accepting second best for your life, for your struggles don't warrant you to live by '*Plan B*'; that's not how God thinks! What you may be going through right now doesn't prohibit God from doing what He wants in your life.

The Lord remains forever able to fulfil every promise, and He has a perfect plan for you; remember, His "perfect plan" is the best plan, not the second best, therefore, take your eyes off your struggles and fix your eyes on that which reflects the motives of God's heart. You need to see the way God sees, and you need to place *value*, as Moses did, on heavenly matters. Yes, your *treasures*, the things you consider valuable, must be in heaven at all times. For "where your *treasure* is, that's where your heart will be also" (Matthew 6:21).

DAY 240

FORCEFUL

βιάζεται = *'biazetai'*
Forcefully advancing, to suffer violence

In Matthew 11:12 Jesus said something quite strange: *"And from the days of John the Baptist until now the kingdom of heaven suffers violence, and violent men take it by force."* The phrase "the kingdom of heaven suffers violence" has been interpreted and translated in various ways. The NIV states that the kingdom "has been forcefully advancing." I believe the verb *biazetai* holds the key to the correct view, since the translation of the passage is in the middle form. The word implies that "the kingdom has come with holy power and magnificent energy and has been pushing back the frontiers of darkness." Furthermore, instead of violent men taking over, in a negative sense, *forceful* men take hold of the kingdom in a positive sense. In my view, the most accurate translation is "the kingdom has been forcefully advancing."

Now, it's up to God's children to adopt a militant spirit and be forceful in how we deal with spiritual opposition. The enemy will always provide violent confrontation to any planned advancement of the kingdom of Heaven. However, the kingdom of Heaven is taken by forceful men and women with a militant and intense attitude! Today, stir up that spirit in you. Don't allow the devil's fierce resistance to put you off, He is a defeated foe.

Each day, you are able to *forcefully enforce* his defeat!

DAY 241

GATES

πύλης = *'pulis'*
A gate, gateway, council, entrance

"And I also say to you that you are Peter, and on this rock I will build My church, and the gates of Hades shall not prevail against it" (Matthew 16:18). In this verse, Jesus speaks of the gates of hell, He was revealing of the plans and strategies of the powers of darkness. As long as these powers remain undisturbed and unchallenged in the gateways of the world, they continue to pose a threat, a hindrance and a bondage to the people of God and their families.

God's word tells us that the weapons of our warfare are mighty, yet we are not plundering hell to populate heaven enough. With the power of the Holy Spirit in us we should be able to win any battle for the hearts and souls of men and women; against the powers of darkness. It is only when we reach the point where we are able to rise up as the mighty army of God and victoriously storm the gates of hell that we'll see a real change in our communities. It is not for us to battle satan alone. Zechariah carried the message that it is: *"...not by might, nor by power, but by my spirit, says the Lord of host."* If you're going to battle you'd better take the Lord of Hosts with you. Further, the Holy Spirit will assure you of your conquest as you storm the gates. Hence, stormtrooper secure the victory today!

DAY 242

COMMANDMENT

ἐντολή = *'entoli'*
Commandment, an injunction, order, law

In Matthew 22:37-38 Jesus answered the stern question, *"What is the greatest commandment in the law?"* with the statement, *"Love the Lord your God with all your heart and with all your soul and with all your mind."* This is the first and greatest commandment; and the second is similar, *"Love your neighbour as yourself."* It's always beneficial to start with the second commandment to love our neighbour!

Whenever you *serve*, you are most accurately reflecting the character and nature of God, which is founded on love. So anything you do, whether it is pouring coffee; or visiting someone in hospital; or helping a student with their studies; or caring for someone who is sick; or teaching others; or playing guitar in a coffee shop; or being part of a sports team; or just spending good time with friends. All of these normal activities are ways of serving others, and therefore, *loving* them. That gives each activity a unique sacredness because God partners with those that *serve*. All of your service in the kingdom is inherently valuable, whether it is in sacred or secular realms, whether it receives a greater or lesser return. Your responsibility is to plan for the long haul and use your gifts to advance to kingdom of God. Consequently, as a servant of Christ, every part of your life is infused with the presence and power of God! His greatest commandment is to love, and to love is to serve!

DAY 243

DREAMS

ἐνυπνίοις = *'enupniois'*
A dream, a vision, an aspiration

Peter, when addressing the crowd in Acts 2, quoted the prophet Joel saying, *"And it shall come to pass in the last days, says God, that I will pour out of My Spirit on all flesh; your sons and your daughters shall prophesy, your young men shall see visions, your old men shall dream dreams"* (verse 17). I believe both young and old, male and female should dream big *dreams* for God. Proverbs 13:19 says, *"When dreams come true... there is life and joy."* That is a good reason to have your dreams come true! God is in the business of making your dreams come true.

Every believer should have a big dream, and every dream should be conceived in the heart by inspiration of the Holy Spirit. The divine seed that creates your dream is planted in your heart by God's Spirit. Therefore, your dream should not be aborted as your destiny in God depends on it. It doesn't matter how long it takes to give birth to your dream, you should not abandon it. Never get tired of carrying your dream.

If that's you, remember this, God would not have birthed a dream in you if you were not able to see it come to fruition. If there's a dream that you've discarded it is time for you to begin dreaming again. Dare to dream big - it's not too late. In fact, I dare you to wake up and *dream* today!

Day 244

Overcome

νικάω = *'nikao'*
To overcome, conquer or prevail

"And they overcame him by the blood of the Lamb and by the word of their testimony, and they did not love their lives to the death" (Revelation 12:11). Did you know that every time you speak a Word from your spirit man you overcome? The tests and trials you're going through are linked to the "word of your testimony" that comes out of your mouth. Your spirit man is like the Ark of the Covenant, where the testaments are placed and kept safe. When you endure the enemy's temptations and quench his fiery darts, your spirit man develops an overcoming attitude that is powerful in God. Testimony is best defined as someone's personal "spiritual narrative" - the story of your spiritual journey. While your testimony may include parts of your biography, that isn't at the heart of it.

To testify means "to express or to declare a strong belief in; to make a statement based on personal knowledge in support of an asserted idea; to declare publicly or make known; and to bear witness or provide evidence for." The word of God is full of people who testified to the power, majesty, grace and mercy of God. Every positive experience you have offers you the opportunity to testify! It's not who you are in Christ, but rather, who you declare you are in Christ that causes you to overcome; that's the word of your testimony.

DAY 245

PROCLAIM

διαγγέλλω = *'thiaggello'*
To proclaim, publish, declare, announce

"For the Scripture says to the Pharaoh, 'For this very purpose I have raised you up, that I may show My power in you, and that My name may be proclaimed in all the earth'." (Romans 9:17). You need to understand the power of proclamation. The most powerful proclamation you can make is "Jesus Is Lord!" The Lordship of Jesus has both future and present relevance. There is coming a day when every person who has ever lived will acknowledge that Jesus Christ is Lord, but for you that great proclamation should be an everyday reality. Live every moment in faithful submission to the Lordship of Jesus; you should announce His Lordship before heaven and earth; you should surrender your life to the sovereign rule and ownership of the Lord Jesus Christ.

The predominant message of the Bible is: "Jesus Christ is Lord." Such a universal truth should compel you to make this announcement a matter of priority and urgency every day. Could it be that the source of defeat, discouragement and despair in the lives of many is down to the fact that they are attempting to live the Christian life in their own authority and power? There can be only one Lord, one true authority, and that is, Jesus Christ! Therefore, you must not fail to communicate the "whole council of God." Jesus Christ is both Lord and Christ, and He has supreme authority and absolute anointing! Proclaim this today - witness His power.

DAY 246

TOWARD

εἰς = *'eis'*
Toward, to or into

"And what is the exceeding greatness of His power toward us who believe, according to the working of His mighty power" (Ephesians 1:19). Here lies evidence of the supreme power of God in Christ Jesus being pointed "man-ward." It's not sufficient that the Divine Fulness is poured out in unlimited supply, it must be accompanied by a receptive heart and attitude on your part. A bottle may be submerged in the waters of a fountain, but if the cork is still on you will wait a very long time and eventually carry it away empty. Many spiritual people are, as it were, immersed in the power of God, yet the cork of unawareness is still to be removed. Because their minds have been blinded as they have read God's word, the simplicity and the glory of this powerful truth has not dawned upon them. That is, all the awesome power that raised Jesus from the dead was directed toward the Church and is therefore available to all of us.

For that reason, you must be fully *open* to the Spirit in order to qualify for Christ's authority. You need to pray continually, with deep heartfelt humility, that "the eyes of your mind may be enlightened"? Whenever the eyes of your understanding have been enlightened your attitudes change. Why? Because when the light gets switched on you see and act different. Today, be open to the Spirit and you will grasp "the exceeding greatness of His power toward you."

DAY 247

THRONE

θρόνος = *'thronos'*
A throne, a kings seat, dominion

Concerning the throne room of heaven, this is what John saw, *"Immediately I was in the Spirit; and behold, a throne set in heaven, and One sat on the throne. And He who sat there was like a jasper and a sardius stone in appearance; and there was a rainbow around the throne, in appearance like an emerald"* (Revelation 4:2-3). Because of the throne in heaven and Who is sitting on that *throne*, we have been given "Throne Rights." The Lord is head over all principality, power, might and dominion and every name that is named in this world and in the world to come. His position and power is supreme! The risen Lord enthroned at God's right hand rules far above every other force which seeks to control and govern the world today.

Within the exceeding riches of His grace in His kindness toward us, God the Father, "has raised us up together, and made us to sit together in heavenly places" with our risen and enthroned Lord (Ephesians 2:5-7). Through the grace of God, every believer is elevated and occupies the Throne. For you to stand victoriously in this hour, when evil forces are coming against you, you must understand the necessity of fully accepting your place of spiritual authority in Christ. That way, you can fearlessly bind these forces of darkness, enforcing their defeat! When you take your seat in heavenly places "in Christ," you can exercise your full Throne Rights.

DAY 248

PERCEIVE

θεωρέω = *'theoreo'*
To perceive, behold, discern, look at, understand

Paul was not a soothsayer or fortune-teller, yet in Acts 27:10 he perceived "in His spirit" that disaster was going to strike, saying: *"Men, I perceive that this voyage will end with disaster and much loss, not only of the cargo and ship, but also our lives."* We can see that perception is not discernment; it is not reasoning or understanding; it is not mind-reading or fortune telling; and it has nothing to do with being psychic. In fact, as a believer, you can perceive or become aware "in the Spirit." Therefore, there is a *perception* that is indeed spiritual, that is made available to every one of us.

You can choose to walk in spiritual perception or you can choose to walk in carnal perception. After fishing all night you can go back out in your boat, and as the Spirit of God directs you, throw out your net for a miraculous catch, or you can fish all night and catch nothing. He who perceives receives! The Lord is calling every one of us to walk in a much higher level of spiritual perception. You cannot draw back from the promptings of the Holy Spirit; the "still small voice." You need to press in to Him, seeking to know more than you know now; seeking to experience more than you have experienced. Today, purpose to become fully aware "in the Spirit" of any difficulties challenging you. For when you do, you will perceive right and receive right.

Day 249

Persevere

ὑπομονῆς = *'ipomonis'*
Perseverance, steadfastness, endurance

Someone once said, "The race is not always for the swift but to those who keep on running, who persevere." Among other things, fulfilling God's will for your life is reaching your total God-given human and spiritual potential. You don't have to be a geniuse to do this, but you do need to persevere, regardless of your circumstances. This applies to securing your physical well-being also.

The Apostle Paul experienced all sorts of trials and setbacks. He was shipwrecked, stoned and left for dead, whipped and beaten, and thrown in jail for promoting Christianity. He knew firsthand what it was to experience loneliness, cold and hunger, yet he penned some of his greatest letters while in prison. Paul maximized all his potential through persevering. Giving up was not an option!

Perseverance has its just rewards: *"A spider can be caught with the hand, yet it is found in king's palaces"* (Proverbs 30:28). What could a tiny spider possibly teach us? It teaches the rewards of perseverance, which takes it right to the top. A spider will keep trying to find a way in, and when it does, it will get to the top. Perseverance will get you to the top as well! *You have need to persevere, so that after you have done the will of God, you may receive the promise* (Hebrews 10:36).

DAY 250

GENTLENESS

πραΰτης = *'pravtis'*
Gentleness, mildness, meekness

"But the fruit of the Spirit is love, joy, peace, longsuffering, kindness, goodness, faithfulness, gentleness, self-control" (Galatians 5:22-23). Gentleness is a fruit of the Spirit and is necessary for God to produce a harvest in your life. Meekness toward God is that disposition of spirit in which you accept all His dealings with you as good, without disputing or resisting Him. In the Old Testament, the *meek* are those wholly relying on God rather than their own strength to defend them against injustice. Gentleness or meekness is the opposite to self-assertiveness and self-interest. It stems from trust in God's goodness and control over the situation. The gentle person is not occupied with self at all. This is a work of the Holy Spirit, not of the human will. A gentle person possesses the rare spiritual strength to restrain himself and to rely on God completely.

Some people equate meekness with weakness, so they explicitly reject and despise it. But a meek or gentle person does not restrain himself because he is timid, but because he trusts in God to vindicate and promote him. In fact, the righteous are more courageous than the wicked because they are confident and secure in God. Why don't you take on this distinctive trait; it reflects the inherent nature of Jesus? By displaying gentleness you place yourself in a position to receive favour from God, and in turn, favour from man.

Day 251

Peacemaker

εἰρηνοποιοί = *'eirinopoioe'*
Peacemaker, making peace, loving peace

"Blessed are the peacemakers, for they will be called sons of God" (Matthew 5:9). Being a peacemaker is risky because it is not natural or normal; most of us avoid confrontation due to the fact that it's risky. Knowingly or unknowingly everyone who chooses to be a *peacemaker* enters into the danger zone. For Jesus Christ it was a cross and that should be true with any peacemaker. When you're called to be a peacemaker one side can't be always right and the other side always wrong, consequently neither side is in the mood for peace.

Everybody who is a peacemaker lives in the *danger zone*; whether you choose to or not. Greece, at its height of glory, had all its gods and goddesses; Athena was the goddess of wisdom. Wisdom was considered the highest value among the Greeks. In the Parthenon, where they built the great temple that still stands today, they chose Athena the goddess of wisdom; who wears a helmet, carries an olive branch and also holds a spear. Wisdom is peace with strength! You need the olive branch but you also need the spear for strength, for peacemaking can be a precarious business. As a child of God you have a ministry of reconciliation: you are to bring *peace* between God and man through Christ Jesus. This alone is what can bring lasting peace; peace with God, peace with man!

Day 252

Hardship

συγκακοπαθέω = *'sugkakopatheó'*
To endure hardship, to suffer ill-treatment

Speaking to Timothy, his son in the Lord, Paul advises him: *"You therefore must endure hardship as a good soldier of Jesus Christ. No one engaged in warfare entangles himself with the affairs of this life, that he may please Him who enlisted him as a soldier""* (2 Timothy 2:3-4). You cannot go into battle unless you truly desire to please your Commanding Officer. There are many things that will seek to distract you, however, what is mentioned here is a little different. It says you should not entangle yourselves with the affairs of life; as a soldier, you have to concentrate on carrying out orders and staying focused in the midst of battle.

If you intend to go behind enemy lines the only way to avoid casualties is to be inconspicuous. If the devil can detect you he will figure out your strategy. This is where the wisdom of God comes in! The enemy cannot *comprehend* the wisdom of God (1 Corinthians 2:8). Are you equipped with the wisdom of God; are you ready to become a good soldier for Jesus Christ; are you willing to go behind enemy lines and set up prayer camps. Are you really willing to please your Commanding Officer, carrying out His orders and staying focused until the battle is won? Are you prepared to take the kingdom of God by force? From your heavenly command post you can find and implement a strategy for each assignment that God gives you, and win every battle.

DAY 253

WORTHY

ἀξίους = *'axious'*
Worthy, deserving, suitable

You should have faith in God's respect for you. Hence, it's not humility to call yourself "worm of the dust." You are a man or woman of God; you are a somebody, a worthy child of God. Jesus said, *"They shall walk with me in white for they are worthy"* (Revelation 3:4). There is no Biblical standpoint from which you should consider yourself unworthy as you have wonderful possibilities. You've been *wonderfully and fearfully* made: God counts you worthy to stand in His presence before His throne. There is therefore no need for you to go through life in sackcloth and ashes; you should recognise that God respects you and esteems you highly. He would not have sacrificed His Son for you had this not been true.

You must stand by *faith*, learn to exercise *faith*, learn to live by faith and judge yourself righteously. Do not let your feelings master your faith; make your faith master your feelings. As a general rule, when you believe right you will feel right. Very often faith is based on feelings instead of on realities, but it does not really matter how you feel. This is to be settled by your *faith* quite apart from your feelings, so when you resolve it leave your feelings out as they are not proof. Faith itself is the only proof! You are worthy, so start building into your life with the confidence of faith and not the uncertainly of doubts, fears, and anxieties. That way all your actions will be praiseworthy!

Day 254

Measure

μέτρον = *'metron'*
Measure, a measuring rod

"Till we all come to the unity of the faith and of the knowledge of the Son of God, to a perfect man, to the measure of the stature of the fullness of Christ" (Ephesians 4:13). What you need to focus on is not a mere truth, or more knowledge of the truth, but Christ Himself. He must take center stage and His full stature should occupy your life. The desire of God the Father is that His Son, the Lord Jesus, shall fill all things and all things shall be filled with Christ. Therefore, the value of anything in the eyes of God is measured according to the manifestation of Christ in it. From that standpoint alone, God determines the importance of everything.

The measure of Christ in you determines your value in the kingdom of God. Now, does God still love you when the measure of Christ in you is small? Yes, but the kingdom cannot truly benefit until the "fullness of Christ" is manifest in you. Can you see that? In the eyes of God the value of everything is determined by the *measure* in which His Son is manifested and glorified; this is God's primary objective. Christianity is not a doctrine, not merely a truth, but the experiential knowledge of a Person. It is coming into contact with the full measure of the Lord Jesus Christ in you. Let the degree to which Christ is manifest in you grow today, and then let it keep growing.

DAY 255

GROW

αὐξάνω = *'auxano'*
To grow, to increase, to grow up

This verse is telling us to grow up! But the Greek word can also be translated "to increase," therefore, it implies that we should increase or be extended into Christ in all matters of life. Growing up or enlarging is always Christ centered. Christ is the aim and object of your growth, or increase, and the sphere of growth is in all things. In every area of life you should be *extending* yourself further into Him.

The Father wants you to come of age; He wants sons and daughters who can take hold of their inheritance, and He has provided a sound process for achieving this. As the gifts that God has placed in the church equip the saints (that's you), and as you enlarge through active and energetic service, you grow up and increase in all matters of life. Resulting in you being transformed into the image of Christ and becoming a true joint-heir with Him - ruling and reigning here on earth. However, growing up into maturity is a definite process, a journey, and it requires thought and determination.

I believe that accomplished maturity is when you start to exercise God's power. Yes, the miraculous achievements and deeds or power that Jesus Himself did you should do also! That is why God wants you to come of age. So this should be your aim, your calling card.

Day 256

Manifested

ἐφανερώθη = *'ephanerothi'*
Manifested, to make visible, to reveal

"For this purpose the Son of God was manifested (made visible)*, that He might destroy the works of the devil"* (1 John 3:8). Our Lord Jesus Christ was manifested in His eternal power and kingdom to destroy the works of the devil, for *"the government shall be upon His shoulders, and His name shall be called Wonderful, Counsellor, The Mighty God, Everlasting Father, Prince of Peace"* (Isaiah 9:6). Kings, presidents, parliaments, poets, leaders, celebrities, and such like, these are visible powers, but there is over them all an invisible power; an all-encompassing power.

Enthroned on high, there is a King of Kings and a Lord of Lords and who is He? It is Jesus, who is ruling and reigning. He is in office governing right now; His kingdom is here. The ultimate destruction of evil on the earth is a certainty and the reign of Him who is righteous and good is manifest. Total dominion is with the Son of God and together we shall terminate the reign of the devil in people's lives.

Constantly remind yourself of this truth: "the Son of God was *manifested* to destroy the works of the devil and that assignment is finished." Now, it's up to you to make sure the destruction of evil continues until His return. Don't let a day go by without playing your part in the devil's demise.

Day 257

Temple

ναὸς = *'naos'*
Temple, shrine, where God resides

God wants to interrupt your life and visit with you, but He cannot manifest His divine presence where any form of iniquity has been practiced. The "law of divine intervention" is solely reliant on you having prepared a sanctified location for God to inhabit. It's a place where spirit meets spirit and righteousness responds to righteousness; never holiness to flesh, which is unacceptable to God. He wants you to be just like His Son Jesus, so that He is be able to visit you anytime He wishes. That means you should always have a holy place of meeting, a tabernacle, prepared for Him.

Divine intervention is the *sovereignty* of God interrupting your daily life. *"Do you not know that you are the temple of God and that the Spirit of God dwells in you? If anyone defiles the temple of God, God will destroy him. For the temple of God is holy, which temple you are"* (1 Corinthians 3: 16,17). Notice, God desires to intervene and fellowship with you because you are His sacred temple. However, your behaviour must be fully acceptable and pleasing to Him.

What you must ask yourself is this: If you want Jesus to come round to your house today and visit, have you *prepared* for Him coming? He may be standing at the door knocking right now! But are you listening (Revelation 3:20)?

Day 258

Worshippers

προσκυνηταὶ = *'proskunitai'*
Worshippers, participants

We are all children of God, but children eventually grow up, and the evolving and advancing you will do when you begin to live according to your divine purpose is part of that growing up. When you choose your divine purpose, you are framing your life with meaning. You are also taking an important step in your spiritual development, and that is, to demonstrate to yourself that you are a chosen vessel, and to prove to yourself that you have the power to affect change.

Once you start down this path you will realise that you are bigger, stronger, more powerful, and more creative than you ever thought. It was Emerson who said, "Oh Man! There is no planet, sun or star could hold you, if you but knew what you are." There is nothing in the universe that could hold you back, if only you knew your true power. In God, all things are possible because we tap into His divine power; in God, we can find the faith to move mountains. In God, your full potential can be realised! In John 4:23-24 Jesus makes an amazing statement, *"But the hour is coming, and now is, when the true worshipers will worship the Father in spirit and truth; for the Father is seeking such to worship Him. God is Spirit, and those who worship Him must worship in spirit and truth."* God is seeking true worshipers because it is in the atmosphere of true worship that you'll find your divine purpose and realise your full potential.

DAY 259

LAVISH

δέδωκεν = *'thethoken'*
To lavish, to give, to pour upon

God loves you not because you are valuable, but rather, you are valuable because God loves you. 1 John 3:1, *"How great is the love the Father has lavished on us, that we should be called children of God!"* A father is always expected to love his children: love is the result of that relationship. But how much better is a relationship that has come about as a result of love. God doesn't love you because it is His duty; He has taken the role of father because He loves you. More importantly, God does not love you because of your role as His adopted child, or anything else in fact, He has given you this privileged position purely because of His pre-existing and unconditional love for you.

How reassuring to know that God had already decided to love you, no matter what! You don't have to perform or prove anything. With foreknowledge, He loves you as you are and His love is not based on what other people think of you. Your true worth is housed in the truth that He loved you first: *"We love Him because He first loved us"* (1 John 4:19). If God didn't choose to love you first, you could never feel valuable and precious; you would still be looking for self-worth in your own endeavours. Today, feel the great love that God has lavished on you; for when you do, you will know how valuable and precious you are!

DAY 260

THROW-AWAY

ἀποβάλητε = *'apobalite'*
To throw-away, discard, get rid of

There're many things you possess that the Bible says you should hold on to; things you should not loose, cast away or get rid of; things that, when retained and maintained have a great reward. One such thing is "confidence." Hebrews 10:35 says, *"Therefore do not throw away your confidence, which has a great reward."* One of the rewards of confidence is strength. Strength to tough it out and stay the course; strength to outlast the battle and still be standing when the victory trumpet is heard. Isaiah 30:15 states, *"Confidence shall be your strength."* There are times then you may feel that you do not have the strength to carry on. Perhaps your problem is not lack of strength but lack of confidence!

Self-confidence is being certain, first in God, then about yourself with regards to addressing certain tasks. Confidence is critical to effective performance in the workplace and in the home, and it is the source of decisiveness. Confidence must be founded and grounded on God's infallible word, and also on your true abilities. With the right amount of self-confidence you will operate in faith, take informed risks, and stretch yourself, consistently trying harder. But never going beyond your strengths and abilities! Confidence is an acute necessity in life, so remind yourself today: "No one can take away my confidence; I alone can throw it away."

DAY 261

WORKMANSHIP

ποίημα = *'poiema'*
Workmanship, a thing made

Ephesians 2:10 says that we are God's workmanship: we were hand-made by the Master of the Universe. *"For we are His workmanship, created in Christ Jesus for good works, which God prepared beforehand that we should walk in them."* Imagine that! The Psalmist said, *"I praise you for I am fearfully and wonderfully made"* (Psalm 139:14). In the same Psalm it says that God made all the delicate and intricate parts of your body while you were in your mother's womb. God knew every fragment of your being as He was meticulously designing you with tender loving care. You didn't just evolve into what you are today, you were created and designed with a purpose; you are unique, *one-of-a-kind.*

You were exquisitely prepared beforehand, given all the right attributes, that you should implement the "good works" which you were created for in Christ. In fact, your destiny involves good activities and assignments, and nothing else! God is only associated with good things and He expects you to do the same, therefore, all your accomplishments must be intrinsically good. Since you are God's *workmanship*, you should always feel like you are wonderfully made. More than that, you've been wonderfully made for a specific purpose which brings glory to the One who created you.

Day 262

Faithful

πιστὸς = *'pistos'*
Faithful, reliable, trustworthy, believing

God's faithfulness is still the single most divine attribute that never ceases to amaze me. In fact, I've learnt to depend on His faithfulness more than anything else. 2 Timothy 2:13 says, *"If we are faithless, He remains faithful; He cannot deny Himself."* Faithful is what God is, not something He possess! That's why God cannot deny who He is: "God is faithful." But what's the magnitude of God's faithfulness? Since God's faithfulness is part of His very essence it affects everything He says and everything He does. This assurance is expressed to the Thessalonians: *"Now may the God of peace Himself sanctify you entirely; and may your spirit and soul and body be preserved complete, without blame at the coming of our Lord Jesus Christ. Faithful is He who calls you, and He also will bring it to pass"* (1 Thessalonians 5:23-24).

God is *faithful* to bring all His promises to pass. He has given you His Spirit to live in you and empower you; He has equipped you with His Word which gives you authority over the devil. God is constantly available for communication through prayer, and whenever you step out in faith, He will meet you there with His strength. These are resources which He has faithfully provided and if you chose to use them you will enjoy His victory. Today, place absolute trust is God's faithfulness.

Day 263

Looking

ἀφορῶντες = *'aphorontes'*
Looking, gazing upon, looking away from all else

What you "behold," gaze upon, you will become. That is why the word of God encourages us to keep our eyes on Jesus. *"Looking unto Jesus, the author and finisher of our faith, who for the joy that was set before Him endured the cross, despising the shame, and has sat down at the right hand of the throne of God"* (Hebrews 12:2). We should look away from everything else and fix our eyes upon Jesus, the author and finisher of our faith. That way we cannot get distracted and miss what God has for us; what God is speaking to us about right now.

As you fix your gaze upon Jesus, becoming still in His presence, you will find that a two-way dialogue begins to flow: spontaneous thoughts direct from the throne of God. Yes, you start conversing with the King of Kings! If you are going to receive a pure word from God, it is vital that you become still and remain properly focused. Whenever you do not remain fully focused, you receive your own thoughts and not God's. But when you're looking at Jesus, and nothing else, you receive a flow of communication that is pure and uninterrupted. Why? Because this instinctive flow comes out of that which you have fixed your eyes upon. I encourage you to look away from everything else today and fix your gaze only upon Jesus. If you do, God's voice shall be heard clearly.

DAY 264

HELPER

Παράκλητον = *'parakleton'*
Helper, called to one's side, comforter, advocate

In John 14 Jesus was preparing His disciples for the crucifixion and His departure; in *verse 16* He says that "another Helper" will come and abide with them forever. In a different verse Jesus states that it is better for Him to go away, because if He doesn't, then the Helper could not be sent. Imagine what the disciples must have thought: better than having the Master alive with us; better than having His personal teaching and counsel day in and day out? No way! Why did Jesus emphasise the function of the Holy Spirit in such a fashion? I believe it's because He wanted to prepare all believers for the vital role which the Holy Spirit is meant to play in our everyday lives.

John 14:15-17, *"And I will ask the Father, and He will give you another Helper* (besides Myself) *to be with you forever, the Spirit of truth."* The Greek word for Helper literally means, "one who is called alongside to provide assistance." Imagine that! Imagine having someone who will draw alongside you throughout the day, someone you can talk to who will listen to you, someone who will help you and comfort you. That Person is already by your side! But, if you do not engage with Him you will never experience the benefits of having a divine Helper. Day-in and day-out remind yourself that He is with you; by your side. And that He will never leave you.

DAY 265

DISCLOSE

ἀναγγελεῖ = *'anaggelei'*
To disclose, announce, declare, report

Romans 8 describes how the Holy Spirit equips us for spiritual warfare; He leads us and guides us, and helps us to effectively engage in spiritual warfare. When you are fully surrendered to the Spirit of God, you are fully equipped for any conflict. Why? Because you are being led by the Spirit, and being led means taking on His divine attributes. By being spiritually minded you can successfully engage in spiritual warfare through having the mind of Christ. When you have the mind of Christ you know exactly what to do when the forces of evil are trying to overwhelm you. In John 16:14 Jesus says, *"He* (the Holy Spirit) *will glorify Me, for He will take of what is Mine and will disclose it to you."* The Holy Spirit equips you with *Christ-like* abilities so that you can become more than a conqueror, and He does this by telling you what is on Christ's mind: disclosing exactly what He has received.

God's Spirit is your Intelligence Agent, gathering and distributing all the intelligence you need. Warfare under the guidance and direction of the Holy Spirit means you fight every battle from a position of victory. With the evidence and counter-intelligence provided supernaturally you have the a strategic advantage. Therefore, you can apply the same divine strategy that Jesus did during His ministry on earth. Yes, this day, you can destroy the works of the devil!

Day 266

Foundation

θεμέλιον = *'themelion'*
Foundation, a foundation stone

God wants to build your life, but He also wants to dwell in it. Yes, God builds a house for Himself to live in. As with any builder God looks for a suitable piece of land in His kingdom on which to build. Quite simply, God builds on your life because this is the land He wants to bless. How you conduct yourself, what crop you produce, and how you walk out your salvation is important to God. Without your testimony God has very little to work with. Just as a builder is interested in physical land, God is interested in physical lives. There is a spiritual dimension to everything God does.

Only after God has found the land, cleared the area, and laid the foundations, does He move on to the business of building lives. With this principle in mind, how can you be sure to receive His blessings? Simply, by building the way He expects you to build. This is how the apostle Paul built his life: *"According to the grace of God which was given to me, as a wise master builder I have laid the foundation, and another builds on it. But let each one take heed how he builds on it. For no other foundation can anyone lay than that which is laid, which is Jesus Christ"* (1 Corinthians 3:10-11). The foundation you build your life on must be Jesus Christ. I encourage you to carry out a building check today; find out what *foundations* have been laid for everything you value in life.

Day 267

More

μᾶλλον = *'mallon'*
More, extra, added, beyond, farther

When Jesus compares the intrinsic qualities and *attributes* of our Heavenly Father to those of natural fathers He uses the phrase, how much more: *"If you then, being evil, know how to give good gifts to your children, how much more will your Father who is in heaven give good things to those who ask Him"* (Matthew 7:11). Jesus uses the example, *"If you, then, though you are evil,"* to contrast mortal and fallible humans with a holy and perfect God.

"How much more" is a true reflection of the Father's heart, therefore, as you reflect on the many aspects of what you do as an earthly parent, it helps you to catch a glimpse of your heavenly Father's heart. It helps you to see in a way that you can understand and relate to Him on a deeper level. Yes, "how much more" your heavenly Father cares for you; "how much more" He feels about you; "how much more" generous He is towards you; "how much more' He loves you; all effect the way He engages with you. Today, you need to really grasp this truth!

When you ask God for His abundant blessings, focus on the fact that He wants to do so much more for you. Far more than you can ever hope, dream or imagine (Ephesians 3:20).

Day 268

Stand

στῆναι = *'stenai'*
To stand, to make to stand

Ephesians 6:13 tells us to stand and keep standing! *"Therefore take up the whole armour of God, that you may be able to withstand in the evil day, and having done all, to stand... Stand therefore!"* What really spoke to my heart was the statement, "having done all!" Often you may think you've done all, when in fact you haven't, and that is probably why your breakthrough has not happened. If you are to have and enjoy the abundant life that Jesus came to secure for you (John 10:10), there are principles you must comply with regularly. One of them is to live in "standing" mode. Yes, it's vital that you learn to stand and keep standing.

Have you ever noticed how much time it takes for God's blessings to manifest? After you've exercised your faith, believing and then receiving, it's often preceded by a period where you come under attack. The devil is bent on stealing the blessings of God, so he tries to highjack your blessings on route. That is the main reason why you must stand and keep standing! It's interesting that the Greek word can also be translated "to make to stand." Yes, you're going to have to command yourself to stand! For if you don't, you may not be present when your blessings arrive.

Today, command yourself to *stand*, and to keep standing!

Day 269

World

κόσμῳ = *'kosmo'*
World, world order, universe, worldly affairs

In Acts 16 a woman possessed by a demon begins to follow Paul, calling them: "servants of the Most High God." This distresses Paul because the Jews might conclude that he consorted with soothsayers so Paul commands the demon to leave the woman in the name of Jesus Christ. However, her employers, who were making considerable profit from her fortune telling were not pleased because her supernatural abilities had disappeared with the demon.

In order to remove an ability that was controlled by an evil spirit, a greater ability needed to present itself. Both these abilities were *supernatural*, but one had much greater authority than the other. *"You are of God, little children, and have overcome them, because He who is in you is greater than he who is in the world"* (1 John 4:4). In you is a greater authority, a greater power, a greater strength, than any spirit who is in the world. In you is the Holy Spirit! Therefore, you've been equipped with a *supernatural* ability to deal with any evil spirit which is manifest in the world. Our scripture says, you have overcome them (past tense). Today, you must deal with the affairs of life as if that were an absolute reality.

Certainly, you have already overcome any opposition to you living a victorious life!

DAY 270

DOUBTING

ἄπιστος = *'apistos'*
Doubting, unbelieving

Then He said to Thomas, *"Reach your finger here, and look at My hands; and reach your hand here, and put it into My side. Do not be doubting, but believing"* (John 20:27). When Jesus spoke to Thomas it was not to counter a misplaced desire but to rebuke a lack of faith. Doubting Thomas had expressly said he would not "believe" until he had *touched* the body of the Lord Jesus. Knowing about Thomas's declaration, Jesus was prepared to offer His body as *living proof* of His resurrection.

Two people who were very close to the Lord, Mary and Thomas needed more faith. Mary needed faith enough to let Jesus go (John 20:17); Thomas needed faith enough to believe without hands-on proof. Mary needed to loosen her grip; Thomas needed to strengthen his grip. The resurrected Christ Jesus gave both parties the faith they needed to fulfil God's plan and purpose for their lives. The difference between Mary and Thomas, and how they responded to the resurrected Christ, accentuates the need for you to either (a) loosen your grip and let God be God, and (b), strengthen your grip and get close and personal with Jesus. But neither approach will work if you do not have faith! If you need more faith to *loosen* or *strengthen* your grasp, simply remember the mustard seed (Luke 17:6). Whenever you do not doubt, but believe, your faith will be effectual.

DAY 271

FOOLISH

ἄφρονες = *'aphrones'*
Foolish, senseless, without reason

"So then do not be foolish, but understand what the will of the Lord is" (Ephesians 5:17). Many believers desire to do God's will, but they struggle because they don't know what God's will is for their lives. *"And do not be conformed to this world, but be transformed by the renewing of your mind, that you may prove what is that good and acceptable and perfect will of God"* (Romans 12:2). God's will can be divided into two headings: God's "general will" (His good and acceptable will), and God's "specific will" (His perfect will). His general will is always clear; we find His general will clearly revealed in Scripture. It is the determining of God's specific will that is most challenging for the majority of believers. One thing is absolutely assured, no one has complete insight into God's will. The soundest, most mature men and women of God can make mistakes about His perfect will.

Even with the best discernment, it is possible to do things that are out of God's perfect will. The key is not to let pride get in the way, rather to admit wrong and then submit to God's new instructions. God has given you gifts and abilities to use in His service. Using them correctly is a good way to protect yourself from stepping out of the will of God. He has given you such gifts to equip you in order to complete every assignment. Plan to operate in your gifting today.

DAY 272

CONVICTIONS

κρίνων = *'krinon'*
To convict, to judge (whether in court or privately)

How do you get to know God's will? Psalm 32:8 promises guidance while seeking God's will; you must immerse yourself in prayer and in the study of His Word. That way, you are able to make decisions that are compatible with God's specific will. However, every decision must meet at least two criteria: first, it must be compatible with God's word (Psalm 119:105); second, it must be compatible with your personal convictions. Some decisions and choices are objective enough to be eliminated on the basis of being in direct contradiction to God's word. Namely, God will not lead you in a direction that will violate His principles.

Many times people believe God is leading them into something, so they lunge forward without getting exact directions. Each decision must always be compatible with your personal *convictions*. Paul wrote, *"The faith which you have, have as your own conviction before God. Happy is he who does not condemn himself in what he approves"* (Romans 14:22). In order to keep your path straight you're being held to the highest standard, which requires constant inspiration from the Holy Spirit (John 16:13). This means that you are accountable if you go against your conscience by doing something you know is wrong. For you to be happy, you cannot do anything that convicts you! Remember, the Holy Spirit never condemns, He *convicts* you to repentance!

DAY 273

LIFE

ζωὴν = *'zoen'*
Life (both of physical and of spiritual), existence

There are countless ways in which humanity searches for happiness. Two of the most common are pleasure-seeking and self-improvement. You can find these pursuits under different names, but many of us are drawn either to the gratification of our lusts or the suppression of those lusts. Neither approach to life leaves us lastingly happy. Those drawn to a celebrity's lifestyle of uncontrolled excess need only look at the latest headline to see that the unrestrained pursuit of pleasure does not fulfil anybody. The quieter path doesn't yield as many page views but it can leave the soul wasted. When we go looking for happiness and do not find the supreme God who created us, we find more questions. Both of these approaches to happiness will no doubt feel good at certain times, but neither provides true satisfaction.

Christians believe that this is because we are made for something greater. That instinct in us is what C. S. Lewis called the "desire for True North." We all want something greater, something pure, a force that restores us; this is God and God alone! He is the cause of true happiness and He is happiness itself. Jesus said, in John 10:10: *"I have come that they may have life, and that they may have it more abundantly."* So the question is: "What good is the full super-abundant life that Christ secured for us if it does not involve being happy?" Never forget, Jesus came that you may live a happy life.

Day 274

Revealed

φωτίσαντος = *'photisantos'*
To reveal, to bring to light, to uncover, disclose

2 Timothy 1:10 states: *"But has now been revealed by the appearing of our Saviour Jesus Christ, who has abolished death and brought life and immortality to light through the gospel."* When Jesus came He brought the light, through the gospel, which revealed all that was hidden in God. The importance of this revelation can never be underestimated. The eyes of your understanding could never have seen anything without Jesus first appearing. Your soul and mind would still be in spiritual darkness.

Jesus said, *"I am the light of the world"* (John 8:12). That means, without Him "appearing" the world would be in darkness. But praise God, Jesus came and brought light and immortality. Christ has been presented throughout the New Testament as the "light" of a believer's entire life, and in this amazing truth is included these representations: (1) Jesus surrounds or embraces you, in His own life; (2) He separates you in Himself from all hostile influences; (3) He protects you in Himself from all perils and foes of life; (4) He provides and supplies in Himself all your need.

Today, let His light shine into your heart and reveal the very things you need to see and understand! This is how Jesus wants to appear to you and bless you superabundantly.

DAY 275

RACE

σταδίῳ = *'stadio'*
A racecourse, a stadium, a racetrack

Many a person has failed in life because he/she has given up too soon. Too many people are not in the race to win it. In 1 Corinthians 9:24 the apostle Paul says, *"Do you not know that in a race all the runners compete, but only one receives the prize? So run your race that you may lay hold of the prize and make it yours"* (AMP). Another translation simply reads, *"Run in such a way as to win."* How are you running your race? Are you in it to win it, or are you simply making up the numbers?

Many of the Bible heroes were "in it to win it!" The story of Caleb records that for forty years he waited for a promised reward. Through no fault of his own the reward was postponed. If Caleb had looked at the circumstances, or listened to the people around him, he would have lost his faith and dropped out of his race. Yet he trusted God and refused to quit! 45 years is a long time to wait for a promised reward! Most people Caleb's age would have just given up and made a graceful exit into retirement, but not Caleb. He wholeheartedly followed the Lord with steadfast faith. He stood on God's Word and held onto God's Promise, no matter how impossible things appeared!

Decide right now to keep competing; the prize is worth it! Don't drop out, and don't get disqualified for not running according to the rules. Run in such a way as to win!

Day 276

Humble

ταπεινόω = *'tapeinoho'*
To humble, to make low, lowly, submissive

After the Parable of the Wedding Feast, Jesus concludes: *"Everyone who exalts himself will be humbled, and he who humbles himself will be exalted"* (Luke 14:11). This *perspective* is especially provocative to the culture and sensitivity of today's society. The humble person is perceived as someone who is not cool; someone who gives up easily, someone defeated, or someone who has nothing relevant to say to the world. Instead, this is the primary way to live. Not only because humility is a great human virtue but because, in the first place, it represents God's own way of acting. It was the way chosen by Christ Himself, who: *"being found in human form he humbled himself and became obedient unto death, even death on a cross"* (Philippians 2:8).

Therefore, this is today's message for you: "do not follow the way of selfishness but rather that of humility." Go against the tide! Don't listen to the persuasive voices that are selling models of life marked by self-importance; by success at any price; by appearances and by having possessions at the cost of having character. Be alert! Be critical! Be real!

You may feel that you are among the ranks of the unknown saints, but you are not unknown to God. For to Him you are unique, and God has plans to prosper you and give you hope and a future (Jeremiah 29:11).

DAY 277

BODY

σῶμα = *'soma'*
Body, flesh, body of Christ

"From whom the whole body, joined and knit together by what every joint supplies, according to the effective working by which every part does its share, causes growth of the body for the edifying of itself in love" (Ephesians 4:16). This scripture talks about the Body of Christ; that is, it talks about the Church. We sometimes fail to understand or act upon the fact that we are the Body of Christ. In other scriptures, Paul reveals how each part of the body plays a certain role in the undivided body. Paul explains that we cannot all be eyes or mouths or fingers.

These teachings of Paul are very important. They mean that you have your own unique purpose; they mean that you should not look with envy on those who are better at certain things than you are. Paul makes it clear that you have a valuable part to play in the Church, what he calls Christ's Body. Sometimes it seems like what you have to offer doesn't really matter, but that is not true. There are parts of the body that seem pointless yet have real significance. You will always have authentic usefulness. This is essential! You should not allow your own feelings of inadequacy or low self-esteem keep you from being an integral part of the plan that God has prepared for you. You're valuable and precious in His eyes, and always will be.

DAY 278

GLADNESS

ἀγαλλίασις = *'agalliasis'*
Exuberant joy, wild gladness, ecstatic delight

When the angel of the Lord appeared to Zacharias and spoke of the coming birth of John the Baptist, he made this exciting declaration: *"And you will have joy and gladness, and many will rejoice at his birth"* (Luke 1:14). The Greek word translated "gladness" means far more than being glad at the birth of a son; it is to be wildly glad, have exuberant joy or ecstatic delight. This sounds like the reaction someone would have when they are told that their barren wife was going to conceive and have a child. It is the same word used in Luke 10:21 when Jesus "rejoiced in the Spirit" after seeing satan fall like lightning from heaven. In fact, Jesus "laughed uncontrollably" because He had sent out 70 rookies and they came back saying, *"Even the demons are subject to us in Your name!"*

"This is the day that the Lord has made; we will rejoice and be glad in it" (Psalm 118:24). This day is God's gift to you. God is the Creator; God made today and today is a precious time-frame that God has given you. While God made today, He has left it up to you to do what you will with this day. Yet God wants you to rejoice and be glad in it! That's an order. Implying that if you do not rejoice and be glad you have wasted this day, and the whole purpose of today. If Jesus can find reason to be *wildly glad* and express *exuberant joy*, I'm sure you can!

DAY 279

JOY

χαρὰν = *'charan'*
Joy, delight, pleasure, joyfulness. happiness

After salutations, James starts his epistle by telling us how we can in fact prosper from trials: *"My brethren, count it all joy when you fall into various trials"* (James 1:2). "Count it all joy," not just a little bit of joy with a whole bunch of sadness and grief. No, a full measure of joy! There are so many things that seek to rob you of your joy. People can discourage you; things can distract you from what God has given you to enjoy; yet God wants you to develop abundant, overflowing joy. That actually involves a choice on your part. I believe that one of the most valuable commodities missing in today's society is *joy*.

There is so much confusion as to what joy really is. A lot of the time even Christians find it hard to express true joy. But God expects you to come to know His joy. So what is joy? Joy is something that you choose to express; it's not pie in the sky; it doesn't come and go like the wind. Where does this kind of *joy* come from? It's a matter of boldness which comes from the Holy Spirit dwelling in you. Your rejoicing is *"in the Lord"* (Philippians 4:4), and in Him lies your joy. Paul learned what every child of God needs to know, there can be rejoicing in God even when outward circumstances are contrary to a spirit of rejoicing. The Holy Spirit is the *spirit* of joy! So today, don't forget to obey the commandment to rejoice! Ask Him to fill you with joy.

Day 280

Power

δύναμιν = *'thinamin'*
Miraculous power, might, strength, force

There is a power that every believer should possess. In Acts 1:8 Jesus says, *"And you will receive power when the Holy Spirit comes upon you."* We know that on the Day of Pentecost this actually happened! The question is, "Have you received this power?" If you have, "What are you doing with it? The power mentioned here was given to equip believers with supernatural abilities to fulfil their calling. You cannot do this without being filled with the Spirit of God. What's more, for this "power" to be really effective in your life, you need to be continually filled (Ephesians 5:18).

This verse doesn't say, "Fill yourself with the Spirit" but rather, *"Be filled with the Spirit."* That's a bit harder to understand. It's like saying to someone, "Be loved." How do you do that? How do you "be loved?" However, this is the key to everything. To "be filled" means that the infilling of the Spirit is a work of God and not man. God intends for you to be continually filled with His Spirit. At any given time, He is ready and willing to fill you to overflowing.

Have you ever driven a vehicle without power-steering? I have and it's not enjoyable! It's hard to maneuver and very difficult to park. Well, that's exactly what your life is like without the *power* of the Holy Spirit at work in you. Make up your mind today to be *continually filled* with His power.

DAY 281

DECLARE

Ἀπαγγελῶ = *'apaggelo'*
To declare, announce, report

Declaration plays a very important role in the Christian life. To *declare* means to proclaim, make known or announce. When talking of bringing many sons to glory, the writer of Hebrews quotes Psalm 22:22: *"I will declare Your name to My brethren; in the midst of the assembly I will sing praise to You"* (Hebrews 2:12). The principle of declaring the Lord's name to others and singing His praises wherever people are gathered is vital to your spiritual health. You cannot silence your declaration!.

In 1 John 1:1-4, John was making known to us someone who he had seen with his own eyes; someone he had chatted with and touched with his own hands; someone who existed from the beginning of time; someone who he declared is the Word of Life; someone who is holding all things together. In this passage, John was declaring the most important Person he had ever met: the Lord Jesus the Christ. And he was doing this publicly so that we could share in the inexpressible joy that he had experienced. The joy of having seen, heard and touched the Living Word. By implication, I believe John was declaring the absolute sovereignty of Jesus. Why don't you follow John's example right now? Declare the absolute sovereignty of Jesus in every area of your life; declare that He is Lord over your circumstances and future.

DAY 282

JUST

δίκαιος = *'thikaios'*
The just, righteous, correct

Galatians 3:11 says, *"But that no one is justified by the law in the sight of God is evident, for 'the just shall live by faith'."* Being "just", morally and ethically correct before God, and living by faith is not optional. Here the apostle Paul is quoting from the Book of Habakkuk to show that God has always justified men by faith and not the law. The original Greek reads, *"The just by faith shall live."* Literally, *"Those whose conduct before God is right, by faith shall live."* Therefore, your conduct before God must first be right if you are to live by faith. Notice, it says "by faith" and not "in faith." You are not asked to live *in* faith but rather *by* faith, which implies that you use faith to live by. It is an instrument for "just" living before God, and this pleases Him!

Hebrews 11:6 states, *"Without faith it is impossible to please Him."* No amount of good works can compensate for lack of faith. Faith is the only thing that gives God His proper place in your life, because it proves that you have more confidence in Him than in yourself. Faith not only believes that God exists, but it also trusts Him enough to know that He will reward those who diligently seek Him. Is it possible to live every moment of every day in faith mode? Yes it is! Because when God is pleased with you every moment of every day, you are living the victorious life.

Day 283

Obey

ὑπακούω = *'hupakouo'*
To obey, to listen to, to attend to

Hebrews 11:8: *"By faith Abraham obeyed when he was called to go out to the place which he would receive as an inheritance. And yet he went out, not knowing where he was going."* There will be times in your life when you must simply obey God's voice; even if you do not yet know where you are going! This is how you will be sure that you are really living by faith. Your obedience and your faith can have a generational effect on you and your family.

In Genesis 26:3-5, when talking to Isaac, God said this, *"I will be with you and bless you; to you and your descendants I give all these lands and I will perform the oath I swore to Abraham your father - because Abraham obeyed My voice."* Notice, obedience is very powerful because it frees God to perform His word - either for you or the next generation!

I encourage you to obey the voice of the Lord today. Don't let it get drowned out by the busyness of life or the noisiness of the world around you! God is always speaking to you! In fact, if He stopped speaking your life would fall apart. Why? Because He is: *"upholding all things by the word of His power"* (Hebrews 1:3). His power has a voice! And that voice wants to speak into your life, every moment of every day. When you obey His voice you release that divine power.

Day 284

Honour

τιμάω = *'tipao'*
To honour, to value at a price, to fix the cost

The fundamental principle of service is centered around this one truth, and that is, you cannot *serve* anyone or anything with your gifts and abilities unless you have first served the Lord with them. Jesus said, *"If anyone serves Me, let Him follow me; and where I am, there My servant will be also. If anyone serves Me, Him My Father will honour"* **(John 12:26)**. Remember, a servant is always with his master; by His side, serving Him. And whenever or wherever you've chosen to serve the Lord with your gifts and abilities, God the Father will promote you to a place of honour.

But there's more! The Greek word for "honour" literally means. "to place a value (a price)" upon something. Hence, when you serve the Lord with your gifts and abilities, God places significant value on them. Implying that until they are operating "in service to Him", they have no real merit, they are deemed worthless. This may be the reason why so many gifts fail to prosper when removed from doing service to God. Your guarantee for success is contained in this one truth. So don't neglect it!

Today, identify just one of your gifts and purpose to serve God with it. I can assure you, you will receive honour. Your gift has incredible value to God and His kingdom.

DAY 285

ADDED

προστίθημι = *'prostithimi'*
To be added, to gain, to be enhanced

If you stood on a mountaintop and faced the same direction day in and day out, you would always see the identical view. It's the same with spiritual matters, if you want a specific view you'll need to be facing in a specific direction. See, it's the particular view or perspective you have that determines your response or reaction to things. I am convinced that a right perspective will help us to live a prosperous and victorious life in Christ Jesus. What's more, the "view" you have may be a serious hindrance to God's plans and purposes. The principle is this, adopt a Kingdom mindset and you'll get Kingdom rewards - it's as simple as that! Matthew 6:33 confirms this, *"Seek first the kingdom of God and His righteousness, and all these things shall be added to you."*

Your rewards, what is added to your life, comes after you get your priorities right. What are they? You must place at the top of your action list the kingdom of God and His righteousness as these are unnegotiable priorities. They must always come first! I love what the Greek implies when it says, *"and all these things will be added."* These are "things" that are important to you which have no significance or value to God's kingdom. Therefore, God is happy to add anything that will satisfy you; He is merely *adding* what you need!

DAY 286

SEASON

καιρῷ = *'kairo'*
Season, appointed time, period of time

The universal law of "sowing and reaping" has some conditions attached. You cannot sow except in the right season. You cannot choose to sow at any time because; *"to everything there is a season and time to every purpose under heaven, a time to plant and a time to reap"* (Ecclesiastes 3:1-2). In most cases the best time to sow is spring time, when things are fresh. Also, there is an amount of time between sowing and reaping - a lag-period. Therefore, you must: *"Not grow weary while doing good, for in due season we shall reap if we do not lose heart"* (Galatians 6:9). Generally, the better the type of harvest, the longer it takes.

God's promise that, *"Whatsoever a man sows that shall he also reap"* (Galatians 6:7), is an exact science. You cannot sow bananas and reap apples. You cannot do bad and expect good to come from it. Are you sowing seeds of materialism which will result in an harvest of material things? You must also be careful of what you sow in your physical body. Are you sowing seeds of ill health; with cigarettes, alcohol, overeating, lack of exercise? Are you sowing seeds of neglect with your loved ones so that you will eventually reap a harvest of neglect for yourself? More importantly, are you not sowing enough spiritual seeds to see you through your season of testing? Sow your seed today and receive God's promise!

DAY 287

PRESS-ON

διώκω = *'thioko'*
To press on, to pursue, to put to flight

"Pressing on" suggests effort and determination. Unless you decide at the start of each day with what you intend to pursue, you are unlikely to achieve your objectives. The apostle Paul knew this principle well: *"I press on, that I may lay hold of that for which Christ Jesus has also laid hold of me"* (Philippians 3:12). If you "press on" there is a trade-off. This verse mentions taking possession of that which Christ has already attained. I'm sure you will agree that is a great and precious reward for your endeavours. Aren't you pleased to know that God is certain to respond every time you *press on*?

Why is "pressing on" so important? Because God has a desire to refresh the hearts of those who would earnestly seek His face. If your life needs to be refreshed, it must begin inside of you. Pressing on to know Him intimately means living in God's presence. The understanding of the Hebrew word for presence is to be given the opportunity to see God "face to face." Therefore, you must get to recognise the Lord! And in order to do that you must keep "pressing on" to know Him completely and acknowledge Him in all your ways.

If that is what you genuinely seek, then I guarantee that God will respond by pouring out His Spirit upon you every single day. Furthermore, I guarantee that you will have a regular "face to face" encounter with God. So press on!

Day 288

Gift

δώρημα = *'thorima'*
A gift, a bestowment, bounty, contribution

"Every good gift and every perfect gift is from above, and comes down from the Father of lights, with whom there is no variation or shadow of turning" (James 1:17). The good and perfect gifts which come down from heaven are as steadfast and reliable as God Himself. When He blesses you with prosperity and good health there is no deviation. He is the same yesterday today and forever (Hebrews 13:8), and so too is the intrinsic nature of His gifts. They don't change! Hence, you must be fully persuaded of this fact at all times.

You need to empty your mind of any hindrances that may prevent you from accepting the truth that God can and will do the impossible today. Jesus is not any different to what He was in Bible times, He is not withholding Himself from you in any way. God requires firstly that you believe Him and then He wants you to let Him be God. In Genesis 17:7 the Lord declares that He wants to be your God. Do you remember any of the miracles mentioned in the Bible? If you do, you would have noticed that in most accounts, there was somebody involved that believed a miracle would take place. Someone expected it to happen! What are your beliefs and expectations today? If you genuinely believe that God wants to bless you with something you are in need of, you will have it. It will be yours!

DAY 289

WORKS

ἔργα = *'erga'*
Works, tasks, deeds or actions

One of the most astounding statements Jesus made is in John 14:12: *"Most assuredly, I say to you, he who believes in Me, the works that I do he will do also; and greater works than these he will do, because I go to My Father."* This declaration came out of the mouth of the very Person who controlled the winds, raised the dead, and healed every kind of sickness and disease. Can it be true? Jesus spoke prophetically of the Body of Christ, that we are meant to continue His early ministry and do exactly what He did.

So what does God want to be doing through you? What mountains does He want moved; what principalities and powers does He want removed; what miracles does He want to perform? Do you ever pray the Lord's prayer? Do you say the part: *"Thy will be done in earth, as it is in heaven?"* You're telling Him that you want His will done here on earth, but are you prepared to be a vessel that will allow His will to be done through you? The *works* Jesus mentions are the very things that reveal the will of God on the earth!

You must allow God to teach you to do His will so that it mirrors heaven. Why don't you start right now: pray the Lord's prayer and ask Him to use you to perform His will in a miraculous way. Request that the very things Jesus did manifest through you to bless someone super-abundantly.

Day 290

Truth

ἀλήθεια = *'ahlethia'*
The truth, but not merely truth as spoken

There is much to be gained by living according to God's plan. True fulfilment and meaning in life is only found in God and the Truth. That's why St. Augustine said centuries ago: "You have made us for Yourself, O God, and our hearts are restless until they find their rest in You." When you make Jesus (*the Truth*) the biggest part of your life, you will discover the very purpose for which God created you. There is no thing and no one else who can do this; no religion, no philosophy, no person. Just Jesus! He said of Himself: *"I am the way, the truth and the life. No one comes to the Father except through Me"* (John 14:6).

Modern society has robbed us of the knowledge of our true purpose in life. We are led to think that it consists of acquiring wealth, leading an exciting life, or climbing the corporate ladder. Most people do not even know that they exist for a greater purpose. Jesus tells us something different: *"I have come in order that you might have life,"* He said, *"...and have life in all its fullness."* Because Jesus alone is the source of abundant life, you can only experience this *purpose-filled* super-existence through knowing God's plans and purposes, and that involves knowing the Truth. How familiar are you with the Truth? Have you spent time with Him today? Can you discern His voice? Can you feel His breath on your brow? Can you hear His heartbeat?

DAY 291

ABOUND

ἐπερίσσευσεν = *'aiperisevsen'*
Abound, lavish, overflow, to be abundantly furnished with

You may not fully appreciate the great generosity God has toward you, Ephesians 1:7,8: *"In Him we have redemption through His blood, the forgiveness of sins, according to the riches of His grace, which He made to abound toward us in all wisdom and prudence."* The Greek word "abound" elsewhere in the Bible is also translated "abundance" and it means to super-abound. Literally, "to have in excess, to acquire an exceeding measure, or to greatly excel." This word implies that there is no restraint, and whenever it is used in the context of God's nature or love, it serves to guarantee blessings that overtake us; truly abounding blessings.

The same root word appears in John 10:10, *"The thief does not come except to steal, and to kill, and to destroy. I have come that they may have life, and that they may have it more abundantly."* A literal translation could read: *"That they may have it superabundantly."* The Lord is telling you that He came in order that you may have a life that is overflowing with blessings! Also, that it will be an *extraordinary life* where there is always a surplus; where you constantly have over and above, or more than enough. This is definitely no commonplace life; there are no skimpy measures in this kind of life; it is over and above anything that you may hope, think or imagine. Live in the reality of this truth today.

Day 292

Anger

οργίζεσθε = *'orgizesthe'*
The wrath of man – the strongest of all passions

Within the family circle one of the most important issues you may have to deal with concerns anger, and the question often asked is: "Is it a sin for a Christian to get angry?" The answer to that is, "Yes and No!" There is anger of which the Bible approves and there is anger that is sin. Mark Twain said: "Anger is an acid that can do more harm to the vessel in which it is stored than to anything on which it is poured." There isn't a person alive who hasn't experienced anger; anger can tear apart relationships. Sadly, most people tend to justify their anger instead of accepting responsibility for it.

The word of God says, *"Be angry, and do not sin: do not let the sun go down on your wrath, nor give place to the devil"* (Ephesians 4:26-27). Notice, there's anger that God approves of called "righteous indignation," but it never involves self-protection. Rather, it is a defence of others or a principle (Galatians 2:11-14; John 2:13-18). Getting angry because someone has offended you is not righteous indignation, it is merely selfish outrage. Anger turns to sin when it is selfishly motivated. Instead of using the energy generated by anger to attack the problem, it's the other person who is attacked. Anger becomes sin when it is allowed to boil over without restraint. Remember, you can always handle anger correctly by simply communicating to solve the problem. So why not keep the peace and seriously think about this right now.

DAY 293

DESTINY

προορισθέντες = *'prooristhentes'*
To be predestined by God for a divine purpose

If you have ever asked the question, "What can I do to achieve my destiny?", my advice is this: "You will never accomplish what you are unwilling to pursue. So hunt down your destiny!" Remember, you have been predestined to fulfil your destiny (Ephesians 1:11). A God-given destiny is not a series of random events, everything He has planned for your life has been predestined and predetermined. God looked out across eternity; He saw you; He saw everything he had created and everything He would create around you; He saw the specific need on this earth that He wants you to meet; He saw the full set of traits and abilities that you require in order to complete His purpose for your life.

Don't forget, God wants you to become who He made you to be; He wants to develop what He put inside of you; He doesn't want you to try to exchange what He gave you for what He gave someone else. You are made up of a unique blend of talents and gifting and character, and you have a unique destiny upon this earth. However, you will never leave where you are until you've decided where you'd rather be. So why not get started today by living your life with a sense of *destiny*, and on route never position your future with the pain of the past. You can build a great future!

DAY 294

EXPERIENCE

ἄπειρος = *'apeiros'*
To be without experience, unskilful

You may feel that you are not experiencing the presence of God, but this is probably because you are without experience; not yet skilful in the word. Hebrews 5:13 says, *"For anyone who partakes only of milk is without experience in the word."* You must fully comprehend that there is never any separation between you and God, even though it may feel like it at times. Yes, you can experience Him anytime and anywhere!

However, whenever you approach God you must do it with confidence, and this highlights the need for an intimate relationship with Him. You cannot fully experience God's presence in a state of negative energy or apprehension. You can only come into His presence knowing that He gladly receives you, as you are: He is your heavenly Father! A father desires nothing else but to experience and share as much as he can with his children. Likewise, God wants to experience everything with you. In John 5:19 Jesus said, *"I only do what I see My Father do."* Jesus shared every *experience* with His Father before He implemented it. You can do the same. So enter the throne room of grace today; in the confidence that you will be received with open arms. Then, *experience* the awesome love of the Father because He wants to share every moment of every day with you.

Day 295

Giving

δοθήσεται = *'dothisetai'*
To give, to render what is due, to pay, to give an account

I'm sure you will agree, giving is always a delicate topic. How often are you expected to give; how do you know who to give to; what is the right amount to give? In answer to the last question I would like to quote C S Lewis: "I do not believe that any of us can settle on how much we ought to give. So I am afraid the only safe rule is to give more than you can spare." According to 2 Corinthians 9:6-7 you ought to give until it brings joy to your heart. Your "giving" must always be a heart decision and not a head decision. If you intellectualise your giving, you will end up doing it grudgingly or out of necessity. God loves a "cheerful giver." It doesn't say God "likes, admires or compliments" a person who gives cheerfully, it says God loves him! Wouldn't you like to do something today that causes the love of God to abound toward you?

Martin Luther said, "When I have tried to keep things in my own hands I lost them all, but what I have given into God's hands I still possess." How true that is! When you place something into God's hands you never lose it. In fact, it is multiplied back: Luke 6:38 says, *"Give, and it will be given to you: good measure, pressed down, shaken together, and running over will be poured into your lap."* Don't ever miss an opportunity to give to God - seize every opportunity.

Day 296

Leadership

ὁδηγῇ = *'othigi'*
To lead, steer, guide or direct

2 Corinthians 3:18 describes the development and transformation that is necessary for good leadership: *"And all of us, as with unveiled face, because we continued to behold in the Word of God as in a mirror the glory of the Lord, are constantly being transfigured into His very own image in ever increasing splendour and from one degree of glory to another; for this comes from the Lord Who is Spirit"* (AMP). A good leader will become identical to the person they want to be like. The highest form of leadership is to be *Christ-like*. The Lord's followers genuinely wanted to become exactly like Him. The apostle Paul caught hold of this and that is why he was able to say, "Whatever you see me do you do also!" The more you imitate Christ, the "Christ in you" will cause others to want to be like you as well.

Jesus was a great leader because He was a great follower (John 5:19). Maybe this is what's lacking with many of us. We are not prepared to follow before we are able to lead. Jesus learnt to lead by fully representing His Father here on earth; He followed His Father's every move. You are meant to do the same with Jesus.

If you decide to follow the Lord's every move today, you will discover that others will find themselves following you as well.

DAY 297

NEAR

ἐγγίσατε = *eggisate'*
To draw near or bring near

In the Bible the responsibility for drawing near is placed on you. James 4:8 says, *"Draw near to God and He will draw near to you."* The same Greek word is repeated in this verse and it implies that you must take the initiative. Since God is eternal, never-changing and absolutely consistent, you must believe that He is always accessible and within reach. If you accept the fact that the Lord is nearby, you should have the confidence to draw-near. In Psalm 73:28 the psalmist says, *"But it is good for me to draw near to God; I have put my trust in the Lord God, that I may declare all Your works."*

There is a strong connection between intimacy and trust. Drawing near to God without trusting Him is pointless; how can you really be intimate with someone you don't trust? Furthermore, as well as putting your trust in God, you must have a genuine desire for relationship, you must sincerely want to be close to Him. Then, when you choose to draw near with that kind of attitude, God will reciprocate and *draw-near* to you. This becomes a wonderful and precious interaction between both parties. So why not make up your mind right now to take the lead and get as close as possible to God? I guarantee that the more you do this, the more you will experience God's presence; then, the more you experience God's presence; the closer you will get to the source of divine power.

DAY 298

PATIENCE

ὑπομονῆς = *'hypomonis'*
Patience, perseverance, steadfastness, endurance

Hebrews 10:36: *"For you have need of patience, so that after you have done the will of God, you may receive the promise."* The Greek word translated "patience" can also be translated "endurance." It describes the unique capacity to continue to bear up under difficult circumstances, not with passive complacency, but with hopeful fortitude that actively resists weariness and defeat. The verb literally means, "to remain or stay under", and is also rendered "to remain behind" in Luke 2:43 and Acts 17:14. It is also transcribed as, "to stand one's ground; persevere; or remain steadfast."

The noun *hypomone* usually denotes a patient tenacity that does not lose hope in the face of obstacles, persecutions, trials, or temptations. Our verse clearly states that we have need of it. Patience can include the calm willingness to tolerate delay. The Greek word usually translated "patience" is more often associated with patience concerning people.

I believe that this is what God is saying today. He wants you to be more patient with the people around you. You may genuinely be in need of patience, but they too have need of patience – your patience! If you provide this necessity, you will find that your relationships will get stronger and you will gain more respect from others. What's more, you will receive the promise!

DAY 299

OPPORTUNITY

εὐκαιρίαν = *'eukairian'*
A fitting time, a right opportunity

"And from the time he was seeking an opportunity" (Matthew 26:16). God is an equal-opportunity God! He doesn't have favourites when dealing with His children, therefore, we should all have equal opportunity to succeed. But we must remember that success in God is fully aligned to each individual's calling and destiny. In this regard, in order for you to prosper and succeed in life, you must be doing what God wants you to do, when He wants you to do it, how God wants you to do it. Then, as you are obedient in the fulfilment of His plans and purposes, distinct and unique opportunities will arise.

There will be open doors! *"See, I have set before you an open door, and no one can shut it"* (Revelation 3:8). The church at Philadelphia had been given an *open door* of opportunity. All they had to do was to walk through it! The church had many opponents; even satan himself had pitted his wits against the small group of believers, but these believers kept true to their Lord and seized the opportunity to draw on His strength and step through those open doors.

God has opened doors of opportunity for you as well! Opportunities to be successful and prosper in all matters of life. It's impossible to stop God from holding this door open for you; so don't stand still, cross over the threshold.

DAY 300

SUCCESS

επιτυχία = *'epitugia'*
To have success, to realise a goal, achievement, to triumph

In Romans 8:31 (AMP) it says, *"If God is for us, who can be successful against us?"* How does God measure success? One answer can be found in the life of the prophet Elijah. Elijah had a big showdown with 950 prophets of Baal; where he demonstrated the power of God. He challenged them with these words: *"If the Lord is God, follow Him; but if Baal is God, follow Him"* (1 Kings 18:21). Winner takes all! Elijah gave them every advantage by letting them go first. He even soaked his bull and the firewood with water, making it seem impossible to win the contest. But when he asked God, God sent fire to consume Elijah's sacrifice and everything else next to the altar. That night Elijah claimed his success.

However, right after this event (1 Kings 19:9-21), rather than Elijah doing his victory salute, we see him fleeing the scene from Queen Jezebel. You'd think that a person who was as devoted to God as Elijah would never have fled from the Lord but in fact he did. He ran like a wanted criminal and tried everything to evade being captured. Just like a defeated soldier, Elijah was ready to raise a white flag and surrender. I'm sure there have been times that you've felt the same. Therefore, I encourage you to stand firm in your faith. Put aside personal failures; don't dwell on the frustrations and heartaches of the past. In spite of your personal flaws, step into success and go from glory to glory.

DAY 301

TRUST

πεποιθότας = *'pepoithotas'*
To trust, have confidence in, to rely on completely

"And we have such trust through Christ toward God" (2 Corinthians 3:4). One of the toughest things to trust God for is your future, and many people have a fear of the future. I firmly believe the key to living a happy and contented life is to plan today as prayerfully and carefully as you anticipate tomorrow, and then trust God for both. If you can trust God with eternity, why can't you trust Him for today and tomorrow? God doesn't want you to trust in your own abilities or your own intellect; He wants you to be totally dependent upon Him. Why is this? It is simply because the more you rely and trust in yourself the less you rely and trust in God. Then the less you rely and trust in God the more fear of the future you will have.

Fear is your greatest enemy. God's Word is filled with powerful exhortations to not be afraid. When you fear, you cannot have believing faith. Fear paralyzes, frustrates and imprisons; fear also involves torment (1 John 4:18); fear is the prison of the heart. Trusting God in hard times requires refusing to be anxious, refusing to be frightened, refusing to be immobilized. Hard times necessitate trusting God, so whatever happens refuse to fear. Instead, trust God: He is the Almighty. No matter what the prevailing conditions are, God is able, and He is willing.

Day 302

Belonging

ἐστε = *'este'*
To be, to belong to

Any feeling of dissatisfaction and disconnection can have an adverse effect on your relationships and your ability to succeed in life. On the other hand, belonging to a religion or local community can influence your sense of identity and the extent to which you participate and positively engage in your sphere of society. There are many reasons why people cannot settle, and as a result, feel that they do not belong or fit in. Most of the time this has to do with not satisfying an emotional need to be accepted. Whether it's family, friends, co-workers, or church members, we all have an inherent desire to belong.

In Mark 9:41 Jesus makes this statement, *"For whoever gives you a cup of water to drink in My name, because you belong to Christ, assuredly, I say to you, he will by no means lose his reward."* Here, the Lord assures us that because we belong to Him whoever blesses us will receive a reward. Jesus is implying that our relationship with Him is so strong that whenever anyone shows any act of kindness toward us, it's as if that person was doing it unto Him personally. Ephesians 1:6 declares that we are; "*accepted in the beloved.*" This means that we are the objects of divine satisfaction. Yes, we are literally His joy! If you are struggling with your sense of belonging, I want to encourage you to keep reminding yourself that you belong to Christ, you are His delight.

DAY 303

DEVOTION

σέβασμα = *'sevasma'*
The object of worship, that to which worshipped is directed

Great men of God were noted for engaging in private devotions; Jesus Himself encourages private devotion. He sought solitary places in the early morning and late at night. You must develop the habit of private devotions, and in order to do this the time and place may have to be the same each day. But the act of devotion must never supersede the *devotion* you have in your heart toward God in everything. Mother Teresa said, "There is always the danger that we may just do the work for the sake of work. This is where the respect and the love and the devotion come in – that we do it to God, to Christ, and that's why we try to do it as beautifully as possible." When your heart is fully devoted to God it will be obvious; you will have a sincere desire to draw near to Him as often as possible and wherever possible.

If David, a man after God's own heart, and Jesus, the Son of God, found it needful to spend time alone with the Father, how much more should you. *"I rise before the dawning of the morning, and cry for help; I hope in Your word. My eyes are awake through the night watches, that I may meditate on Your word"* (Psalm 119:147-148). When you are stressed and you cannot find inner peace, I encourage you to lay everything aside and make an effort to spend time with God. Drawing nearer and walking closer to Him should be a way of life. An everyday custom.

DAY 304

MISTAKES

πλανᾶσθε = *'planasthe'*
To make a mistake, be in error, deceived, or led astray

In 1818 a nine-year-old French boy was watching his father at work in his leather shop: "Someday," said Louis, "I want to be a harness-maker just like you." The father took a piece of leather and drew a design on it. "Now, my son, take the hole-puncher and a hammer and follow this design, and be careful you don't hit your hand." Excited, the boy hit the hole-puncher hard, but it flew out of his hand and pierced his eye! He lost the sight of that eye immediately. Later, sight in the other eye also failed. The boy was now totally blind. A few years later, Louis was sitting in the garden when a friend handed him a pinecone. As he ran his sensitive fingers over it an idea came to him; it wasn't long before he created an alphabet of raised dots on paper so that the blind could feel and interpret what was written. Thus, Louis Braille opened up a whole new world for the blind. All because of a dreadful mistake he had made.

God can turn a tragedy into a blessing, mistakes into miracles! Deuteronomy 23:5 tells us why this can happen: *"Instead, He changed the curse into good* (a blessing) *for you, because the Lord your God loves you."* God loves you, He cares for you, and that's why He is willing to turn your mistake into the greatest miracle in your life. No matter what you've done today, give it over to God. Then stand back and watch what He does: He wants to turn your mistake into a miracle.

Day 305

Promises

ἐπαγγελίαι = *'epaggeliai'*
A promise, pledge, an undertaking to do or give something

Over the years I've seen so many people hurt through broken promises. Unfortunately, this happens and it only serves to break down relationships. My advice is, "God's love never fails" It's only people who sometimes fail. They can fail to keep promises; they can fail to tell the truth; they can fail to trust each other. But this does not negate God's promises. They are "Yes and Amen!" For that reason, keep a good attitude and do the right thing even when it hurts. If you do this you are passing the test and God's promises will make sure His blessings arrive on time. Corrie Ten Boom said, "Let God's promises shine on all your problems." Whatever challenges you may be facing, remember that God's promises have the power to shine His glorious light into every one of them.

In a world of too many broken promises, you have a God who keeps His! In a world where it is easy to believe one can count on no one, you can count on God. The central fact that proves God's faithfulness in the midst of a faithless world is Jesus Christ. As Paul puts it in 2 Corinthians 1:20: *"For no matter how many promises God has made, they are 'Yes' in Christ."* God promised that Christ would be heir to the throne of David (Isaiah 9:7); He promised He would be born in Bethlehem (Micah 5:2); He even promised the exact time of the birth (Daniel 9:25). It all happened as He had promised!

DAY 306

BAPTIZE

βαπτίζω = *'baptizo'*
To dip repeatedly, to immerse, to submerge

Acts 1:5: *"For John truly baptized with water, but you shall be baptized with the Holy Spirit not many days from now."* The New Testament speaks explicitly of people being "baptized in" or "with" the Holy Spirit. *Baptism* in the Holy Spirit is compared and contrasted with the water baptism of John using almost identical dialogue. The language is important to those who wish to understand what baptism "in" the Holy Spirit means. The baptism of John and that in the Spirit is alike in that both are accomplished by full immersion. The Greek verb used to describe these baptisms is *baptizo*, meaning to bathe or immerse, however, the baptism of John is performed through the use of water (physical substance) and the other with the Spirit Himself.

Baptism with the Holy Spirit, then, is being completely immersed in the Spirit, and this should be 'visible' after the event. What you have to ask yourself today is this: "Have I been baptized with the Holy Spirit?" For if you have, there will be evidence and it will be visible. After Pentecost, great and powerful things started to happen through the hands of those people that had been fully immersed in the Spirit. I am convinced that God wants to do the same through your hands, so why don't we agree together, that you will see evidence, visible proof, that you've been baptised in the Holy Spirit. After which, powerful things will happen.

DAY 307

DWELL

ἐσκήνωσεν = *'eskinnosen'*
To dwell, abide, tabernacle, to fix one's abode

John 1:14: *"And the Word was made flesh and dwelt among us, and we beheld His glory, the glory as of the only begotten of the Father, full of grace and truth."* The original Greek text reads, *"And the word flesh became, and tabernacled among us, and we discovered His glory, a glory as of an only begotten with a father, full of grace and truth."* John wants to connect the abiding presence of God in the Old Testament with the glorious presence of God in Christ. This is confirmed when we *accept* that somewhere in the history of ancient languages, both the Hebrew word and the Greek word must have had a common ancestor. After all, were they not both written by the same Holy Spirit?

Therefore, in my mind there is no doubt that John was thinking about the Shekinah Glory (God manifesting Himself physically); when he confidently declares, *"The Word became flesh, and tabernacled, among us."* One of the early promises of God was that He would dwell or glory among us! Jesus was a complete representation and manifestation of that promise. God's glory is dwelling in our midst through Jesus Christ! What an incredible truth. Jesus Christ, the "hope of glory" is here with us today. Yes, He is here with you in full glory. What that means is that every inherent characteristic of God is here as well; His love, His mercy, His grace and His power.

DAY 308

MOUNTAINS

ὄρει = *'opei'*
Mountains, foothills, highlands

There are many obstacles in life; some small and some large, but the mountains that confront us are the most challenging. You can't go around them, you can't go over them, and you can't go through them. So how do you deal with them? In Mark 11:23 Jesus assures that question: if you command this mountain to be removed it shall happen. But there is a condition, you must not doubt but believe that those things you have commanded will be done. How is it that you have such great authority over something as gigantic as a mountain? I believe it's because this mountain is of your own doing.

There are things that we permit in our lives that eventually become major obstacles. The only thing left is to remove them; cast them into the sea. Therefore, if you are standing in this valley, start speaking to the mountain before you. *"So Jesus answered and said, 'Have faith in God. For assuredly I say to you, whoever says to this mountain, 'Be removed and be cast into the sea', and does not doubt in his heart, but believes that those things he says will be done, he will have whatever he says'."* Today, you can have whatever you say! Provided (1) you have faith in God, (2) you do not doubt in your heart, and (3) you believe that what you've said will be done. Go on... speak to your mountain right now.

Day 309

Redeem

ἐξαγόρασώ = *'exagoraso'*
To buy out or purchase a slave with a view to his freedom

In the ancient world men, women and children were routinely bought and sold. They were owned, traded, purchased, to put to work. They could be handed down from one generation to another. You might be born into slavery or you might go into debt and legally fall into slavery. The purchase price for a slave was called the redemption money. To *redeem* means to see a slave, to pay the price, to take them off the market and then set them free. In redemption there is an *exchange*; one man pays the price so another man can go free.

There are three primary Greek words that are used for redemption. The first comes from the Greek *agora* which means the market place. In its secular sense, it means to go into the marketplace and buy something. When applied to redemption, it means to go in and purchase a slave who is on the auction block. The second word means to go into the slave market; to pay the price and to take somebody off the slave market and out of that area altogether. The third word means to save, set free or deliver somebody from captivity. Note, these three words are used to describe what Jesus did on the cross: Ephesians 1:7 says, *"In him we have redemption through his blood."* To live in this truth means always living in total freedom, so enjoy your freedom and the liberty you have in Him.

Day 310

Drink

ποτίζω = *'potizo'*
To drink, give to drink, to furnish drink, to water

1 Corinthians 12:13: *"For by one Spirit we were all baptised into one body - whether Jews or Greeks, whether slaves or free - and have all been made to drink into one Spirit."* This word literally means "to make to drink," and it has to do with infilling. In the Modern Greek it is used most often in relation to watering plants, fields etc. and for pouring liquid into another vessel. It's where we get the word *ποτήρι*, which means glass. It also has to do with "being made full" with that which is being poured out.

Drinking the Holy Spirit is the intentional act of receiving that which the Spirit is pouring out. You "drink" by simply believing wholeheartedly that the Holy Spirit wants to pour Himself into human vessels. Therefore, learn to trust in His grace, and in doing so, God will flood you with the presence and power. Keep in mind that God designed you to be continually filled (Ephesians 5:18). Why? By virtue of the fact that He will never stop being a fountain of life to you.

Just as water gives life physically and is integral to one's physical life, so the spiritual water you are told to drink gives life to your spirit man. Are you thirsty today? In John 7:37 Jesus says, *"If anyone thirsts, let him come to Me and drink."* Accept the Lord's invitation and you won't thirst again; accept His invitation and you will be quenched.

DAY 311

TROUBLE

θλῖψιν = *'thlipsin'*
Trouble, tribulation, affliction, distress

In John 16:33 Jesus said, *"These things I have spoken to you, that in Me you may have peace. In the world you will have trouble; but be of good cheer, I have overcome the world."* This verse doesn't apply only to the major troubles you have as it also deals with everyday life. It is the kind of victory you have been given to guide you through each day. One in which you can have confidence for the future, no matter what it may bring. Most of us live in two worlds; one bound by time, with all of its limitations, and the other eternal; unlimited and full of hope. Don't be torn between two worlds, they both have a part to play. In one world Jesus is the "Prince of Peace," yet in the other He is "Ruler" the Lord of Lords. That's why He says, "Cheer up, I have conquered the world!"

When Jesus was in the world, He always did everything with the excellence that heaven demanded. If you do a small thing as though it were a great thing, God will let you do the great thing as though it were a small thing. Jesus had the ability to fully relate one world with the other, despite the trouble He was having to face. Heaven was always the Lord's measure!

Let heaven be your measure today: "Let it be on earth as it is in heaven!"

Day 312

Unbelief

ἀπιστίαν = *'apistian'*
Unbelief, distrust, unfaithfulness

Most of us have some understanding of the laws of gravity; we have it firmly implanted in our minds that gravity will cause everything to fall to the earth. Unless the object could be propelled out of the earth's gravitational pull, it will eventually fall back to the earth. Do you know? God is not ruled by the laws of gravity: God is not bound by its influence. As the creator of gravity, if He chooses, God can make an axe head float on the surface of water. We all know from experience that if we put a heavy steel object in water it will sink every time. It is imperative that you view the laws of physics; the laws of gravity in a whole different light. You need to open your mind to allow God to work. If not, He is unlikely to do anything! With unbelief, very little is going to happen: *"Now He did not do many mighty works there because of their unbelief"* (Matthew 13:58).

In Matthew 17:20 Jesus said, *"Because of your unbelief, I say to you; 'If you have faith as a grain of mustard seed, you shall say to this mountain, move from here to there; and it will move; and nothing shall be impossible to you'."* This statement must be accepted as being absolute truth – without any unbelief! So make up your mind today to open you mind. Take the lid off your thinking and let God do the miraculous!

If you have faith as a mustard seed, nothing is impossible.

DAY 313

EARTH

γῆς = *'geis'*
Earth, physical land, soil

Have you ever wondered exactly what God wants to be doing through you; what mountain does He want moved; what principalities and powers does He want removed; what miracles does He want to perform? Do you ever pray the Lord's prayer; do you say, *"Your kingdom come. Your will be done, on earth as it is in heaven"* (Matthew 6:10)? Note, you're telling Him that you want His will done here on earth, but are you prepared to be a vessel that will allow His will to be done through you?

You need to allow God to teach you what to believe and what to expect in your life. When you were in school you probably accepted every word that came out of your teachers' mouths as being factual. Now, you may have to discard many of the things you learned and relearn them in a new way, in *a spiritual way*, allowing the Holy Spirit to teach you all things concerning matters of importance.

Man was told to subdue the earth (Genesis 1:28), and maybe God wants you to command the rain to fall or to stop it falling. It could be your personal assignment. Ask Him? For what He commands He will deliver on; that is an absolute certainty. God wants His will to be done on earth, and He wants to use you to perform it.

DAY 314

VIRTUES

τούτοις = *'toutois'*
These virtues, these things, qualities

Become a loving person is more important than having great faith. How can that be possible? Colossians 3:14: *"And over all these virtues put on love, which binds them all together in perfect unity."* Here's your answer: love is the realm where all the other virtues should be experienced. Love is the glue that holds them all together; love is the power behind everything else we do; love is like the hub of a wagon wheel, the spokes are all the other virtues that find their origin in love. What is kindness without love?

Without love you just go through the motions as it's not real, genuine or authentic. Do you see the significance of love? You can leave out a lot of things in this life and still be fine. But, if you neglect this you are truly wasting your life. You can be the most successful person in the world, but without love, it amounts to nothing! It is the greatest virtue you can possess.

1 Corinthians 13:7 tells you to have enduring love. But how can your love be long-suffering? How is it possible? The only way to love like this is through Christ. You cannot love like this in your own strength. If you are willing to surrender yourself, and your relationships to God, He will empower you to love this way. It is possible only if you get yourself out of the way and let God's love permeate into every area.

Day 315

Shine

φαίνει = *'phainei'*
To shine, to gleam, to bring to light, to cause to appear

In order to see the blessings of God in your life you may need to look back, but when you look back you must be able to see exactly where God's light has shone. *"In Him was life, and the life was the light of men. And the light shines in the darkness, and the darkness did not comprehend it"* (John 1:4-5). If you do not recognise precisely where the "light of God's presence" was manifested, you risk remaining in darkness. Looking back and seeing is the key to future success.

In order to help you position yourself to receive the fullness of God's blessings, I want to encourage you to look back and see where His light was shining. If you don't know where you've come from, you won't know where you are going. As you move forward from one day to another, it is a good idea to look back, provided you do it in a positive and spiritual way. You can look back at where His glorious light has shone in your relationships, finances, achievements, milestones, and so much more. However, when it comes to your faith you need to look back at your relationship with God: all the God-encounters you've had. There's no point in looking back at your negative circumstances, staring into the darkness, because they have no power over your future. Every day, try to identify exactly where God's light was shining brightly; where His light had brought about blessings.

DAY 316

GAVE

ἔδωκεν = *'ethoken'*

To give, to offer, to flourish, to give from oneself

John 3:16 says, *"For God so loved the world, that He gave His only begotten Son, that whosoever believes in Him should not perish, but have everlasting life."* Wrapped up in that little word "gave" is a powerful truth: it means "to furnish, to give forth from one's self." In the Greek it's the past tense of a verb meaning; "it has no starting point or ending point." The love of God is a giving love, a furnishing love, a love which does not contain any reference to duration or completion of the action. It is unconditional and eternal! But the gift that God gave was also a sacrificial gift.

How far are you prepared to go for love? I heard about a man whose wife left him and their children and moved in with another man. The husband took the role of both mother and father, did the housework, paid all the bills, and waited for his wife to return. After living with the man for over a year, she decided she wanted to go back home. He had been praying for her and so he gladly welcomed her back. Many of his friends told him he was crazy for taking her back. "Jesus doesn't quit on me - no matter what I do! I can at least treat my wife the same way," he said. He truly *gave* the unconditional love he had received from Jesus to his wife. What are you ready to give to bring glory to God today?

DAY 317

PURGED

καθαρίζεται = *'kathapizetai'*
To purge, make clean, purify

In the days of Moses, God instituted the system of sacrifice for His people. There were decrees, regulations and commands to sacrifice animals. Hebrews 9:22 has this in mind when it says, *"And almost all things are by the law purged with blood; and without shedding of blood is no remission."* Old fashioned Christianity is out of vogue today. Fewer people want to worship a God who demands sacrifice. It is an offence to most of them. Yet, in the Garden of Eden, after Adam's sin, an animal was killed to provide a covering for Adam and Eve. Who do you think provided the coats of skins? It was God Himself! You're not expected to shed your own blood, but you are expected to recognise that blood was shed for you! Who could love you more than Christ; who willfully shed His blood so that your sins could be purged.

Living your life in that truth brings about a correct view and understanding of what it is to be a sanctified child of God. Because Jesus shed His blood, you have been *purged* from all unrighteousness. That puts you in a very favoured, privileged and honoured position, but more than that, your life is now "out-of-bounds" to the devil. All evil forces have no access to you except by invitation. So today, make sure you have not inadvertently left the door open. If you have, simply plead the blood over that situation.

DAY 318

HUNGRY

πεινῶντας = *'meinontas'*
The hungry, those hungering, the needy

In Mary's Song she makes this statement, *"He has filled the hungry with good things, And the rich He has sent away empty"* (Luke 1:53). It's comforting to know that the Lord will meet our needs when we are hungry. However, in today's affluent western society not many people will do hungry. But that is not the point being made here. Mary's words reveal that God responds in two ways to the two different kinds of people in the world. There are those who fear God and obey Him, and those who are proud and conceited. The ones who fear God and obey Him receive His mercy and provision for their needs. They are exalted; they are made full.

In her song, Mary states that this news is not just for her, but can be passed down from generation to generation. The good news is for all people. The blessings of God through Jesus Christ are for everybody, if they will just believe in Jesus. Mary begins her song by magnifying God. If you have trouble magnifying God, it is probably because you are magnifying yourself; if you have trouble praising God, it is probably because you are trying to sit in His seat. Remember, God opposes the proud but gives grace to the humble. He fills all those who are "hungry" with good things. What are you hungry for? Are you hungry for companionship, love, affection, respect, recognition, or anything else? If you are, you can be satisfied today – so let Him fill you.

DAY 319

TRUE

ἀληθινόν = *'aleithinon'*
True, genuine, correct, factual

"And we know that the Son of God has come and has given us an understanding, that we may know Him who is true; and we are in Him who is true, in His Son Jesus Christ. This is the true God and eternal life" (1 John 5:20). The word "true" is mentioned three times in this verse. Jesus came to give us the ability to know Him completely and understand that He is the Truth. We are in fact living "in" Him who is Truth. The true God who has given us eternal life considers us to be His dream team. This is the best combination to perform His will on earth. What's more, such a powerful union brings glory both to the Father and to the Son.

The possibilities are endless! The truth is, your affinity with the Holy Spirit means there is no where you cannot go, nothing you cannot do, and not a thing is challenging enough. Maybe you should start re-educating yourself to embrace the outlook of: "Continue to amaze me, Lord!" In other words, not to be limited in your thinking as to the possibilities for your life in God, but rather to: *"enlarge the place of your tent, to stretch your tent curtains wide, to not hold back, to lengthen your cords, and to strengthen your stakes"* (Isaiah 54:2). Because you are divinely connected to the Truth, you can confidently operate in all the spiritual principles that are true; that are "yes and amen!" So right now, accept the fact that you and the Holy Spirit are God's dream team.

DAY 320

SACRIFICE

Θυσίαν = *'thysian'*
Sacrifice, an offering, gift

"I urge you therefore, brethren, by the mercies of God, to present your bodies a living and holy sacrifice, well-pleasing to God, which is your spiritual service of worship." (Romans 12:1) When an Israelite had received a blessing from the Lord, he would have the priest offer up a "whole burnt offering" to show his gratitude. God was pleased by this precious sacrifice and expressed this by calling it a "soothing aroma" (Leviticus 3:5,16). You too must express your gratitude to God by offering yourself as a living sacrifice. You may think that a personal sacrifice is not very great because you have so many faults, nevertheless, God says that it is "holy and well-pleasing to Him." According to the apostle Paul, such a sacrifice is your "spiritual service of worship."

"Through Christ then, let us continually offer up a sacrifice of praise to God, that is, the fruit of the lips that give thanks to his name." (Hebrews 13:15) Here is another spiritual sacrifice which pleases God: "praising Him and thanking Him" for all that He is and all that He does for you. The practice of thankfulness to God is emphasised over and over again in the Bible. As you choose to recall God's blessings and then thank Him for them, you are keeping yourself properly aligned with the reality that you are wonderfully blessed; blessed beyond anything that you could ever deserve. Start thanking Him and enjoy the absolute liberty it brings.

Day 321

Boast

καυχάομαι = *'kauchaomai'*
To boast, brag, glory, exalt proudly

If you want to procure the full benefits of a "supernatural life" in Christ, you must get accustomed to not operating in the natural realm with everything. God wants to add to your "natural" His "super" so that His mighty deeds of power may be exhibited. But when experiencing the supernatural life, the degree to which the natural is operating can affect the measure of super-power which God is adding. Like everything with God, He desires all the glory. Therefore, when there's less of you; less of those natural abilities you possess; there will be more of Him; more of the supernatural power He is able to add.

We see this principle operating in 2 Corinthians 12:9: *"But He said to me, 'My grace is sufficient for you, for My power is made perfect in weakness.' Therefore, I will boast all the more gladly about my weaknesses, so that Christ's power may rest on me."* Another translation reads, *"My grace is all you need, for My power is greatest when you are weak."* Clearly, God's mighty power is perfected in human imperfections: all your natural limitations or frailties. It's only when you recognise this, and boast in it, that Christ's power is able to rest on you. If you truly understand grace, you will know that His grace is more than adequate, and you'll be able to *boast* in your weaknesses. Today, when you feel weak confess that you are strong, and God's power will *rest* on you every time.

DAY 322

HUSBAND

ἄνδρας = *'andras'*
A husband, spouse, partner

In John chapter 4 Jesus meets a Samaritan woman at a well. Imagine unexpectantly meeting Jesus as you go about your daily chores! I'd like you to put yourself in this woman's place. Do you regard Christ as a kind of mystic who can show you what's wrong with you; do you treat Him as another therapist from whom you can get a second opinion; or is He truly the Christ, the Lord of your life?

"You've had five husbands," says Jesus, "and the man you now have isn't your husband" (John4:18). This woman is a symbol for all people who worship falsely. The Samaritans were easy prey for the many cults that had spread across the Graeco-Roman world. In confronting this woman with her marital history, Jesus is also, at another level, raising the issue of true worship. He is asking, "Who are your *husbands*, your idols?" Yet, He is asking the same of you: what do you devote yourself to in place of worshipping God? What values have you embraced that take the place of Jesus? Values that keep you from being "the bride of Christ." Even good things can be false *husbands*. If the living Christ cannot be found at the center of your life, generating your vision and your priorities, you need to reexamine yourself. Focus on worshipping God in spirit and in truth; drink of the living water that only He can provide. Do that today and every day.

Day 323

Launch

ἐπανάγω = *'epanago'*
To launch, to put out to sea

After teaching the multitudes from a boat, and having stopped speaking, Jesus said to Simon, *"Launch out into the deep and let down your nets for a catch "* (Luke 5:4). Here, Simon Peter had been washing and mending his nets; after addressing the crowd, Jesus asks Simon to launch out into deeper water. This is an analogy of what Christ wanted to do in Simon's life: Jesus was intending to take Simon to a deeper, more personal relationship with Himself. He asks Simon Peter to do something contrary to his own professional expertise. Peter is reluctant because he can't see why it would work. The best fishing on the Sea of Galilee was at night, close to shore, yet Jesus asked him to launch out into the deep in the middle of the day.

Jesus was in effect asking Peter to try again even though he had failed. God may ask you to try again even if you have failed! The circumstances of the past evening indicated that further fishing would be fruitless. Yet Jesus was asking them to take the freshly cleaned nets and row out to the deep water and go through the strenuous process of letting out the nets all over again. These disciples needed to learn that obedience to Jesus should not hinge upon favourable circumstances. Do you allow circumstances to dictate your obedience? No matter how many times you've failed, today, launch out and try again! There's a miracle catch waiting.

Day 324

Centurion

ἑκατοντάρχης = *'ekatontarchis'*
Centurion, a captain of one hundred men

In this story, Jesus had intended to go to the centurion's house, in fact, Luke tells us that He was already not far from the house. Luke 7:6: *"The centurion sent friends to Him, saying to Him, 'Lord, do not trouble Yourself, for I am not worthy that You should enter under my roof'."* Now, this might seem like a minor point but it isn't. The centurion had already expressed a clear recognition of the Lord's superior *authority*; we can see this just in the way he approached Him. He addressed Him as "Lord"; He pleaded, not demanded; he simply stated the facts and left it to Jesus to choose what to do. That's how he confessed Jesus' superiority over himself.

I believe this *centurion* had come to terms with who Jesus really was, and humility was an important part of his faith. But there's one more aspect of his faith which caught the Lord's attention the most, in fact, the Bible tells us that Jesus "marveled" at the man's faith. He said to Jesus, *"But only speak a word, and my servant will be healed"* (Luke 7:7), because this man was under authority and fully understood the power of authority, he recognised that all Jesus had to do is "say the word" and the miracle he wanted would take place. Today, I'd like you to ask Jesus to "say a word" over your troubling circumstances. Psalm 107:20 says, *"He sent His word and healed them!"* Ask Him to send His word right now!

Day 325

Garment

ἱματίου = *'imatiou'*
A outer garment, a cloak, a robe

Luke 5:36 says, *"No one tears a piece of cloth from a new garment and puts it on an old garment."* It would be ridiculous to try to mend an old garment by destroying a new one. If any piece of cloth is to be cut out from a garment it would be the other way around. We always seek an older, discarded garment as a source of material for patching newer ones. A devotional routine or doctrine from the Gospel of Grace could not be inserted back into Judaism and it be legitimate or admissible. Therefore, the gentile believers could not find ready acceptance in the synagogues of the Jews. No, they would need to organise new ways to "gather together" in their own homes, as in the Book of Acts.

The truth being, a new building block has now become the "cornerstone" of a whole new religious order. The very stone which the builders rejected has become the Chief Cornerstone (1 Peter 2:7-8). The building methods of the past are no longer applicable; God is doing a new thing, and in doing a new thing, God does not patch up the old with the new. If He did it would not be a new thing. It's the same with your life, God does not take your worn past and use it to build your future. Everything He does, is always "new!" He uses what has never existed before to build every day of your life. Today's building materials are entirely and uniquely fresh, so stay away from what is old and used.

Day 326

Seed

κόκκον = *'kokkon'*
Seed, grain, kernel

Jesus said to them, *"Because of your unbelief; for assuredly, I say to you, if you have faith as a mustard seed, you will say to this mountain, 'Move from here to there,' and it will move; and nothing will be impossible for you"* (Matthew 17:20). A mustard seed is one of the tiniest of seeds, but it grows quickly into a large plant. Suppose we had faith that believes in the far-reaching effects of tiny little efforts, what difference it could make! But that's not necessarily the kind of faith that a mustard seed has; its own size has nothing to do with the outcome.

Jesus invites you, in the shadow of your mountains, to remember the little mustard seed; to remember that it's always hard to see potential until you plant it in the soil of faith and water it with the love of God. Things you never even noticed suddenly become the most impressive plants in the garden. I encourage you to think about ways that your faith might become more like the faith of a mustard seed. Are you expecting too little; are you dreaming too small; does a problem seem insurmountable? Your life cannot be enriched until you release the divine nature of God that is in you. For His power to be released all you need is a little drop of it. Today, you may be feeling small, weak and insignificant, but you have the full potential of God Himself in you. You have faith as a mustard seed - use it!

Day 327

Keys

κλεῖδας = *'kleithas'*
Keys, an implement that locks and unlocks

In Matthew 16:19 Jesus mentions the *keys* of the kingdom of heaven: *"And I will give you the keys of the kingdom of heaven, and whatever you bind on earth will be bound in heaven, and whatever you loose on earth will be loosed in heaven."* In the previous verse, Jesus mentions that the gates of hell shall not prevail against His church; implying that His church has the authority, freedom and ability to unlock the gates of hell. But with what? The answer is found here: "I will give you the keys of the kingdom of heaven." The gates of hell cannot prevail, prove superior to, the church of Jesus Christ because it has the *keys* of the kingdom. Yes, you have the authority to unlock (loose) everything that the gates of hell are keeping imprisoned. Therefore, whatever is kept bound by the gates of hell can be *loosed* by the church.

You already possess the keys which establish all-inclusive victory in both the natural and spiritual realms. Whatever you permit on earth is *released*, and whatever you forbid on earth is *bound*. Absolutely nothing, can oppose or reverse this authority. Revelation 5:10 declares: *"And have made us kings and priests to our God; and we shall reign on the earth"* With the *keys of the kingdom* in your hands you rule and reign on this earth! So don't be neglectful, use these keys wisely; use them every day of your life. Remembering that you've the authority of a king and the anointing of a priest.

DAY 328

MOTHER

μητέρα = *'mitera'*
Mother, a woman related to her children

Ephesians 6:2 gives us this sound advice, *"Honour your father and mother," which is the first commandment with promise: "that it may be well with you and you may live long on the earth."* Very good reason to respect your mother! The word "mother" or "mothers" appears in the Bible almost 300 times. Much importance is attached to the mothers of kings; often the queen-mother is more honoured than the queen-wife. A mother's influence is also revealed in Ezekiel 16:44, where the phrase, *"as is the mother, so is her daughter"* is found. I have seen this spiritual truth displayed clearly in my mother-in-law Mary, my wife Loraine and our daughter Xana; where we can find five generations of godly women!

With Timothy, the devout influence of his mother Eunice, and her mother Lois was also visible. Faith is certainly not inherited, but it is surely passed from one generation to another through godly influence. Wives and mothers, you must understand that you are the most influential people in the entire world. That is the role God has assigned you in life. Don't let the modern mindset rob you of your calling as a woman and mother. If you desire honour and respect, that is the best place to find it. In Biblical times, mothers were held in great esteem, so let's do the same. Whether your mother is still alive or she has gone to be with the Lord, remember her today in such a way that will bring honour to her.

Day 329

Much-More

πολλαπλασίονα = *'pollaplasiona'*
Much more, many times more, manifold

We must get to know the importance of working together with God as Jesus worked together with His Father. Didn't the Lord make a promise that He would never leave us or forsake us? Maybe if we all truly believed in the divine hope that is present in this small statement, we would begin to see the rule of God's Kingdom present with us. Maybe our lives, the church, our community, our nation, and even the world would be transformed. After all, "with God all things are possible!" The reverse is, "without God nothing is possible!"

Jesus boldly states, *"what is impossible with man is possible with God"* (Luke 18:27). Then Peter jumps in and says, "See we have left all and followed You" (verse 28). Jesus replies by stating that no one who has given anything up for the sake of the kingdom of God will go unrewarded. His exact words are: *"Who shall receive many times more in this present time, and in the age to come eternal life"* (verse 30). The New Living Translation says, *"Will be repaid many times over in this life, and will have eternal life in the world to come."* The Lord promises to multiply back everything that you have given up for Him, but also note where these rewards are going to manifest "in this present time - in this life!" Don't let the devil lie to you about the seed you've sown in God's Kingdom.; what you have given up will be bountifully rewarded. Therefore, start rejoicing in this day!

Day 330

Cornerstone

κεφαλὴν-γωνίας = *'kefalin-gonias'*
Cornerstone, headstone, foundation stone

Luke 20:17-18: *Jesus looked directly at them and asked, "Then what is the meaning of that which is written: "'The stone the builders rejected has become the chief cornerstone'? Everyone who falls on that stone will be broken to pieces, but anyone on whom it falls will be crushed."* What is a cornerstone? The cornerstone concept is derived from the first stone set in the construction of a masonry foundation. It's very important since all other stones will be set in reference to this stone, thus determining the position of the entire structure. Jesus said, the stone that the builders rejected has become the *Chief Cornerstone.*

God has laid this Cornerstone firmly on which the whole building rests, His Church, built not with brick and cement, but with living stones - His children. There is no other stone as firm as this Stone anywhere to be found. Even if the whole world should move and be shaken, this Stone will not tremble. Anyone who builds on this foundation will never be disappointed. If you wish to build your life, there is no other *foundation* to build on; everything else will disappoint. Who is the cornerstone of your life? If you are married, is Jesus Christ the Cornerstone of your marriage? What stone is your ministry or business built on? No person can prosper or succeed if he/she doesn't build on this Foundation, the Chief Cornerstone. Examine your building plans today.

DAY 331

WINE

κάμπέλου = *'ampelou'*
Vine, grape vine

As they were eating, Jesus took bread, blessed and broke it and gave it to them saying, *"Take, eat; this is My body."* Then He took the cup; when He had given thanks He gave it to them and they all drank from it. Jesus said to them, *"This is My blood of the new covenant, which is shed for many. Assuredly, I say to you, I will no longer drink of the fruit of the vine until that day when I drink it new in the kingdom of God."* Afterwards, they sung a hymn and went out to the Mount of Olives (Mark 14:22-26). There is an element of the Lord's Supper that is often overlooked, an element which is referred to as the "lifting up of the hearts." This element is common among most early Christian traditions: the "*Sursum Corda*" (Latin for "*Lift up your hearts*") is the opening dialogue to the Eucharistic Prayer dating back to at least the third century. The dialogue is recorded in many of the earliest worship ceremonies.

Note, "lifting up your heart" does not mean you feel uplifted; it means that, by faith, you are lifted up into the presence of Christ in heaven itself. The "lifting up of hearts" is like the lifting up of the wine cup. The cup symbolises the heart because wine represents the blood, which denotes life. Every time you lift up your heart, you are in fact lifting up your life in total surrender to our Lord Jesus Christ. Why don't you have Holy Communion today and lift up your heart; holding up the precious wine towards heaven.

DAY 332

THIRST

Διψῶ = *'thipso'*
To thirst, to desire earnestly

On the cross Jesus whispered, *"I thirst"* (John 19:28); meaning that Jesus was thirsty and experienced the physical pain of life. Again, it reveals the humanity of Jesus; it's the shortest of His seven last words. In English, it is two words long; in the Greek language, it is only one word. It means that Jesus knew physical pain. His physical pain was not make-believe or pretend it was real. This single word focuses on the intense physical pain of Jesus: Jesus experienced the enormity of human pain. There were 39 lashes across His back; there was a crown of thorns stuck into His head; there were ten inch spikes through His wrists, and He was hanging on the cross for three hours.

"Emanuel" (God with us) experienced the enormity of human pain because He became human flesh and suffered on the cross. The Son of God, the Mind of God, the Heart of God, was fully human just like we are. Jesus was a true incarnation of God: He was fully God but also fully flesh, or fully human. He suffered intense emotional pain and He suffered intense physical pain. That means that God knows and truly understands physical and emotional pain.

There are times in life when you may feel physically dreadful. However, it's comforting to know that God knows exactly what you are going through. He has been there!

DAY 333

VOICE

φωνῆς = *'phonis'*
Voice, speech, sound, language

The most important and beneficial *voice* you can hear is the Lord's voice. Revelation 3:20 reads as follows, *"Behold, I stand at the door, and knock: if any man hear My voice, and open the door, I will come in to him, and will dine with him, and he with Me."* What an astonishingly sad concept of Jesus. He stands at the door knocking; softly yet persistently He is seeking entrance. In the book *Christ And The Fine Arts*, someone had written about a picture depicting this verse. It was found on a stained-glass window in a famous cathedral: "The picture of a door with no handle portrays the moment when human destiny hangs in the balance, when Divine Love patiently waits upon human reluctance. Here is the perpetual issue between heaven and earth - choice. Here is the continual challenge of Christ to mankind. Here we see the ever-present appeal of love. It's a call to decision in stained-glass."

As beautiful as this window is, its somber message can never be ignored. God, in all His love and persistence, will never cross the line of human freedom. Jesus the Savior stands at the door of your heart and knocks, waiting for your response. Not even God's great love will force open the heart's door. Ultimately, the decision to open your heart to Him, or to leave it shut tightly against Him, rests with you. Take note, the door is shut! Jesus is standing behind a closed door without a handle waiting for you to hear His *voice* and open it. Are you prepared to let Him in today?

DAY 334

TRIALS

πειρασμοῖς = *'peirasmois'*
Trials, temptation, experiment, calamity

Your faith in God has incredible potential to make your life complete. Faith can take you from the place of deficiency to the place of being quintessential and accomplished. James puts it this way, *"My brethren, count it all joy when you fall into various trials, knowing that the testing of your faith produces patience. But let patience have its perfect work, that you may be perfect and complete, lacking nothing"* (James 1:2-4). Faith in God can make you perfect and complete, however, your faith will be challenged. Your faith will go through the fire of trail. The up-side is this: whatever you are in need of, your faith in God has the potential to take you from where you are right now, a place of lack and insufficiency, to this place the Bible calls "being perfect and complete." That is, lacking nothing! Nevertheless, the downside is that your faith must first be put to the test.

This being the case, the path to perfection and wholeness is one of serious trials and stern opposition. Your faith cannot get you anywhere until it has been authenticated. The devil knows exactly what's at stake and he will do all he can to keep you from trusting God and His word. Therefore, as your faith encounters the turbulence of tests and trials, do what James says and "count it all joy." This is the first step to becoming perfect and complete in Christ Jesus. Take the first step today, consider your tests and trials a joy, and let the devil know you will not be defeated.

DAY 335

HEALTH

ὑγιαίνειν = *'hygiainein'*
To be in good health, to be sound, healthy

Does God want you to prosper? Definitely! He wants you to prosper in all matters of life, and be in good health. God takes a holistic view of prosperity, for without it you will struggle. You are meant to prosper emotionally, materially, physically and spiritually. God's Word declares: *"Beloved, I wish above all things that you may prosper and be in good health, even as your soul prospers"* (3 John 1:2). Prosperity is not an accident but the result of the Word of God being received and correctly applied in your life. True scriptural prosperity is the ability to use God's ability in you to meet the needs of others. As mentioned, divine prosperity involves Spirit, Soul and Body; it is the will of God for all believers.

To prosper implies "to excel in something desirable." The Greek word literally means "to help on the road" or "to succeed in reaching." Hence, prosperity is not a momentary passing phenomenon, but rather, an ongoing state of success and wellbeing, and it is fundamental if you are to attain true happiness. Prosperity is always measured against the health and wealth of your soul: "As your soul prospers!" The only way this can happen is to feed your soul on the word of God. Your health is totally dependent on what you feed your soul. In that respect, you are what you eat! Therefore, make sure you are eating a good helping of the Bread of Life – God's infallible word!

Day 336

All-Things

πάντα = *'panta'*
All-things, every kind, the whole

You must take *ownership* of what God has given you; of what you already possess. You have been given great and powerful tools, which much of the time are not recognised and seldom used. 2 Peter 1:3-4 declares, *"His divine power has given to us all things that pertain to life* (the natural) *and godliness* (the spiritual)*, through the knowledge of Him who called us by His own glory and virtue, by which have been given to us exceedingly great and precious promises, that through these* (promises) *you may be partakers of the divine nature."*

"All things" in the Greek is one word and it refers to all things both spiritual and material; "every requisite" means every necessity of life. Therefore, God's divine power has catered for every necessity of life and godliness. Another way of putting it is this: "God has already given you every conceivable thing that is essential to living both an abundant and a righteous life." You have no excuse for living below par, because you have been fully equipped. The Greek word used for "all-things" implies "always!" God's divine power has given you all things that pertain to life and godliness, *always*! There should not be a moment in any day when you feel ill-equipped to achieve your goals; when you feel a lack of confidence in the abilities you possess. You have it all because God's divine power has *always* supplied *all* of it.

DAY 337

WILLING

Θέλω = *'thelo'*
I am willing, I am desirous to do, I want

George Washington Carver said, "How far you go in life depends on your being tender with the young, compassionate with the aged, sympathetic with the striving and tolerant of the weak and strong. Because someday in life you will have been all of these." Compassion empowers you to make a difference. Wherever you are and in whatever you're doing, compassion is waiting to release God's love and power. Mark describes a desperate solitary leper coming to Jesus, begging Him on his knees: *"If you are willing, you can make me clean." Moved with compassion, Jesus stretched out His hand and touched him, and said to him, "I am willing. Be made clean!" And immediately the leprosy left him.* (Mark 1:40-42). The man was not only healed of this dreaded disease, but in the process he was loved and affirmed as a valued member of the community. I believe that compassion must have been a key in Jesus' miraculous healings. That said, Jesus is the same yesterday, today and forever!

Therefore, the same Jesus, with the same level of mercy and compassion is here today, and He is *willing* to do what is needed in your life to bring about the victory. Don't forget, Jesus will continue to have compassion until compassion is no longer needed. The Lord is near and He is willing!

DAY 338

KINDNESS

χρηστότης = *'christotis'*
Kindness, loving kindness, goodness, uprightness

Titus mentions God's *kindness* made visible in Jesus, *"But when the kindness and the love of God our Saviour toward man appeared."* God's loving kindness was made manifest in the Lord Jesus. The extraordinary scripture in 1 Corinthians 13 has a bearing on this as Love Personified. You can give to charity, surrender your body to the flames, do things that everyone would applaud, *"but if I have not love I am nothing,"* says Paul. It is the same scripture which tells us that *"love is kind."* However, if you are to really experience Divine Grace, you must first recognise that you are undeserving and that God has found you, drawn you and given you a place at His table as a son or daughter. God has exhibited undeserved and great *kindness* toward you.

Let me assure you of this, whatever your state if you turn to Him; every time you turn to Him, I promise you He will deal kindly with you. Look at this scripture: *"God, who is rich in mercy, for His great love with which He loved us, even when we were dead in sins, has raised us up together and made us sit down together in heavenly places in Christ that in the ages to come He may show the exceeding riches of His grace, in kindness towards us through Christ Jesus"* (Ephesians 2:4-7). God, who is rich in mercy, came that He may display the exceeding riches of His grace in kindness toward you. Express gratitude this day.

Day 339

Careless

ἀργὸν = *'argon'*
Careless, thoughtless, unprofitable

Do you know that all of your words, day in day out, are recorded? Do you know who does that recording? The Lord does! He keeps a record of each word that you speak; He monitors your conversations every day. He is always listening, and He holds you accountable for every word you utter. The Lord Jesus Himself made that very clear when He said in Matthew 12:36, *"But I tell you that all men will have to give account on the day of judgment for every careless word they have spoken."* Therefore, I suggest you speak and act as though you are already having to give an account.

"Death and Life are in the power of the tongue: they that love it shall eat the fruit thereof" (Proverbs 18:21). We often say that a man will eat his words, in fact, this is a spiritual truth. You are what you eat, and with regards your words, you will eat the fruit thereof. If your words have been good words, they will yield good fruit and bring satisfaction to you. However, if your words are bad, they will yield bad fruit and become toxic to you. Remember, you are always rewarded according to the nature of your speech. Your words have the power to produce *life* or *death*. Therefore, I challenge you today to watch over every word that leaves your mouth. Try to monitor your speech and conversation toward others. Also be aware of what you say about yourself as that will have a profound effect on your life.

DAY 340

PURSUE

διώκετε = *'thiokete'*
Pursue, to hunt down, to put to flight

Diligent believers pursue good, for doesn't the Bible say; *"Always pursue what is good both for yourselves and for all"* (1 Thessalonians 5:15). It is this quest that will tug on your heart strings; a quest which you genuinely consider honourable. But be careful, your primary pursuit should still be the *pursuit* of God Himself, and not merely becoming a good person for God. God, and not good, is the ultimate thing you should be chasing after. You can often miss God by seeking His by-products; by seeking His provision, His gifts, or seeking His fruits independent of Him. If you genuinely pursue God and seek His presence, all His fruits and His mighty power will be available to you without striving or great effort.

King David declared in Psalm 27:8, *"When You said, 'Seek My face', my heart said to You, 'Your face, O Lord, I will seek'."* You must seek His face with such heartfelt tenacity as to find Him in every situation, and in finding Him, you will discover a whole new source of supply: new love, new peace, new joy, new strength, new inspiration, new hope, new faith and new horizons. Your life will truly be refreshed. But can you meet this standard? Are you willing to pursue Him with all your heart and with all your soul; have you prioritised this pursuit; will you genuinely delight yourself in Him and Him alone? Seek God's face and diligently *pursue* His heart today.

Day 341

Ministry

διακονίαν = *'thiakonian'*
Ministry, service, ministration

You have been summoned into His Majesty's service so He expects you to complete His plans and purpose for your life. I like what Colossians 4:17 says, *"Take heed to the ministry* (official service) *which you have received in the Lord, that you fulfil it* (complete it to His satisfaction)." If you think that being just a homemaker, just a labourer, or any other position is acceptable, you are wrong. You need to acknowledge the fact that you serve in a very lofty position; you have a "royal calling" that is important enough for the King of Kings to summon you personally.

There is an abundant life which He pre-arranged for you to walk in. Therefore, genuine fulfilment only comes from understanding your ministry – official service to God. What you must first understand is that you have been created for a purpose that's so much bigger than just doing the right thing. After that, you can discover the joy that comes when you own the assignment you have been given. Yes, peace and joy will come to you when you take "full ownership" of your appointed service to God. The good news is God has already provided everything you will ever need to successfully navigate and complete your mission. Are you willing to do whatever He asks you to do? Have you already made that life changing commitment to trust Him with your future? If you haven't, today is your day!

Day 342

Save

σῶσαι = *'sosai'*
Save, heal, preserve, rescue

In 1 Timothy 1:15 the apostle Paul makes this statement: *"This is a faithful saying and worthy of all acceptance, that Christ Jesus came into the world to save sinners, of whom I am chief."* Jesus came into the world to save sinners. Salvation matters! In the Old Testament "salvation" refers to: deliverance from danger; deliverance of the weak from an oppressor; the healing of sickness and disease; and deliverance from guilt and its consequences. But salvation finds its deepest meaning in the spiritual realm. Mankind's universal need for salvation is one of the clearest teachings in the whole Bible.

The salvation that comes through Jesus Christ may be described in three tenses: past, present and future. When you believe in Christ, you are *saved*, but you are also in the process of *being saved* from the power of sin. Finally, you shall be saved from the very presence of death and sin. God has released into your life today the power of Christ's resurrection and this gives you a foretaste of your future life as a child of God. Your experience of salvation will only be complete when Christ returns and the kingdom of God is fully revealed. Until then, you are able to experience heaven here on earth. That is why you must thank God every day for your salvation, for sending Jesus to *save* you.

DAY 343

SEEK

ζητεῖτε = *'ziteite'*
Seek, search, desire, demand

"Seek first the kingdom of God, and His righteousness; and all these things shall be added unto you" (Matthew 6:33). The Jews were greatly mistaken in respect to the nature of the kingdom that their Messiah was going to set up. They expected a kingdom like the kingdoms of this world, infused with earthly splendor. But Jesus sought to change their view. He told them that His kingdom did not come with outward visibility which existed among men. He wanted them to understand that it was spiritual and not temporal.

The simple idea of this kingdom is that Christ Himself reigns in the hearts of His people, securing the perfect submission of the human will, and the setting aside of every power to Himself. His kingdom is "within," therefore, it is invisible; it puts on no outward expression. The subjects of this Kingdom abide in no particular location. Every citizen dwells where they first met with Christ; where salvation was received; where they became a legitimate resident of His invisible kingdom. The Lord rules and reigns over you so that you may truly be a citizen of the kingdom of God. It is this kingdom that you are told to seek - the kingdom that exists *within*! Are you seeking first the kingdom values that have been written on your heart? Look within today and prioritise all those things your heart wants you to follow. Yes, seek them first!

DAY 344

GOSPEL

εὐαγγελίου = *'evaggeliou'*
Gospel, good news, the good news of the coming messiah

The gospel is "good news!" The apostle Paul said, *"For though you might have ten thousand instructors in Christ, yet you do not have many fathers; for in Christ Jesus I have begotten you through the gospel"* (1 Corinthians 4:15). Are you serving up the good news? In this verse, Paul had in some way participated in the spiritual birth of the people he was addressing. Not only did he see himself as having a father's responsibility for their overall well-being, but he fully acknowledged that they would not have been birthed without his direct involvement. Can you see something? Spiritual birthing, as with physical birthing, requires the participation and co-operation of two parties.

When planning to birth spiritual offspring, God restricted Himself to "the preaching of the gospel of Jesus Christ." However, this birthing could only take place with the deliberate involvement of two parties. One party, who has been equipped, is willing and able to deliver the "good news." The other party, possessing the divine power necessary to impart new life. We know the Holy Spirit is willing and able to bring new life to all of mankind. Therefore, the only question is whether the first party is willing to bring the good news. You may not think you've been called as an evangelist but that is not the point, you are only meant to carry the gospel. So share it with a lost soul!

DAY 345

JERUSALEM

Ἱερουσαλήμ = *'Ierousalem'*
Jerusalem, the capital of Israel and Judah, a future heavenly city

In Luke 9:51 we learn, *"When the days drew near for Him to be received up, He set His face to go to Jerusalem."* Note, Jesus was not accidentally entangled in a web of injustice. The saving benefits of His death were not an afterthought. God planned it all out of infinite love for us, and He appointed a specific time. Jesus, who was the very embodiment of His Father's love, saw that the time had come and "set His face" to fulfil His mission - to die in Jerusalem for our sake.

You should set your face toward Jerusalem every day, the place where the ultimate sacrifice was made; you should be doing something radical with your life, something radical with your income, something radical with your free time, something radical with your job. The more secure you are in God, rather than material things, the more open you are to meaningful involvement with those people who are most needy. As this happens, your witness with family and friends will become more striking and fruitful. Jesus expects you to go out into the market place and meet the needs of others. You are to "set your face toward Jerusalem" and pick up your cross to follow Jesus. As Christ set His face to *Jerusalem* each day, you ought to follow Him on the road to Calvary. It is on this rugged road that you will fulfil your destiny and bring most glory to God.

Day 346

Uncertainty

ἀδήλως = *'athilos'*
Uncertainty, without certain aim, obscurely

Successful people have a clear sense of direction in every area of their lives; they have the ability to plan ahead and focus on the right things at the right time. Jesus was a prime example of this. You'll be surprised how many of your problems can be put down to lack of direction. The apostle Paul said, *"I do not run with uncertainty, and I do not fight as one who beats the air"* (1 Corinthians 9:26). The Greek word used literally means "to be aimless," something Paul avoided! He was decisive and he always had a target that he was aiming at.

To be fruitful you must do something every day, no matter how small, that moves you toward your objective. You must celebrate every achievement. Also, you need to accept responsibility for where you are right now, because you are where you are and what you've become, due to the decisions you've made. Greater progress in your life is possible only to the degree to which you accept a higher level of responsibility in that area. No one else can or will do this for you, and no one is coming to the rescue. It's entirely up to you! If you want your situation to get better, you must get better. If you want things to change, you must change. If you want things to improve, you must improve. Taking responsibility is your personal tool for going to the next level. Therefore, except responsibility for the choices you make and the direction in which they take you. The next level awaits!

DAY 347

GOOD-PLEASURE

εὐδοκίας = *'evthokias'*
Good pleasure, good will, satisfaction

In Philippians 2:12 the Apostle Paul writes, *"So then, my beloved, just as you have always obeyed."* The framework here is always obeying the instructions God gives you. It is your responsibility to work out your salvation, but with eyes wide open. You are to apply all diligence in implementing and carrying out the wishes of God in your life. Note what Paul says in the next verse, *"for it is God who is at work in you, both to will and to work for His good pleasure."* There is the balance, you are working out your salvation with God working in you. Therefore, you can lean on this truth; the truth that you have been saved for a reason, for a great cause, and for His good pleasure.

Obedience to what God is doing in you is pleasing to Him. Everything He does in you will be accompanied by Holy Spirit energy, therefore, you have a responsibility to apply this energy to your service for the living God. It ought to be conspicuous. You must expect your life to reflect the fact that you are very energetic, and you must believe that you're here to fulfill a God-given assignment. Time is rushing by and there are things to do, but without enthusiasm you're going to run out of steam. Research has discovered that most people find lack of enthusiasm unattractive. In pursuit of God you must infuse every day with a kind of energy that is whole-hearted and irresistible - for His good pleasure!

Day 348

Anything

τι = *'ti'*
Anything, all, whatever

God's word reveals His will, and His will and His word are one. Many believers do not have because they do not ask according to the will of God. 1 John 5:14-15 says, *"Now this is the confidence that we have in Him, that if we ask anything according to His will, He hears us. And if we know that He hears us, whatever we ask, we know that we have the petitions that we have asked of Him."* Besides cultivating a proper attitude in prayer, you also need to pray for the right things. Asking according to God's will involves focusing on God's priorities and not your own. When you do, you can ask anything and He hears you. What's more, when God hears God responds.

The more your perspective is soaked in God's Word, the more you will pray according to its priorities, and the more you will see God answer your requests. If you don't know God's priorities you will naturally pray for your own priorities. If this is what dominates your prayer requests your success rate is going to be low and your motivation to pray more is going to diminish. Therefore, it really benefits you to pray according to the will of God; this demonstrates the confidence you have in Him. Right now, God is listening, so pray for anything according to His will and be certain that God hears and responds. Not tomorrow or the next day, but today.

DAY 349

DELIVERANCE

σωτηρίαν = *'soterian'*
Deliverance, salvation, preservation, safety

Philippians 1:19: *"For I know that as you pray for me and the Spirit of Jesus Christ helps me, this will lead to my deliverance."* When the Spirit of Jesus Christ is with you, He will lead you into complete liberty; delivering you from all your burdens. There are different mentions concerning the Lord's Spirit: the "Spirit of Jesus" is related mainly to the Lord's humanity; the "Spirit of Christ" is related mainly to the Lord's divinity. Therefore, to experience the Lord's humanity, you need the "Spirit of Jesus." However, to experience the power of the Lord's resurrection, you need the "Spirit of Christ."

To receive help in every situation in life, you need the Spirit of Jesus Christ: *"...And the Spirit of Christ helps me."* In his own suffering the apostle Paul experienced both the Lord's suffering and the Lord's resurrection. Hence, the Spirit to him was the "Spirit of Jesus Christ." The compounded, all-inclusive, life-giving Spirit of the Triune God. Such a Spirit was in bountiful supply for the apostle Paul, who was experiencing and enjoying Christ in every area of his life, but God wants to do the same with you. To experience freedom and deliverance, you not only need the "Spirit of Jesus" or the "Spirit of Christ," you need the amalgamation of both: the "Spirit of Jesus Christ." It's this duo-functional Spirit that helps you to achieve victory in every situation. May the Spirit of Jesus Christ help you today.

Day 350

Spiritual

πνευματικὸς = *'pnevmatikos'*
Spiritual, unworldly, holy

Have you ever wondered what an "acceptable sacrifice" to God is? The apostle Peter, in his first letter, refers to believers as a royal priesthood (1 Peter 2:9), and that they should offer up spiritual sacrifices which are acceptable to God (1 Peter 2:5). In the same verse, he refers to the saints also as members of a holy priesthood: *"You also, as living stones, are being built up a spiritual house, a holy priesthood, to offer up spiritual sacrifices acceptable to God through Jesus Christ."* Peter states, as members of a royal and holy priesthood, we should offer up spiritual sacrifices which are acceptable to God. Just what are spiritual sacrifices?

I have found four spiritual sacrifices which are acceptable to God: (1) "generosity" [Philippians 4:18], (2) "service" [Romans 12:1], "praise" [Hebrews 13:15], and "love" [1 Corinthians 13:13]. I encourage you to offer up all these sacrifices continually. Let God witness your generous heart; let Him acknowledge your service to Him; let God hear your praises in heaven; and let God see the love that you give Him and share with others. Let this all happen today!

Spiritual sacrifices are not meant to be demanding and dreary. They are meant to be an overflow from your heart toward the Lord; a fountain that is full of thanksgiving and adoration to the Most High God. It is an act of true worship.

DAY 351

VESSEL

σκεῦος = *'skeuos'*
A vessel, implement, container

Often God talks to us using different measures; whispers, dreams, intuition, a knowing; calling us to take new steps in preparation for His plans. But are we listening? Do we take the required actions; do we get to stay focused and participate the way Jesus did? For many of us there is much reservation about getting ready to do God's will. With others there are feelings of unworthiness; being not good enough, not humble enough, not holy enough. But if God has faith in you, who are you to doubt yourself? If He believes in you, who are you to say, "I am not able?"

Preparation can sometimes seem laborious. Yet, even in your preparing you are honouring God. Don't forget, none of us can learn through another's journey. Your season of preparation is exclusively your own. Why? Because you are being individually prepared for His glory: *"That He might make known the riches of His glory on the vessels of mercy, which He had prepared beforehand for glory"* (Romans 9:23). You are the unique vessel through which God has chosen to make known the riches of His glory. Today, prepare yourself to have His glory poured into you; prepare yourself to have His glory shine through you; prepare yourself to have His light come, that the glory of the Lord may rise upon you (Isaiah 60:1). Prepare for an outpouring of God's blessings.

Day 352

Surrounded

περικείμενον = *'perikeimenon'*
Surrounded, encompassing, clothed with

"Therefore we also, since we are surrounded by so great a cloud of witnesses, let us lay aside every weight, and the sin which so easily ensnares us, and let us run with endurance the race that is set before us" (Hebrews 12:1). For the sake of all those heroes of faith who surround us, let us never give up. These are difficult times in which we live: times that make us want to give up on our dreams; give up on looking for a job; give up on finding the right mate; give up on trying to live healthy; give up on buying a home; give up on improving our lives. But I want to encourage you today, do not give up, stay the course. The game is not over until God says it is over.

A good coach encourages his team to never quit trying, never quit playing because you never know what may happen to your opponent. A lot of games have been won in the last minute. Your victory is just around the next corner; your deliverance may come with the next sunrise; your answer may come with the next prayer; your healing might be in your next praise. Winners never quit and quitters never win. So stay the course and do not give up. If God says you are a winner, who can convince you that you are beaten? If God says you are chosen to be more than a conqueror, who can make you a loser? Don't give up!

Day 353

One-Accord

σύμψυχοι = *'sympsychoi'*
One accord, united in soul, of one mind

"Fulfil my joy by being like-minded, having the same love, being of one accord, of one mind" (Philippians 2:2). The original Greek says, *"Fulfil my joy that you may be of the same mind, having the same love, united in soul, minding one thing."* Does this mean that we are all expected to think and act the same? Definitely not, for there is nowhere in God's word that suggest this. Uniformity and unity is not the same thing. It is possible to attain unity without uniformity. We have the right to choose unity or discord, therefore, it's up to each of us to exercise our will to be unified and likeminded. Where there is like-mindedness you will find unity, and where there is unity the Lord will command His blessing (Psalm 133).

Being in *one accord* (united in soul) means having the same love, the same spirit, and the same purpose. When you were reconciled to God in Christ you became one with Him, and therefore, the bond that unites you with God unites you with others. You are one with Him and one with others! Grace renews not only your relationship to God but to man as well. You are a member of one family, and also of one body. It is the symphony of love that unity has created, in which the Spirit manifests His full power. Live every day in the full knowledge that being of like-mind and like-heart (united in spirit) is where God commands His blessing.

Day 354

Laying-On

ἐπιθέσεώς = *'epitheseos'*
A laying on, an assault, an attack

Hebrews 6:1-3: *"Therefore, leaving the discussion of the elementary principles of Christ, let us go on to perfection, not laying again the foundation of repentance from dead works and of faith toward God, of the doctrine of baptisms, of laying on of hands, of resurrection of the dead, and of eternal judgment."* The Bible considers the "laying on of hands" as part of the ABC's of doctrine - along with repentance and baptism.

Jesus dwells in you, and He will use you as His hands to touch those in need. It is not that you wield the power, but that you yield to the power of Christ who is able to heal. He is the healer, you are the hands! Jesus lives in you, and therefore, He cannot help but manifest His presence to the person for whom you are praying.

You need not worry about how much faith you need, just remember that it is not your faith which transmits or effects the healing power of God, it is His faithfulness. Your faith simply opens the door and invites Him to enter in. In the laying on of hands there is divine communication; the love of God flows through the touch of one person to another. The laying on of hands can be a source of comfort as well. Be His hands today, and let Jesus touch those around you.

DAY 355

AFFLICTIONS

μαστίγων = *'mastigon'*
Afflictions, sufferings, scourge, severe pains

Some have suggested the possibility that Jesus did not know where *afflictions* came from. If Jesus didn't know the cause of sickness, it creates a huge problem for us believing anything else He said. What if He was incorrect about other matters He spoke of? But this simply doesn't make sense! Jesus displayed complete authority over sickness and disease, and even historians agree that He was a miracle worker. Why would demons be in submission to someone who didn't know what he was talking about? Let me tell you why, because Jesus knew what was behind sickness and disease: *"And that very hour He cured many of infirmities, afflictions, and evil spirits; and to many blind He gave sight"* (Luke 7:21).

Today, doctors look at someone with a medical problem and they order tests to find out what is physically causing the problem. Once they find what is physically causing the problem they assume it is also the source of the problem. But many times it is not the true source of the problem. The problem may lie somewhere else. But no matter its origins, Jesus has the authority to deal with every infirmity, and that authority has been passed on to His Church. Yes, you have the same authority over sickness and disease that Jesus has; He has given you His name and said "use it.' If you know of anyone that is struggling with an *affliction* use the prayer of faith – in Jesus' name – and see God's healing power at work.

Day 356

Approved

δόκιμος = *'thokimos'*
Approved, tested, tried, acceptable

Romans 14:16-18 says, *"Therefore do not let your good be spoken of as evil; for the kingdom of God is not eating and drinking, but righteousness and peace and joy in the Holy Spirit. For he who serves Christ in these things is acceptable to God and approved by men."* In the four Gospels, Jesus referred to the "kingdom of God" or the "kingdom of heaven" 106 times, so it must be important that we gain insight into the operations and governance of God's kingdom. *"The kingdom of God is ... righteousness and peace and joy in the Holy Spirit."* This means that the Holy Spirit is manifesting these attributes right now. He is continually working in us to make us more righteous, more peaceable, and more joyful.

In other words, the working of the Holy Spirit and the advancing of the "kingdom of God" are one and the same. Why? Because it is the Holy Spirit who brings about God's sovereign rule and dominion. As the Spirit establishes God's sovereign rule in your life, He will establish the sovereignty of God everywhere else. This is the way God has chosen to display His might and power to a lost and dying world. For more miracles and greater demonstration of God's supreme authority to materialise the realm of the kingdom of God must manifest first. When it does, so too does the "presence" of God's Spirit. Yet this will not happen until the things you do today are both acceptable to God and *approved* by men.

DAY 357

EXCEEDING

ὑπερβάλλον = *'hyperballon'*
Exceeding, surpassing, superior, exceptional

In the New Testament the "yardstick" of God's power, is the Resurrection of Jesus Christ. I don't think it put any strain on God to make the world: He just created it. It did not put any strain on God to create light: He just spoke the word, "Let there be light" and there was light. But I believe it put a considerable demand on God's power to raise Jesus from the dead. In Ephesians 1:19-20 it says, *"The exceeding greatness of His power to us all who believe according to the working of His mighty power when He worked in Christ when He raised Him from the dead and seated Him at His own right hand in heavenly places."*

There are different measures of God's power, and there may be things that draw on His power more than others. Look at it this way, when God said, "Let there be light" and there was light, I don't think He said, "let there be Calvary" and there was Calvary! What I love about this passage is how it reveals that all this power is pointed at us. Once the resurrection power of God raised Jesus from the dead, it was then directed toward the Church. Why? So that we may live an abundant and victorious life. Whatever situation you are facing, and however tragic it may appear, there is a power directed toward you today that cannot be denied. It is the immeasurable and surpassing power that God used to raise Jesus from the dead. This power is overwhelming!

Day 358

Conform

συμμορφόω = *'summorphoo'*
Conformed, fashion, to bring to the same form

In Philippians 3:10 the apostle Paul says: *"That I may know Him, and the power of His resurrection, and the fellowship of His sufferings, being conformed to His death."* Paul was in prison when writing this letter to the church in Philippi. Here is an ageing apostle, battle-scarred and gaunt, but observe his prayer! His longing never died; his vision never became dim; the fire in his belly never got dull. He was as focused on knowing God as never before. He did not pray to be released from prison, he might have done that; He did not pray that he might have a ministry there, though I am sure he aspired to that; He did not pray that his body may be healed, he was possibly weak from the suffering he had endured. His genuine aspiration was this: "That I may know Him!" It isn't that Paul does not know Him, rather, there is a fuller revelation of Christ that he is now seeking.

But how exactly was Paul to know the Lord, and the power of His resurrection? By being *conformed* to His death? When you genuinely identify yourself with the Lord's death on the Cross, you will get to know Him better, and thereafter, experience the power of His resurrection. You will be astounded at what the Holy Spirit can do when you truly understand this principle. He can bring new-life into every dead situation! Do this today, invite Him to breathe new-life in your unresponsive and lifeless situation. Do this right now.

DAY 359

FOOLISHNESS

μωρία = *'moria'*
Foolishness, folly, absurdity

What exactly is the power of God? The mighty power of God is not especially physical, even though it can be and has been displayed in this way. The most amazing and awe inspiring display of this power takes place in the spiritual realm. This is the realm where no nuclear explosion can have any effect. It is in this realm that the "power of God" has been unleashed for our eternal benefit. I Corinthians 1:18 declares, *"For the message of the cross is foolishness to those who are perishing, but to us who are 'being saved' it is the power of God."* And 1 Corinthians 15:57 says, *"Thanks be to God, who gives us the victory through our Lord Jesus Christ."* This is the "mighty power" that was released which no man and no invention of mankind could ever begin to match.

However, to many this power is mere foolishness. For if you do not accept the message of the Cross you can never comprehend the magnitude of God's sovereign power. The good news is, if you have received the message of the Cross and have embraced it, it becomes the power of God. At the Cross all of God's power was made manifest to mankind. That is why you should come to the Cross every day of your life. Visit the very place where resurrection power was released. When you come to the Cross you can then go through the Cross to all of God's promises. For they are "yes and amen." Come to the Cross today – encounter the power of God.

DAY 360

WORD

Λόγος = 'logos'
Word, statement, speech

In Leviticus 26:11-12 the Lord says, *"I will live among you, and I will not despise you. I will walk among you; I will be your God, and you will be My people."* One of the clearest revelations God has given us is His desire to dwell with His people. His presence appeared many times in the Person of the "Angel of the Lord." He was also seen in the Burning Bush by Moses, then in the Fire by night and the Cloud by day to the children of Israel. He dwelt in the Ark of the Covenant and inhabited the Temple with His Glory after the dedication offered up by Solomon (2 Chronicles 7:1,2). He dwelt among men in Christ, fully and bodily, and now dwells in us by His Holy Spirit.

"In the beginning was the Word, and the Word was with God, and the Word was God... And the Word was made flesh and dwelt among us, and we beheld His glory, the glory as of the only begotten of the Father, full of grace and truth" (John 1:14). What becomes obvious here is that John wants to connect the "abiding presence" of God in the Old Testament with the "glorious presence" of God in Christ. There's no doubt that God wants His presence to increase in your life. Are you ready and willing to live in the glory cloud? What an awesome place to be! If you are ready, then first you must hunger for God's presence. This is what the Living Word wants you to do right now!

Day 361

Sheep

πρόβατα = *'probata'*
Sheep, little sheep

People regardless of age, education, race, colour, looks, economic standing, past or present condition, all actually matter to God. *"What do you think? If a man has a hundred sheep, and one of them goes astray, does he not leave the ninety-nine and go to the mountains to seek the one that is straying? And if he should find it, assuredly, I say to you, he rejoices more over that sheep than over the ninety-nine that did not go astray"* (Matthew 18:12-13). What we have here is a lost sheep, so let me ask you, what do you think the odds are that this sheep will make it back home on its own? Not very good. Bottom-line, sheep are not bright animals; sheep are not leaders, they are followers. What is the only hope this lost sheep has? That the Shepherd will search and find him.

That's it! That's the sheep's only hope. Why would a shepherd do this? Because that lost sheep matters to him! Here's the point... Why did Jesus come to seek and save the lost? Because people matter to God; you matter to God. Let me tell you, you are priceless, and you are worthy of the precious lifeblood of Jesus Christ. Don't let anyone or anything tell you otherwise. Not your parents, wife, husband, children, boss, friends, enemies, society - or your past, or your present. To God you are truly valuable, and no matter what, He will find you when you are in trouble.

Day 362

Groanings

στεναγμοῖς = *'stenagmois'*
Groanings, sighing, utterings

I'm sure we've all used a satellite navigation system. Now there's one thing you are probably sure of before you log in your information, and that is, the SatNav knows the route better than you do. You don't ever expect it to lead you astray otherwise you may as well embark using your own directions. It is the same with the Holy Spirit. You must fully accept that He knows the path ahead better than you do, and in everything He will guide you using God's plans and purposes as coordinates for your future. So be aware, whenever you do not know what the will of God is, He does! Romans 8:26-27 says, *"Likewise the Spirit also helps in our weaknesses. For we do not know what we should pray for as we ought, but the Spirit Himself makes intercession for us with groanings which cannot be uttered."*

The Spirit does this through intercession or intervention. While you are praying, He intervenes and takes over. How you know that He is at the steering wheel is through the groanings taking place inside of you. He knows God's mind and will concerning all things. God's Spirit will always make sure you receive instructions in a way that you can understand them. He doesn't want you to try and figure out how to get there using your own directions. That ought to give you absolute confidence in His guidelines for your life. Ask the Spirit of God for directions for this day.

DAY 363

AMBASSADOR

πρεσβεύω = *'presbeuo'*
Ambassador, elder, representative

In order to understand what God discloses about Himself we must allow God to speak for Himself and be who He said He is. Let's stop misrepresenting Him by voicing our own opinions and politically correct views. I am always amazed at how many false statements people make about God; about what God does or thinks. I can understand non-Christians having a tainted view of the nature and character of God, as they are ignorant of the Truth, but believers have no excuse. We have God's Word to lead us and guide us.

2 Corinthians 5:20 says, *"Now then, we are ambassadors for Christ, as though God were pleading through us: we implore you on Christ's behalf, be reconciled to God."* What a great honour, we are ambassadors for Christ. We are His appointed representatives in today's society and our position sits above any political nomination. Note, a good ambassador must speak on behalf of whom he represents. We represent the Lord of Lords and we must proclaim His Word and His Word alone. Therefore, let's be sure that when we speak about God we say exactly what He says about Himself. And let's be bold enough to sympathetically correct others who misrepresent Him. Forget about being politically correct, let's be Biblically correct. It's what God says that matters. It's what God says about Himself that's crucial. Today, represent the Truth and introduce Him to someone in need.

Day 364

Works

ἔργων = *'ergon'*
Works, task, action, deed

What is a miracle? The dictionary definition is: "an extraordinary and welcome event that is not explicable by natural or scientific laws and is therefore attributed to a divine agency." The word of God directs us to, "One who must be worshipped as having supernatural powers and abilities!" Hence, every time we mention God we are talking about the One who must be worshiped as having abilities that go far beyond the laws and powers of this natural world in which we live. When God provides miracles they are spontaneous, they cannot be summoned but come of themselves. Miracles are part of His sovereign rule.

Most believers agree that God is still in the business of working miracles, and Galatians 3:5 confirms this, *"Therefore He who supplies the Spirit to you and works miracles among you, does He do it by the works of the law, or by the hearing of faith?"* That being the case, the God who so graciously supplies us with "supernatural power" (by His Spirit) persists in performing supernatural deeds on behalf of His children. And He does this by hearing their faith. Notice, works or human endeavour is in direct opposition to miracles. The moment you get into works, God cannot hear you. He only hears your faith! Today, take God's word, wrap it up in faith, and then hold it up to Him. God loves to hear faith-filled words, for when He does, He is obliged to release miracles.

Day 365

Riches

πλοῦτος = *'ploutos'*

Riches, wealth, abundance, materially or spiritually

Philippians 4:19 talks about God supplying your need according to the riches of Him in glory: *"And my God shall supply all your need according to His riches in glory by Christ Jesus."* The original Greek says, *"And my God will fill up all your needs according to the riches of Him in glory in Christ Jesus."* God wants to "fill up" all your needs today. What a lovely picture this creates! Our Heavenly Father is able to pour out blessings from heaven that will fill up every single need to the brim.

God has promised to supply your need according to His riches. This confirms that you cannot have a need too great for God to supply. Your Heavenly Father knows what your need is, and all His riches are made available to His own. *"He that spared not his own Son, but delivered him up for us all, how shall he not with him also freely give us all things?"* (Romans 8:32). Never question or doubt this great truth. God's unlimited supply and His unfailing word should satisfy your need now and for all of time. God's wealth is at your disposal, and this is a provision beyond calculation. Don't deprive yourself by refusing to take God at His word; don't miss the blessing by pushing this promise into a future time.

Let God *fill up* all your needs today. Then let Him *fill up* all your needs tomorrow, and the next day, and the next!

Biography

Christos Demetriou is the founder and Senior Pastor of CornerstoneTheChurch, a vibrant multi-cultural community with members from over 40 different nations based in Surrey, United Kingdom. Born in Cyprus, his fluent understanding of the Greek language enables him to convey unique insight into the New Testament scriptures. In this, Christos' forth publication, it's his unique understanding of the original Greek text that has enabled him to unlock and expound on the profound Biblical principles used in this book to encourage its readers.

Christos began his career in the music industry aged 17 where he was a successful songwriter and record producer; associated with over 160 recordings and a number of top five hits. Having worked in different capacities with artists such as Cat Stevens, David Bowie and Mike d'Abo, one of his songs was used during the Opening Ceremony of the London 2012 Olympic Games and it appears in the Guinness Book of Records as the first time a "sample" was used on a music track.

Christos is also a notable media entrepreneur; his LinkedIn profile was in the top 1% of the most viewed contacts globally. He presently lives in West Sussex with his wife Loraine and daughter Xana.

Index

THE AUTHOR

Christos Demetriou
Senior Pastor
CornerstoneTheChurch

A special and heartfelt thanks to the following people for helping, encouraging and inspiring me during the creation of this book:

Ward Simpson
James Measures
Canon J John
Bayless Conley
Jerry Savelle
Canon Andrew White

Ayia Panagia tou Sinti Monastery in Cyprus

greektome.co
Original series on God TV

ACTS International
9 780955 728075